Dante

Dante

A LIFE

ALESSANDRO BARBERO

PEGASUS BOOKS

NEW YORK LONDON

DANTE

Pegasus Books, Ltd.
148 West 37th Street, 13th Floor
New York, NY 10018

ISBN: 978-1-64313-913-5

10 9 8 7 6 5 4 3 2 1

Printed in the United States of America
Distributed by Simon & Schuster
www.pegasusbooks.com

CONTENTS

GLOSSARY

Captains of the War: twelve experienced knights who acted as a general would in directing the battle; each of the six *sesti* would appoint two Captains of the War.

citizen knights (*cittadini con cavallate*): those who came from wealthy families but did not wish to become dubbed knights were still obliged by the city government to provide a war horse, military equipment and a rider, who in practice was nearly always the owner himself or a member of the family (see 'dubbed knight').

Council of the Hundred: the council elected from wealthiest citizens who were paying the most tax – 'possessing greater riches [they] carry a higher burden of expenses', as stated in its charter.

dubbed knight (*cavaliere di corredo*): anyone who belonged to a rich family and was willing to spend large sums on the ceremony of becoming a knight and then maintaining the required lifestyle; during the popular regime this status excluded them from the councils of government (see 'citizen knights').

fat commoners (*popolo grasso*): wealthy commoners, socially not much inferior to knightly families but still involved in business and not necessarily keen to have their young men dubbed as knights and to maintain an aristocratic lifestyle.

gold florins: originally a gold coin minted in Florence and worth one pound of smaller silver coins (*lira*), but as time went on, it came have to have an even greater value as the rate of exchange between gold and silver changed.

government of the First People: form of popular government (involving greater participation by commoners) from 1250 to 1260.

government of the Second People: the government of the Republic of Florence from 1266, with businessmen and artisans in power and noble families gradually excluded.

Kingdom of Italy or *Regnum Ytaliae*: following the break-up of the Carolingian Empire, this disputed entity came into being and continued until the early eleventh century, after which the kingship became no more than an appendage of the Holy Roman Emperor, and was only a reality in as much as the emperor could exert his power over the Italian peninsula, which was not very often.

magnates: members of families who followed a chivalric lifestyle; a group mainly composed of longer noble lineages, but open to those who acquired wealth more recently if they chose to cease their lesser business activities, although they often retained large holdings assets in banking.

Office of Rebel Assets: government department responsible for the management of assets confiscated from exiled members of the party not in power.

Ordinances of Justice (*ordinamenti di giustizia*): laws devised by Giano della Bella in 1293 that excluded the magnates from government posts in consequence of their frequent resort to violence.

priors: six priors elected for two-monthly mandates, who constituted the government for that short period.

small florins: silver pennies minted in Florence, whose rate of exchange steadily deteriorated in relation to gold florins.

supreme magistrate (*podestà*): each medieval city-state appointed a supreme magistrate who held a large part of the executive and judicial power and was a professional, but his mandate usually lasted for one year; he administered justice and commanded the army, but he came from another city and was subject to an inquiry on termination of his contract.

Tuscia Alliance (*Taglia di Tuscia*): an alliance that united all the cities governed by Guelphs, and which also had an international reference point – the papacy – whose wishes could not be ignored.

Some terms have remained in Italian, because the use of an English equivalent would probably have confused readers rather than aided them:

feditori: knights chosen by the Captains of the War to join the first rank of knights on the battlefield;

gonfalonieri: standard-bearers, of which the most important was the *Gonfaloniere di Giustizia*, who oversaw the procedures of the six priors who constituted the government;

sesto (plural: *sesti*): one of the six administrative districts Florence was divided into.

WHY DANTE MATTERS

This is the life of the man whom T. S. Eliot placed on a par with Shakespeare: 'Dante and Shakespeare divide the modern world between them; there is no third' (in truth, Eliot went even further on the radio, when he claimed that 'Dante is at least as great as Shakespeare', which is self-evident for an Italian but provoked a little resentment among anglophone men and women of letters). James Joyce, another of the twentieth-century greats, put him on an even higher pedestal: 'I love Dante almost as much as the Bible. He is my spiritual food, the rest is ballast.' We should be put on our guard about all the prejudices against the Middle Ages by a voice that can hail from that epoch and still speak with such intensity to the modern world: it was no more a dark age than the twentieth century, by which I mean that it was an era of great violence, but also of extraordinary creativity and intellectual subtlety. It was a modern age in every sense of the term, and not without reason did Eliot assert that Dante had shared out *modernity* with Shakespeare between themselves.

However, this modernity – the very same which had medieval intellectuals referring to themselves as 'modern' – does not mean that a little preparation is not required if we are to measure up to Dante's contemporaries and understand them. We are inclined to value them and enjoy their company, just as we value – or rather revere – the magnificent cathedrals they built, but which the Renaissance humanists and the seventeenth-century Enlightenment thinkers considered to be the products of a barbarian culture – of Goths, and hence a 'Gothic' architecture. Their world – the medieval world – was full of institutions and regulations whose names in themselves tell us nothing, and yet we need to be introduced to them if we are to share the journey Dante undertook or was obliged to follow amid the temptations and dangers of his times.

Europe and Italy at the Time of Dante

Dante was born in 1265 in Florence, Tuscany, and died in 1321 in Ravenna, Emilia-Romagna, exactly 700 years ago. When he was born, King Henry III of England was busy suppressing the Second Barons' War, which culminated with a decisive royal victory at the Battle of Evesham and the death of Simon de Monfort, when Dante was three months old. Most of Dante's life corresponded to the reign of Edward I. During the years in which the Florentine poet, having passed his thirtieth year, was politically active in his native city, King Edward had to tackle William Wallace's rebellion, which became famous after the film *Braveheart*, and defeated him in 1298 at the Battle of Falkirk. When Wallace was finally captured and executed at Smithfield in 1305, Dante was forty years old and already in exile. He was starting to write *The Divine Comedy*, the work that would bring him his enduring fame.

Did Dante come to hear of these distant events? He most certainly did, as European Christendom was a single vast religious and cultural community held together by the immense multinational organisation that was the Church of Rome, whose seat of power was in Italy. All its intellectuals spoke, wrote and thought in the same language, Latin, and they meditated on the same problems. News travelled quickly. But Dante was not overly concerned about such events, because the Italy in which he lived was very distant and very different from those northern kingdoms. Dante was an Italian, even though this name had not yet been firmly applied to the inhabitants of the peninsula; he preferred to call them 'Latins'. However, they knew very well how to distinguish between those who were born in Italy and those who came from the countries on the other side of the Alps. The French were disliked for their arrogance, the Germans for their coarseness and violence, but the English were not so well known because their mercenaries had not yet made their presence felt and come to be feared for their cruelty, as they would in the fourteenth century, long after Dante's death.

Italians were a nation, and spoke the same language in a myriad of dialects. This was the language that Dante would study in his treatise *De vulgari eloquentia* and call 'the language of the *si*', meaning the language in which the word for 'yes' was '*si*'. It was not yet referred to as 'Italian'. They were a nation, but they were only aware of this when they had to engage with the foreigner: for example, when their merchants from Genoa, Venice or Sicily met up in an eastern Mediterranean port or in 1309, when Dante was forty-four and the French pope Clement V transferred the papacy from Rome to Avignon, which initially went unobserved as it was considered to be a provisional move, although as time went on it caused increasing disquiet about an Italy bereft of that Christian capital Italians looked on as their birthright.

Italians were a nation but not a state, nor were they a kingdom like England or Scotland. In those countries, as in France, Germany and Castile, power was held by the king, even if their territories were not only administered by royal functionaries but also by a warlike aristocracy of barons who were vassals of the king and derived their power from their fiefdoms (hence the term 'feudal monarchy'). Kings did not enjoy absolute power, as they would attempt to obtain in the seventeenth and eighteenth centuries, which would occasionally end in disaster (as in the case of Charles I, who was executed at Whitehall in 1649). Medieval kings accepted that they couldn't rule without the consent of the barons, the clergy, the gentry and the merchants in the cities. In England there was even Magna Carta, which obliged the king to regularly consult his parliament, which included representation of at least part of its people.

Italy was completely different: there was no king, or if there was, then only on paper. In theory there was a *Regnum Ytaliae*, which like France and Germany was the product of the subdivision of the great continental empire of Charlemagne and corresponded to what is now central and northern Italy (the south, the Neapolitan lands and Sicily, would have a long and separate history of their own, even though they were undoubtedly part of Italy). While other European countries always had their own king, the season of independent kings of Italy had been a brief one, and came to an end shortly after AD 1000. The king of Germany claimed to be the true heir to Charlemagne, and through the Middle Ages and beyond he continued to observe the ancient ritual whereby he would travel to Rome and have himself crowned emperor by the pope, just as Charlemagne had done in AD 800, and he would stop along the route in Milan or adjacent Monza, where they kept the iron crown of the kings of Italy, and would also have himself crowned king. In other words, Italy had a king, who moreover boasted the glorious title of emperor, but he was a German king and almost always lived north of the Alps and came to Italy only once in his life for his coronation, if that. The country could do without him, and in Dante's time the German king's capability to intervene in Italian affairs was practically non-existent.

Italian Politics and the Republics or 'Comuni'

Who then was ruling the country? Italy was a country made up of cities, as it still is today, and each city had its own political organisation, the *comune*. This institution had existed when it was subject to a kingdom or empire, and it has continued to this day after returning to a more modest role, but we should remember that in the Middle Ages each of these *comuni* was to all effects and purposes an independent state that treated the other Italian cities as foreigners, and could enter into alliances and go to war. On occasion, an emperor would attempt to reassert his authority over Italy by force of arms, while claiming to be a guarantor of peace and respect for the law. He would find cities willing to support his plans, but each time the cities that refused to submit to his claim proved to be stronger and more numerous, and thus he would be defeated on the field of battle. The Peace of Constance in 1183 obliged Emperor Frederick I to acknowledge that each city could legally exercise all the powers over its own territory that theoretically pertained to a sovereign. The last emperor to make a serious attempt to subjugate the republics was Frederick II, who died in 1250, fifteen years before Dante's birth.

The Italian cities had succeeded in transforming themselves into independent city-states because for a few centuries Italy had taken over the role of principal centre for trade with the east and become the richest country in Christendom. There was more money, merchants, literacy and competence in business affairs in the Italian cities than anywhere else in the world. Moreover, there was, as previously mentioned, the presence of the pope, who governed the Church as an autocrat. He considered himself to be Christ's representative on earth and superior to all monarchs, and he had always assisted the Italian cities in their struggle for independence, because it was in his interest to weaken the only other authority that could challenge his own, that of the emperor and successor to Charlemagne.

As can be imagined, 'peaceful' is not a term that could be applied to this Italy, subdivided into dozens of city-states full of money and ambition in which the pope and the emperor, two supreme authorities that were militarily weak but loaded with ideological significance, jostled for position. The cities were continuously at war to assert their own economic and territorial aspirations to the detriment of their rival cities. Dante's Florence was one of the more powerful ones, and during his life it was decisively asserting its hegemony over Tuscany. But there was also warfare within each city, and this was even more devastating. Within a city there were rival power brokers – family alliances primarily made up of nobles, but also important bankers and the wealthiest businessmen – whose objective was to gain government posts and take control of public expenditure. They wanted all the power to themselves and had no intention of sharing it with anyone. The inevitable corollary of these pressure groups was the creation of larger and larger coalitions until there were two opposing parties, which rarely managed to co-exist: when one was in power, the other was usually persecuted and forced to flee into exile. The modern concept of an opposition fully entitled to exist and to oppose government policy was entirely unknown to them: rivals were criminals and enemies who had to be eliminated.

The opposing parties had appeared spontaneously in every city, and by Dante's time they had taken on the names we know them by today, and which seem so exotic to us: the Guelphs and the Ghibellines. They had discovered the ideological divide around which they could consolidate their own identity: the Guelphs supported the pope and the Ghibellines the emperor. The most difficult political decision every city had to make was whether it should place its trust in the emperor's repeated attempts to assert his authority or to defend its own full independence, whatever the cost, by invoking the protection of the pope. And this was a decision that had to be ceaselessly revised. The two opposing alliances in every city would go in one or other direction in an entirely spontaneous manner, acquiring an ideological stance they had not originally shared. Given that one of the two parties was in power in every republic, the Guelphs and Ghibellines in each city got into the habit of seeking the military and financial support not only of the pope or the emperor but also of all the cities in which the same party was in government. Thus the Guelphs and the Ghibellines became two international alliances capable of assisting their adherents even when they had been defeated in their own republic and sent into exile, and of supporting any attempt to repossess their city by military force.

This was the world in which Dante grew up and in which he was politically active up to the age of thirty-six, when the faction of the Guelph party he belonged to was defeated and he had to abandon his native city and spend the rest of his life in exile, as happened to thousands of Italians at the time. The Florence he grew up in was the richest Italian city, which meant that it was the richest in Europe. It was a Guelph city protected by the pope, a friend to the king of France, and full of money, immigrants, trade and building sites: at the time they were building the cathedral, the churches of Santa Croce and of Santa Maria Novella and Palazzo Vecchio, which was the seat of government. What did it mean to be politically involved in such a city?

Like all Italian cities, Florence was governed by an intricate concatenation of councils, committees and boards which mobilised a broad participation of a great number of citizens. In order to make any decision, committees and boards were summoned by the ringing of bells, agendas were presented, speeches for and against were minuted, and votes taken (by either public show of hand or secret ballot). This system produced an enormous quantity of written documents (for some time Europeans had developed the technology for manufacturing paper, which replaced much costlier parchment), and this means that we can observe the complex workings of government. It was also a surprisingly modern system: success in politics was based on the ability to gain the confidence of the party and create a consensus. You had to know how to speak in public, support a motion and guide the debate and the vote. Dante had studied this art, and he applied it expertly.

While in most cities this participation in councils was for life and more or less openly restricted to membership of a few influential families, this was not the case in Dante's Florence. In Florence councils were open to everyone, by which I mean every adult male citizen who owned a house or a business and paid tax. It was what they defined as a 'popular government', that is to say a government of people who worked – or in other words, large and small entrepreneurs, from the wealthy banker to the humble craftsman. The councils were renewed every six months in order to involve the maximum number of citizens, and this they called a 'broad' government. A democracy? Yes, if the anachronism doesn't perturb us too much. It was a democracy comparable to that of Great Britain in the late nineteenth century, which was restricted to manhood suffrage with a property qualification. The poor were not entitled to vote, but the system still aspired to an ideal of shared, participatory power.

To be clear, citizenship alone was not sufficient for inclusion in political activity, as ideological credentials were also required. You had to be a Guelph, and hopefully the member of family that had always been Guelph. There was no place in Florence for a Ghibelline, for someone who thought that Italy would be better off if the emperor had a little more power and prevented the endless warfare between one city and another, as well as the bloody clashes between factions within the same city. Such nostalgia for central government would have made Italy slightly more similar to the kingdoms of England and France. The Ghibellines had been defeated for good; many were in exile, and those who had remained in the city had to keep their heads down and their mouths shut.

Clearly Dante was a Guelph, otherwise he could not have developed a political career. But by that time, being Guelph was no longer enough, because conflicts between parties did not arise simply from ideological differences, such as support for the pope or the emperor. Far from it: they arose above all from the craving for power, government positions, the control of public funds and the ability to make your friends prosper and to crush your enemies. In Florence the Guelphs, who had once been a single party, split into two rival power brokers, each of which demanded all the power for themselves. They were called the White Guelphs and the Black Guelphs. Dante always argued that he had adopted an impartial position above the scrum, and that he cared only about unity, consensus and the common good, but in reality he too enrolled in one of the new parties, the White Guelphs, and sometimes it was in the wrong. He briefly found himself at the centre of power in 1300, the year in which he held important political positions, but then the White faction was overthrown in a coup and its leaders sent into exile.

Dante was one of them and he lost his house, his lands, his social status and his wife. For the last twenty years of his life he no longer had a home. Part of the time, he lived in the mountains as a guest in the castles of noble lords, because in Italy an aristocratic warrior class of counts and nobles, similar to the one in power everywhere in the rest of Europe, only survived far from the cities in the mountain ranges. But he was also the guest of dictators in some of the cities in northern Italy where absolute power had been superimposed on the complicated mechanisms of a council-based democracy by manipulating the desire for order and peace which was widespread among the citizenry. These societies were, for different reasons, very different from the tumultuous Florentine democracy. Dante was a very welcome guest in these courts because he was a poet and literary figure of considerable fame, as well as a master in the art of writing letters and giving political speeches, but he was always painfully aware that he owned nothing of his own and was dependent on other people's benevolence.

Dante's Literary Works

Exile destroyed Dante's life irredeemably and also shortened it. He died at the age of fifty-six, and in the final years he talked of himself as an old man with white hair. But the period of his exile was also the time in which he wrote the greater part of his works, including the *Divine Comedy*, the one that earned him international fame. Before that he had already created a body of writings that would have gained him a place in literary history. Since adolescence he had had a passion for writing love poetry not in Latin but in the everyday language or vernacular, which had already been the practice elsewhere in Europe for some time. These are known today as Dante's *Rime* and include over one hundred songs and sonnets, mainly composed in his youth and almost immediately in circulation even outside the city. This turned him into a well-known poet in Italy, albeit among those who were interested in such things. Once they were set to music by professional composers and sung in public where they could be transcribed by listeners and sent from one friend to another, these poems could circulate with a rapidity that seems unbelievable to us, as there were no mass media at the time and no printing. And yet we have the proof: a notary in Bologna transcribed one of Dante's sonnets on a blank page of his register in 1287, when the poet had barely reached the age of twenty-two.

Many of these songs examined Dante's love for Beatrice, a girl of his own age whom he had met in childhood and fallen in love with forever. At the time early death was common, and the woman Dante loved, and who was married to another man, died in 1290, when both of them were twenty-five. To survive that bereavement Dante did what writers and poets do in such circumstances: he increased his literary output. Between 1292 and 1293 he told the story of his love for Beatrice in *Vita Nuova*, in which he reworked his writings about her and mixed them into a prose commentary and narration. This was a revolutionary work without any precedents, which has been defined as the first novel in modern literature and a *Bildungsroman*. It produced an immediate response and discussions among other poets. Forty-eight of these manuscripts have survived, of which two were written in the hand of Giovanni Boccaccio, the author of the *Decameron*, and this is clear evidence of the wide circulation of *Vita Nuova* in Italy at the time.

Dante subsequently stopped writing in order to devote himself to politics. It took a coup, his party's disastrous fate, the destruction of his previous life and the sudden shock of exile to get him to immerse himself in literature once more. He was not short of ideas: he started with three stunningly diverse treatises and worked on two of them at the same time for many years, and only completed the third one. The first, *Convivio*, was to have consisted of as many as fifteen books, which would have covered all the major themes of contemporary intellectual debate: philosophy, ethics and politics. He wrote it in the vernacular (Italian) and could thus speak to everyone who didn't know Latin and was excluded from these more sophisticated matters. The title, meaning 'banquet' or 'feast', conjures up an image that we would consider clichéd but which the Middle Ages would have found extremely agreeable. If we struggle to see it through their eyes, we can start to perceive his vocation to be a great populariser. Dante was inviting noblemen and -women to dinner to share with them in their own language the knowledge they did not normally have access to. Thus Dante knew how to popularise, but he was not the first. The Middle Ages were drawn to popularising works and encyclopaedias: the Florentine Brunetto Latini, who had been one of Dante's teachers, had written something similar, entitled *Tresor*. We can only marvel at the ambition of Dante's *Convivio*, but it is worth reminding ourselves that he suspended his labours on completing only the fourth of those fifteen books!

The second project he committed himself to, during that period, was his treatise on linguistics, *De vulgari eloquentia*, which he began around 1304. What did it mean for an intellectual to examine linguistics in the Middle Ages? We have to imagine living in a world in which all educated people from Sicily to Scotland knew the same language, Latin, which was taught at school but never used at home. It was spoken at scientific conferences, university lessons and diplomatic encounters, and it was the language used in almost any text worth writing. Unlike what is happening today with the English language, Latin was an artificial language for everyone, and did not disseminate the cultural and economic hegemony of one or more countries. It did not favour anyone, but was instead an extraordinary instrument of cultural equality, albeit within an elite which had access to a superior culture. However, Dante at the age of eighteen was thrilled to discover that in his city he could write love sonnets in quotidian language that was understandable to housewives and porters. In *Convivio* the people he wanted to invite to dinner were not exactly porters, it's true, but knights and their wives who also knew little or no Latin. The question of the vernacular was therefore of great importance to him, and he decided to adopt a systematic approach.

And so he decided to analyse language by writing in Latin, which demonstrated that here he did not want to popularise but rather to research and reflect on a subject. Everyone knew that the spoken languages differed, and the Bible explained why this had happened. It was the fault of human ambition, which had led to the catastrophe of the Tower of Babel, but there weren't even the names to denote the languages it created. Dante wrote a treatise on linguistics in an era in which there weren't even the foundations of that science, and he began with our hearing which tended to perceive languages as remarkably similar, as in the case of English and German, as he wrote in *Convivio*, I.6.8 ('someone accustomed to Latin, if he comes from Italy, cannot distinguish between the English and German vernaculars'), and then he investigated the subject in greater depth with an extraordinary description of the differing sounds of the vernacular in various Italian regions. Then he lost the thread of his argument and started in the second book to discuss the use of the vernacular in poetry, clearly a subject closer to his heart, and once again he interrupted his work.

The concept of publishing a book existed long before the invention of printing. Just as they do today, authors wrote in solitude until they considered their work to have been perfected (fortunately there were no editors in those days), and had it read by competent people. It then would be copied to those who were interested and perhaps a particularly elegant copy would be gifted to some powerful person (but this courtly habit was not yet frequent in Dante's time, though it would be shortly afterwards). Obviously *Convivio* and *De vulgari eloquentia*, both unfinished works and therefore not published by the author, never achieved a wide circulation. A very different fate awaited *De Monarchia*, Dante's last treatise, which was also written in Latin and the only one he completed.

He wrote during an exceptional moment in Italian history. As we have said, theoretically Italy was a kingdom, but the king was a foreigner and of no importance. For Dante's generation an effective intervention by the king belonged to their historical past. But during the years 1309 to 1313 the past suddenly made a reappearance: the newly elected emperor Henry VII came over the Alps with the explicit political intention of re-establishing his control over the country and limiting the autonomy of the city-states. Dante was one of those for whom this was not a sinister revival but rather the promise of a better future. So he wrote *De Monarchia* as a utopian political manifesto in which the kingdom of a Caesar blessed by the pope would witness a future Italy that would finally be at peace with itself.

De Monarchia was the product of a febrile interlude of intense industry. But why were the other two treatises left unfinished? The fact is that he had got involved in writing something quite different, which he found much more engrossing. This something quite different was the *Divine Comedy*, the long poem in which he imagined a journey into the next world, initially through hell, then purgatory and finally paradise, and which contained a huge cast of characters both ancient – such as Virgil and Ulysses – and contemporary – such as popes, emperors, kings, politicians, men of letters, musicians, corrupt business-men, lovesick young women, saints, criminals, famous people and people that only he knew. It is an extraordinary portrait not only of humanity in his own time but also of humanity *tout court*.

Is it possible to explain the *Divine Comedy* in a few words? Of course, the literary genre can be defined as that of a vision-ary work, whose protagonist is accompanied on a visit to the realms of the hereafter, which was already a well-established Christian tradition. We should recall that at the time everyone was a Christian in an extremely tangible manner. Everyone really did believe in the existence of heaven and hell, and in the rewards and punishments that would be meted out after death. It had become even easier to believe in this since the two biblical realms had been joined in popular convictions by another one, purgatory, in which whoever had repented of their sins would be able to atone for them in the serene certainty of eventually gaining salvation. No one could seriously hope to go directly to heaven, but thanks to purgatory, they could hope to avoid hell. The Church would start to persuade the people that they could redeem years in purgatory – their own or those of the deceased they had loved – by paying the clergy to the melodious sound of ready money. There was nothing strange in this because every-thing could be bought and sold in the Middle Ages, but in the long run this practice would give rise to an increasing unease until, one day, Luther would spark off the conflagration that would forever fragment Christian Europe, but that is another story.

So Dante conceived a journey through the three realms of the afterlife, devoting thirty-three cantos to each one, plus the introductory canto: 100 cantos in all and a total of 14,233 lines. It was a journey from the depths of evil up towards the light, and through all the horrors and marvels of history, through the infamies and glories of human nature. And here we require particularly rich and well-chosen words to explain the nature of the *Divine Comedy*, because it is such an important work in the history of the world … The author of these lines, who writes in the comfort of his study, will be forgiven for choosing another infinitely greater writer who had to do this in unthinkable circumstances. When he befriended the Alsatian Jew Jean Samuel, whom he called Pikolo, in the mud of Auschwitz, Primo Levi struggled to recite from memory the canto of Ulysses, that is Canto XXVI of *Inferno*, in perhaps the most poignant moment in *If This Is a Man*, and he understood that first he had to explain what it was about, for Pikolo, who before the war had been a student at a prestigious French lycée, had never heard of it!

> Who was Dante? What was the *Comedy*? What a curiously novel sensation it was to be attempting to explain briefly the nature of the *Divine Comedy*. How hell is structured, and what is the *contrapasso* [a punishment based of the opposite of the crime, giving it a particular didactic quality]? Virgilio is Reason, Beatrice is Theology. Jean is extremely attentive …

Jean Samuel's homeland, France, had always struggled to admit the greatness of Dante. In the Soviet Union during the 1930s, however, two of the greatest poets of the twentieth century, Anna Akhmatova and Osip Mandelstam, had learned Italian so that they could read Dante, although Mandelstam was soon to die in one of Stalin's labour camps. Akhmatova did survive, and when in old age she was asked if she had read Dante, she replied that she had done nothing else.

The fame of Dante and his poem spread quickly. In 1314 a writer, one Francesco da Barberino, referred for the first time to a book by a certain Dante Alighieri 'which is called the *Comedy* and tells of many things concerning hell': at that time Dante had both concluded and published the first canticle and already some people had read it and were discussing it. *Purgatory* was published shortly afterwards, and before Dante's death the first cantos of *Paradise* were in circulation: who knows whether he put them out for others to read because of his concerns over the proximity of his death or whether he had submitted to pressure from literary circles throughout Italy who had read the first two canticles and were anxious to have the third? When he died, thirteen cantos were still missing, and for a few months it was believed that he hadn't had time to write them. But then they were found in circumstances immediately obscured by the mist of legend, and his sons, heirs to a spectacular literary triumph, took on the task of having them published. This triumph was not confined to Italy. Seventy years after Dante's death, in distant England, Geoffrey Chaucer imagined a monk among many other pilgrims on their way to Canterbury telling his fellow travellers a story taken from the *Divine Comedy*, and advised them to read the original if they wanted to know more:

> Redeth the grete poet of Itaille,
> that highte Dant, for he can al devyse
> fro point to point, nat o word wol he faille.

On the other side of the English Channel, Christine de Pizan, a contemporary of Chaucer and the first professional female writer – that is to say, the first woman in history to have made a living out of writing and publishing books – invited her contemporaries to read Dante in preference to any other writer.

In reply to a friend who had praised the vision of hell in the thirteenth-century best-seller *Roman de la Rose*, she replied that if he wished to hear something really great, deep and moving about that theme he should read Dante, or have it translated to him,

> as it is written in the Florentine language. There, I hope you don't mind, you will find more substance, which is more authoritative and subtler, and you will profit far more from it than from your Roman de la Rose, and the writing is a hundred times better. There is no comparison, and don't be angry!

Since then the *Divine Comedy* has been acknowledged as one of humanity's masterpieces and the work of a man who can only be compared to Homer and Shakespeare, in spite of the changing tastes whereby Dante was criticised in eras more partial to classical tastes for being a poet who mixes the lofty and the demotic, who describes the choruses of angels and the farts of devils and who in *Paradise* grapples with theological questions of unheard-of sophistication and in *Inferno* stoops to such terms as 'whore' and 'shit'. His verses have never failed to be repeated wherever the spirit is enlivened, be it in the reading-rooms of the great universities or the barracks of the death camps. The purpose of this book is not to explain why we should read Dante 700 years after his death, because it is a historical work that describes the life of a particular medieval man who had parents, uncles and grandfathers, who went to school, fell in love, married and had children and who fought in battle, got involved in politics and came to experience successes and failures, and wealth and poverty – and yet this man was also one of the greatest poets who ever trod the ground of this planet, 'this paltry plot of land that makes us act so brutally' (*Paradise*, XXII, 151).

CHAPTER ONE

ST BARNABAS'S DAY

On Saturday, 11 June 1289, St Barnabas's Day, the Florentine army, which was marching across the Casentino Valley to invade the territory of Arezzo came into sight of Poppi Castle, which stands on an isolated rock the River Arno circles around. It had departed from Florence nine days earlier, to the sound of the city's bells, and set up camp outside its own city walls to await the arrival of its allies from other Guelph cities. Then it resumed its march until it was half-way between Florence and Arezzo, having travelled fifty kilometres over difficult mountain roads at the slow pace of carts loaded with victuals and drawn by oxen. Below Poppi the valley widened into a plain, which at the time was called Campaldino. It was the first location suitable for deploying and manoeuvring cavalry that the invaders had encountered along their mountainous itinerary. Their enemy was waiting for them, having punctually sealed off the valley floor by lining up its army next to the Franciscan monastery called Certomondo.

Rather than a general, the Florentine army had a management committee, because the world of the medieval city republics abhorred power overly concentrated in the hands of the few, or indeed one man. The leadership consisted of the twelve 'Captains of the War', who were expert knights chosen to represent each of the *sesti*, the six districts Florence was subdivided into. However, their decisions were taken after lengthy discussion which also involved the leaders of the contingents sent from allied cities, as well as those feudal barons who had chosen to side with the Florentines and whose experience of warfare was held in high regard, such as Maghinardo da Susinana, 'a good captain and wise about military matters'. When they sighted the enemy and it was evident that they could go no further without engaging in battle, the captains halted the column and organised a line of defence before meeting to decide on their battle plan.

At the time, the offensive impact of any army depended on the heavy cavalry, wearing chain mail and armed with lance and sword. According to Dino Compagni, who during those months was one of the six elected priors who governed the city and must have known, the Florentine army with its Guelph allies counted 1,300 knights, but they were 1,600 according to Giovanni Villani, who at the time was a small child but was able to collect information and listen to eyewitness accounts. In both cases this was a high figure: in the Middle Ages you could conquer a kingdom with 2,000 knights. There were 600 Florentines, all of whom were wealthy citizens who had to provide their own war horses (citizen knights): 'the best armoured and mounted' that ever came out of Florence, in the opinion of Villani. Not all of them were young and willing. A quarter of them were chosen by the captains, and these 150 *feditori*, as they were called, were placed in the front rank, where they would be the first off if the decision was to charge or the first to suffer the impact of any enemy attack.

We can infer from Villani's narrative that the way these men were chosen provoked a good deal of agitation: everyone understood that it was the most dangerous position to be in. Fortunately there was time: medieval battles only commenced once all the formations had been leisurely put in place. No one wanted to take on such an important challenge without preparing properly, discussing tactics and praying to God for victory. Given the shortage of volunteers, a captain in each *sesto* was charged with ordering some citizens to become *feditori*. Vieri de' Cerchi, the captain of the district of Porta San Piero, caused a sensation by appointing himself, his son and his nephews, and 'because of his good example, he shamed other noble citizens into joining the ranks of the *feditori*'.

Most of the cavalry were positioned at the rear of this vanguard, and the baggage train was drawn up behind them to prevent them from escaping. The rest of the army was made up of citizens of more modest means and peasant contingents organised by the parishes. These fought on foot with pikes, bows or crossbows. Individually they were of little importance, and a knight could rout a dozen of them, but in their thousands they could play their part, particularly in defence and just as long as they could hold together and not break ranks. According to Villani, there were 10,000 of them. There were specialists who held up *pavesi* – large, cumbersome, rectangular shields made of wood; planted on the ground, they served to form a barricade which could shield the bulk of the infantry. Consequently the captains deployed the infantry and the crossbowmen on the flanks to cover the cavalry, and ordered the shield-bearers to place their *pavesi* in front of everyone. These shields were painted white with a red fleur-de-lis, the emblem of the Guelph government in Florence. On the other side, the enemy army had seen the column emerge on the plain and then come to a halt, and among these leaders was the bishop of Arezzo, Guglielmino degli Ubertini, of whom Dino Compagni wrote: 'he knew much more about the business of war than he did of the business of the Church.' Apparently he couldn't understand how this glistening wall had suddenly sealed off the plain. 'Hence the bishop, who was short-sighted, asked, "What are those walls?" And the answer came, "The enemy *pavesi*".'

Once the position had been fortified, the captains and their advisers came together to decide on the plan: essentially it was a question of whether to attack or wait for the enemy to make their move. Being in some doubt, they decided to wait. After the event, it was said that this was a carefully considered decision, on the basis that whoever could hold on would win the day. The infantrymen, who were only lightly armoured, could sit down and take a swig from their marrows, filled with wine, which hung from their belts. The knights, at the most, could dismount, but it would not have been prudent to leave their horses and the majority remained in the saddle. They didn't yet have the heavier articulated armour that European blacksmiths would learn to produce in the following century, but once the fifteen or twenty kilos of chain mail had been put on, it was impossible to remove it until after the battle. Only the huge helmet, which was hot and suffocating, could be left to the final moment and entrusted to a servant, along with the lance, shield and, in the case of the wealthiest knights, the reserve horse.

Dante was among those knights; in fact he was one of the *feditori* in the first line of battle. This is stated in all the text-books on Italian literature, but how can we be sure? The first mention of it appeared in 1436, when the then elderly human-ist Leonardo Bruni wrote a *Life of Dante*. The memory of the Battle of Campaldino was still very much alive as that day con-tributed decisively to Florence's hegemony in Tuscany, and that Dante had fought there was for Bruni something more than a biographical detail. He returned to the question again and again, not without a degree of discomfort because Bruni came from Arezzo and the defeat of his fellow citizens still rankled a little. Yet he was explicit in asserting that this must have been an extremely important event in Dante's life. So much so that he reproached Boccaccio, who wrote one of the first biographies of the poet, for making no mention of it. It would have been better if he had, rather than writing so much nonsense about Dante's love affairs (this could only be expected of Boccaccio, Bruni added maliciously, because this was the argument he was most interested in: 'the tongue goes where a tooth hurts, and those who like drinking talk about wines').[1]

His involvement in the battle demonstrates that, in spite of his life of scholarship, Dante did not live in an ivory tower and once was a young man like all the others – and being a young man also meant going to war when the fatherland required it. 'He was to be found in every youthful activity; so much so that in the great and memorable battle that was fought at Campaldino, he was as well respected as any young man who was to be found under arms and fighting vigorously on horseback in the front rank,' Bruni wrote. The man who selected him to be one of the *feditori* was very probably Vieri de' Cerchi, the future leader of the White Guelphs and a neighbour of the Alighieris in the district of Porta San Piero. Bruni explained how he came to know this: 'Dante wrote about this battle in one of his letters, and he said that he fought there, and set out the battle plan.' Does this note refer to a sketch? Some people interpret it in this sense, given that Bruni elsewhere assures us that Dante 'could draw skilfully with his own hand', and Dante in *Vita Nuova* recalls the moment following Beatrice's death in which 'thinking of her, I drew an angel on a few tablets'. It is, however, more likely that it was merely a passage in which Dante described the battle. We no longer have the letter, but we can certainly rely on Bruni, who was familiar with several letters written in Dante's hand, and he even described the handwriting ('and his writing was thin and long and very correct, as I have seen in some other letters written in his own hand').

Dante scholars, unaware of how a medieval battle was actually fought, have generally imagined that the *feditori* were some kind of light cavalry engaged in skirmishes, but this fantasy is completely misleading. Before battle commenced, it was normal for commanders to allocate specific tasks to particular contingents of knights selected at that moment. This was the case at Campaldino both for the 150 *feditori* in the vanguard and for the 200 knights under the command of Corso Donati, who were held back in reserve, as will become clear later. These different tasks did not imply any difference in weapons and armour or any specialisation: all the knights were armed in the same way. The rules that governed the citizens' military obligations stipulated the equipment in detail, and they were the same for everyone. Each knight had to be equipped, and there were heavy fines for not doing so. A difference in quality and the amount spent was admissible and indeed the norm, but only for the horse.

For this reason there can be no truth in recent arguments that Bruni must have invented the claim that Dante was fighting 'in the first rank' because the poet would not have had sufficient means to own the arms and horse required for a position of that prestige. Dante was profoundly interested and personally involved in the chivalric way of life, which has to be understood as a military and sporting activity for the elite, and his literary works abound with images taken from that world. When he explained that all the artisans working in a particular field had to take instruction from the end-user, the first example that comes to mind is that 'the sword-maker, bridle-maker, saddle-maker, shield-maker and all the trades engaged in supplying the art of chivalry must put their faith in the knight'.[2] We can be certain that he had good horses when we think of the passage from *Convivio* in which he follows the way human desires evolve from infancy to adolescence in terms that may not have been autobiographical but which do reflect the experience of his generation and his social class: 'Thus we can see that small boys at the most desire an apple, and then as time passes they desire a little bird, and then later smart clothing, and then a horse and then a woman.'

Besides, Dante laments in a letter after his exile from Florence that he was 'without arms and horses' because of the unexpected poverty into which he had fallen, and this means that previously he had owned both. As we have seen, at Campaldino he was one of the 600 that Villani had defined as 'the best armoured and mounted' that ever came out of Florence. And he was deployed under the yellow banners of the *sesto* of Porta San Piero, where even in the past they had recruited, according to the chronicler, 'the best cavalry and men of arms in the city'.

Later on, Bruni would quote from a letter in which Dante makes clear that he fought in the battle, but we don't know whether it is the same letter he referred to earlier, as Bruni apparently had read quite a few of these letters. Dante, according to the biographer, spoke 'in one of his letters' of the two months in which he was a prior, and to demonstrate that he was not too young to hold that position Bruni pointed out that, according to the letter, ten years had already passed since the Battle of Campaldino. We don't have the original text, but Bruni quotes the most significant passage (or rather, he translated it, because the original was probably in Latin, as in the case of all Dante's extant letters, even if he did add 'These are his own words'):

ten years had already passed since the Battle of Campaldino, during which the Ghibelline party was nearly all dead or undone. I found myself there bearing arms yet no longer a youth and was very fearful, but in the end overjoyed by the vicissitudes of that battle.

So Dante really did fight at Campaldino. Should there still be some lingering doubt, the *Divine Comedy* provides decisive proof in the twelfth canto of *Inferno*:

I saw the knights strike camp,
commence the battle and parade their valour,
and those who fought as they were fleeing;
I saw the skirmishes across your country.
Oh Aretines, I saw the pillagers sweep through it,
fight tournaments and engage in jousting ...
(*Inferno*, XXII, 1–6)

The first three lines refer to moments in the military campaign and the combat, and the last three describe the devastation inflicted on the territory of Arezzo once the battle was over: the forays in search of plunder and the jousting and competitions played out below the city walls to humiliate the defeated enemy. Everything suggests that Dante was in the army that won on that day at Certomondo, and following the victory he exultantly pushed on as far as the enemy city.

Besides, in the previous canto Dante speaks as an eyewitness to another military encounter during that adventurous summer. He and Virgil are surrounded by devils who have allowed them to pass by but continue to show their hostility, and to give an idea of the terror these travellers suffered, he makes this comparison:

> … thus saw I the fear of soldiers
> who accepted terms in Caprona,
> and found themselves among a hostile horde.
>
> (*Inferno*, XXI, 94–6)

This episode occurred two months after the Battle of Campaldino. Florence sent 'four hundred citizen knights and two thousand foot soldiers' to assist Lucca, which had invaded Pisan lands. Caprona Castle surrendered on 16 August 1289, and the garrison came out with guarantees that their lives were not in danger. Dante, who saw them coming out, was definitely one of the Florentine knights who took part in the expedition, so he must have been called up twice in a couple of months, which only confirms that he was well armed and equipped, and ready to fight.

It was only human to be afraid in the midst of the Malebranche (the demons who appear in Cantos XXI, XXII and XXIII of *Inferno*), but Dante, as we have seen, admits to having been very frightened at Campaldino. And he recalls having seen knights escaping in search of safety. This is not surprising: expert knights had always taught impulsive youths that in war you have to know how to escape from danger, and there's nothing shameful in confessing to being afraid, as long as you know how to keep that fear under control. When, in the *Chanson de Guillaume*, the youthful Vivien vows never to take a step backwards when faced with the enemy, his uncle Guillaume coolly warns him: 'Nephew, you won't last long. Only youths are unafraid at their first battle, because they are still ignorant of danger.' (Philippe de Commynes would say this two centuries later, when he recalled the Battle of Montlhéry, where 'I was less afraid than I have ever been since in combat, because I was young and had no knowledge of danger'.) By declaring his fear, Dante is confirming what he had just asserted and what was most important to him: when he fought at Campaldino, he was no longer an inexpert youngster.[3]

Bruni went further and suggested that Dante had found himself in 'serious danger', and he implied that at the beginning he had fled, as did all the others. The captains had decided to let the enemy attack, and this meant that the line of *feditori* was pushed ahead to take the impact of the enemy charge without being able to counter-attack. It was not easy for the cavalry to stay put and cushion the blow of a charge at the gallop, and the Aretines had decided to stake everything on this initial clash by sending in as many as 350 *feditori*. Consequently the Florentine cavalry was pushed back. 'The Florentine line recoiled dramatically,' Compagni dryly observed. Villani went into more detail: 'the first blow was so powerful that most of the Florentine *feditori* were unhorsed.' A knight was rarely killed or even wounded at the first blow in a clash between two of them, but anyone hit by an enemy lance that came in at the gallop risked flying out of their saddle. This is what happened to most knights obliged to brace themselves in a stationary position and await an attack at the gallop. Was this what happened to Dante? Statistically we would be inclined to say yes, and whether or not this occurred, we can understand the 'serious danger' Bruni referred to and the 'very fearful' state Dante confessed to being in.

Villani claimed that once the *feditori* had been swept away, the main body of the Florentine cavalry was also pushed back but not routed: 'the bulk of the cavalry was pushed back a good part of the field, but they didn't lose heart and they didn't break, but constant and boldly they received the enemy.' Bruni, who had read Dante's letter, was less benevolent and repeated several times that the Florentine cavalry was not only pushed back but routed: 'once routed, they had to flee back to the line of foot soldiers.' However the impetus of the Ghibelline cavalry abated, the wall of shield-bearers absorbed some of it and, having reached the baggage train, the Guelph cavalry recovered its breath. Then the battle transformed into a confused free-for-all in which the Florentines gradually gained the upper hand. This was the only way it could turn out, because the enemy had distanced itself from its infantry and its crossbowmen, while the Florentine crossbowmen were all engaged. Corso Donati, who led the 200 knights held in reserve, charged without awaiting the order, striking the enemy on its flank. As Villani emphasised, the Guelphs had twice the number of knights, as the enemy had no more than 800.

In spite of this, the battle was fiercely fought. Dino Compagni has provided us with a memorable description:

> The crossbow arrows rained down: the Aretines could not respond in kind, and were struck on their flank where they were unprotected. The air was filled with great clouds of dust. Aretine foot soldiers crawled under the horses' stomachs and disembowelled them, while their *feditori* fought so hard that in the midst of the field of battle there were many dead on both sides. That day, many of those who had been known for their bravery were cowards, and many of those who had not been spoken of were brave.

Eventually the inevitable occurred. 'The Aretines were routed, not for cowardice and not for lack of valour, but because they were outnumbered by the enemy. They were put to flight and cut down as they went: the Florentine soldiers, who were accustomed to victories, killed them. The peasants had no pity.' This is what is being said here: for most of the combatants, who were not professionals, it was enough to have routed the enemy, but the *soldiers* (etymologically this word means 'mercenaries'), who knew the common practice for an enemy fleeing the field, pursued them and killed them, as did the local peasants when a fugitive fell into their hands. The clear implication here is that the peasants stood to gain from stripping their victims.

The clouds that had covered the sky during the afternoon, as Dante recalled, were not only of dust. In Canto V of *Purgatory*, Buonconte da Montefeltro, one of the enemy captains killed that day at Campaldino, tells the poet how he died. Dante is all ears, as Buonconte's body was never found and he is curious to know what actually happened to him. The dead man remembered being wounded to the neck and wandering through valleys until he lost his strength. He recalled the humidity of that hot summer afternoon, which increased until, just after sunset, the area filled with fog from Pratomagno to the Apennines. This triggered a thunderstorm, and the mountain streams immediately overflowed and carried the now cold body of Buonconte as far as the Arno, where it decomposed.

Why have we started with this memorable battle? If we want to tell the story of who Dante was, we have to ask the fundamental question of his social position. Now, if the army that had deployed on the plain of Campaldino had been a foreign one – let's say a French or German one, rather than Florentine – it would have been easy to identify his status with certainty. Did the combatant arm himself almost certainly with the assistance of one or two servants? Did he wear chain mail, carry a sword and mount his horse ready to place the large helmet on his head?

And did he insert his left arm behind his shield carrying the colours of his family? Outside Italy, those who fought on horseback were all nobles – that is to say, members of families who handed down land and peasantry from father to son, along with the power of command and the chivalric ideology of courage, comradeship and loyalty. At the very most there could be some doubt about whether the knight belonged to the even more restricted circle of princes and feudal lords who in France were called *li riche home* ('the rich men'), all of whom were related to each other, or to the wider circle of knights in their service. The uncertainty, however, would soon be resolved because the truly wealthy would have more expensive horses, whose price tags could be compared with a luxury car, and carried a flag on their lances, which served as a reference point during battle for those in their service. But both kinds of knights had undergone a ceremony restricted in law to the nobility. Every effort was made to enforce this law, and therefore they were all lords or *domini*, or at least 'little lords' or *domicelli*, as they came to be called once the prohibitive costs of the ceremony of knighthood prevented the head of the family from arming all his sons as knights.

In Italy, however, things were more complicated. It's true that even in the city republics the population was divided between those who fought on horseback, *milites*, and all the others who fought on foot, *pedites*. In Italy the ritual of knighthood still guaranteed admiration, respect and privilege, which included the right to be addressed as *dominus*, which became *messere* in the Italian vernacular. This term is used mistakenly in Italian fiction almost as a universal form of address, when in fact it was reserved for knights, doctors in law and ecclesiastical dignitaries. Thus no one in Florence, where they knew him, would have called Dante *messer Dante* as does a Genoese in one of the stories by Franco Sacchetti, who is overcome by Dante's fame as a poet.[4] In Italy there was no king to impose a law that restricted knighthood to members of particular families, which would have created an exclusive nobility based on law. In Florence anyone who belonged to a rich family and was willing to spend a great deal of money could pay for the ceremony of becoming a knight with all the rights and duties this entailed: a dubbed knight (*cavaliere di corredo*). On the other hand, those who had the money but had no intention of spending it in that manner could be obliged by the republic to provide a warhorse and therefore preferred to mount it in person: these were the citizen knights (*cittadini con cavallate*), of which Dante was one on the day of battle.[5] They were armed and mounted in the same manner as the others, and collectively they were referred to in the sources as knights or *milites*, even though everyone knew that in battle the real knights were slightly more valuable, if only because they identified fully with the role and usually rode on better chargers.

The fact that Dante mounted a horse, put on his helmet and took up his lance before lining up with the other knights in the front row during that anguished moment when they realised that the enemy was advancing and would shortly come crashing into them does tell us, it's true, that he belonged to the upper stratum of urban society, but it doesn't tell us whether he was a noble. We need to be clear about this question too, as it confuses quite a few Dante scholars. Florence did not have a nobility in the sense of a legal entity, as it would have had under the *ancien régime*, before the *comuni* started to become increasingly independent. There were no registers of noble families or of those authorised to display a coat of arms, nor were there trials to demonstrate whether a family was noble, or official acts of ennoblement, all things that in the following centuries would make it a little less difficult to identify who was of noble rank. Nevertheless, whoever was rich in Florence liked to make it known that he wasn't a parvenu, but had respected ancestors, a *gens*, and was therefore *gentile* ('gentle', as in 'gentleman'), which was a word much more current in the vernacular than 'noble'. These were not the heirs of some kind of 'feudal' nobility that had survived preceding centuries, but rather they were citizen families who tended to parade their aristocratic prejudices gradually with each passing generation and increasing antiquity. The *omo altèr* ('proud man') who in one of Guido Guinizzelli's famous songs ('Al cor gentil ...') boasted of being of noble blood ('Gentle because of long lineage') was not a leftover from previous times but, on the contrary, the product of spectacular economic growth in the Italian city-states. But not all those who were dubbed knights and insisted on being called *messere* were noble in this sense: that is, descendants of families who had provided consuls in the city back in the times of Emperor Frederick Barbarossa. They also included people who had made their money more recently, such as the previously mentioned *messer* Vieri de' Cerchi, who was the richest banker in Florence: everyone remembered that it was not long since his people had moved in from the country. All the more reason for there being many new people among common citizens subject to the rule on providing citizen knights. Ultimately, what have we learned about Dante's social status from the fact that he was one of the 150 'best *feditori* in the cavalry'? That he was well armed, had a good horse and was therefore fairly rich, as well as being youngish, sturdy and well trained, but we still don't know whether his family was noble (in the non-juridical sense of *gentile*) and had therefore been rich and powerful for several generations or only in recent times.

There is another detail on this subject that cannot be ignored: among the other preparations for battle, the captains knighted a number of young men on the battlefield, who were thus officially proclaimed dubbed knights. This honour was an expedient for postponing the traditional costs of the ceremony of knighthood and, above all, injecting an extra degree of aggression into the citizens' army, for it was taken for granted that these 'newly appointed knights' would do all they could to avoid

CHAPTER TWO

DANTE AND THE NOBILITY

The question of whether Dante was noble or not remains, and it is not easy to find the answer precisely because the concept itself lacks a rigorous definition. The leading fourteenth-century jurist Bartolo da Sassoferrato wrote unequivocally, 'the word "noble" is ambiguous'. We have clarified that being noble did not mean having a legal title that had been ascertained and was verifiable, but was instead associated in somewhat vague terms with the antiquity of a family and the respect it enjoyed in the city. Besides, these things don't necessarily go together: someone who could have boasted ancient lineage but had no money would have provoked pity or derision. We have no evidence of what the Florentines thought of the Alighieris, but we do know what Dante thought of his family. And this was very important – something that determined his position in Florentine society and his relationships with his friends. This, then, will be our starting-point.

When, in Canto X of *Inferno*, Dante encounters Farinata, the best-known exponent of the Uberti family, which in Florence was considered to be the city's proudest and most ancient nobility, the first thing the man does is ask Dante who his ancestors were, because he doesn't recognise him (*Inferno*, X, 42). It was not the case that any Florentine on meeting someone they didn't know would ask that question, but naturally for nobles, or rather 'gentle men', society was split between those who had ancestors and all the rest. To be clear, it was not necessary to be *very* ancient to nurture such pretensions. During the thirteenth century, families considered noble in Italian cities could almost always trace their ancestry back to someone of the same name who lived some time between the end of the eleventh century and the first half of the twelfth. The Ubertis, who along with the Donatis were among the most ancient factions in the city, were descended from Uberto son of Benzone, a *causidicus* or expert in law, of whose existence there is written evidence from 1085 to 1098.[1] In other words, they too were city-dwellers who had grown wealthy and adopted a chivalric lifestyle. After a few generations they had forgotten their origins and believed themselves to be much more ancient – Villani mentions a rumour that the Ubertis were descended from Catiline![2] They felt entitled to look down on those who only then were setting out on the same trajectory.

Did Dante share these prejudices? Those who recall the arrogance with which he condemns 'the new people and their sudden earnings' will answer in the affirmative. According to the poet, such people were the cause of the moral decline of Florence. Dante was born and lived until he was thirty-five in a city that was immense for the times: with its 100,000 inhabitants it was one of the largest cities in Europe. Its merchants were active in all the cities of Christendom, and its bankers managed the finances of the papacy, a colossal multinational organisation unrivalled in the world for its size. The profits were staggering, vast riches could be quickly accumulated; social mobility was uniquely important and yet greed, envy and fear were increasingly vicious among Florentines, which poisoned their collective existence. Understandably someone like Dante who lived on the margins of this frantic commerce, immersed himself in books and was happy to get by comfortably on unearned income would observe the protagonists in horror. However, this argument is even more complicated, and during his life Dante expressed contradictory ideas about the nobility – that is to say, the importance of having ancestors – suggesting that his ideas on the subject were evolving, and depended on whether he was examining the question in theoretical terms or discussing very practical matters concerning himself and his family.

When he was involved in Florentine politics, Dante wrote the *canzone* (a long poem usually in hendecasyllables) 'Le dolci rime', and a few years later, when he was already in exile, he commented on it in Book IV of *Convivio*. Here he declares that there's no such thing as nobility of blood: nobility means a predisposition to virtue, piety, compassion and valour. This is a gift that belongs to single individuals and not families. This idea is a variant – a very ingenious one because it doesn't firmly identify nobility with virtue but rather with an innate predisposition to behave nobly – of a very old and threadbare cliché widely explored in antiquity by Aristotle, Seneca, Juvenal and Boethius, among others. It resurfaced in the Provençal troubadours and the countless moralists who reflected on the true nature of nobility. It was discussed in schools. Brunetto Latini, who was Dante's teacher, dwelled on it, and Guinizzelli returned to it in the previously mentioned poem 'Al cor gentil'.[3] Like Guinizzelli, Dante was well aware this was a debate between men of letters: for the people who didn't reason but 'barked', nobility meant membership of a family that had been rich for a long time, and virtue had nothing to do with it:

> It is known that Frederick of Swabia, the last of the Holy Roman Emperors, [...] when asked what gentleness consisted of, replied that it was ancient wealth and upright behaviour. And I would say that others were of slighter knowledge, because they thought over every aspect of this definition and removed the second detail, which is upright behaviour, but held on to the first, which is ancient wealth. In my poem, I wonder if someone who did not display upright behaviour himself but didn't want to lose the name

of gentleness, might define it as best befitted him, that is to say the possession of ancient wealth. I would say that this is almost everyone's opinion – everyone follows those who say that people are gentle because of a long lineage of being rich, given that this is what nearly everyone has been barking out.

(*Convivio*, IV, iii, 6–8)

A little further on, Dante confirms once more that this is the universal opinion:

I argue then that this opinion of the people has lasted so long that without other factors or application of reason, 'gentle' applies to anyone who is a son or grandson of some outstanding man, even if he himself is worthless.

(*Convivio*, IV, vii, 2)

Then he goes further still and claims that even ancient lineage is not that important for the people: someone is noble if they are rich, powerful and well connected through their family ties:

Because they see the kinships making society weddings, marvellous buildings, enormous possessions and exten-sive manors, they believe these things to be the reasons for nobility, or rather they believe them to be nobility itself.

(*Convivio*, IV, viii, 9)

Clearly Dante is not a little irritated by this confusion, but he doesn't like the opinion that nobility is based on ancestry either. Further on, in fact, he embarks on the decidedly unrealis-tic argument that nobility cannot depend on antiquity. It cannot commence from a particular moment, which would mean that someone who wasn't noble could suddenly become it, and still less could it depend on people forgetting with the passage of time that a particular family once had humble origins. If it were true 'that nobility starts at the time people forget the low social position of ancestors', this would produce the surreal outcome whereby 'the more forgetful men were, the more they would be noble' (*Convivio*, IV xiv, 5–8), although we know that this was exactly what happened.

However, Dante argues this because he is playing with an ambiguity. In the language of the time, the word 'nobility' was rarely used in the social sense and 'gentleness' (*gentilezza*) was specifically used to indicate the superiority of those who were of noble blood. On the one hand, Dante declares that he is speaking of nobility in the general sense of a predisposition to excelling and standing out, in line with common usage:

> … if we examine the customary usage of speech, this word 'nobility' is understood as perfecting one's own nature in every aspect. Thus it doesn't only refer to man, but to everything: consequently one can talk about noble stones, noble plants, noble horses or noble falcons.
>
> (*Convivio*, IV, xvi, 4–5)

On the other hand, he refuses to acknowledge the difference between the two words and the two concepts: 'gentleness and genuine nobility, which I understand to be the same things' (*Convivio*, IV, xiv, 8). Clearly he plays on this ambiguity between nobility as the world understands it and nobility as the moralist intends it, pretending that they are the same and concluding that in no circumstances can nobility have anything to do with ancestry. He quotes Guinizzelli's song and agrees with him: nobility is a predisposition to virtue, and God plants the seed of this good disposition in individuals, not in lineages. 'So the Ubertis of Florence or Viscontis of Melano shouldn't say, "I am a noble, because I'm of such-and-such descent"; for the divine seed is not sown into a whole family, that is to say a lineage, but is instilled in individual persons' (*Convivio*, IV, xx, 5).

This was a bold statement. The Dante of 'Le dolci rime' and *Convivio*, who was then in his thirties, was a convinced disbeliever in noble blood, and it would be hard to resist the temptation to speculate on the motives for such an extreme position. Was it because he was fully aware that his family was not one that people admired and considered to be noble? Was it perhaps that friends like Guido Cavalcanti and Forese Donati were noble, and he needed to defend his entitlement to exchange sonnets with them and go to social events where most of the guests had pedigreed surnames? Or was this due to the political climate of those years – of the popular government in which Dante played a fairly important role and which made great display of its distrust and fear of noble families? The latter argument initially appears to be the most persuasive, but on further investigation we may be less convinced. In *Convivio*, Dante does not exclude the idea that individual members of the great families could be predisposed to virtue – perhaps even more so than the average passing cobbler. Indeed there's one passage that admits that in some families the number of noble individuals could be higher, and this leaves the way open to the concept of the nobility of families but not the nobility of blood.

We have no reason to believe that this was an attempt by the merchant class to displace aristocratic ideology, as has been too often claimed by commentators who are always ready to attribute to the Italian city-states the rejection of that ideology along with its chivalric culture in the name of bourgeois ideals and virtues. Quite the contrary: all the evidence shows that the urban elite continued to be fascinated by such things, even when they challenged the nobility for the political control of the republic. Dante undoubtedly shared that fascination. Nor am I persuaded by more sophisticated readings of 'Le dolci rime' which claim that Dante had a straightforward political intention – that the song was meant to dispute the legislation excluding noble families from power and sought to 'redefine and renegotiate' the concept of nobility, so as to allow 'media-tion between the people and the magnates'. The reason why Dante wrote *Convivio* in exile was to confirm point by point and expand on the arguments expressed in 'Le dolci rime' a few years earlier. The purpose was not to confirm a theoretical posi-tion that no longer had a political context but to resolve his own existential situation: that of a young man who felt he belonged spiritually to an elite but wasn't too proud of his own relations. Besides, he was active in politics during a period in which there was nothing to gain from claiming to be of noble blood.[4]

However, in *De Monarchia*, which he wrote later (not before the reign of Emperor Henry VII), the tone was very different and the ancestors are back in play:

> Men owe their nobility to virtues, both their own and those of their ancestors. Indeed nobility consists of virtue and ancient wealth, as Aristotle explains in *Politics*, and as Juvenal says, 'Nobility of the mind is only and uniquely virtue.' These two assertions refer to two kinds of nobility: one's own and that of one's ancestors.[5]

We have returned to the definition of nobility found in *Con-vivio* and attributed to Emperor Frederick II, and here Dante correctly takes it back to Aristotle, whose *Politics* he may have just read.[6] In the previous work he developed his argument to the point of denying the importance of the second element, 'ancient wealth', and asserting that the predisposition to virtue was purely individual (man cannot inherit nobility from his ancestors), whereas here the conclusion is somewhat different. We can be noble in two ways: either because we are virtuous or because our ancestors were virtuous. This last nobility is inherited and confers rights. 'Therefore nobles are entitled to precedence for a just reason.' In *De Monarchia*, Dante exalts the figure of Aeneas and concludes that the founder of the empire was noble both because of his own virtue and because of that of his ancestors. Moreover he gained further nobility from prestigious marriages: 'not only on the basis of his virtue, but also that of his progenitors and of his wives; the nobility of the former and the latter merged in him through hereditary right'.

Here Dante was discussing nobility without bringing his own personal story into play – at least not explicitly. On the other hand, he, his family and his ancestors are centre stage when it comes to the theme of nobility in the *Divine Comedy*. The meeting with Farinata degli Uberti is the first occasion, but Dante does not exploit the moment to pursue the argument. The poet, who elsewhere is so willing to reveal his direct speech, here refuses to tell how he replied to Farinata. He only suggests that his reply was to the satisfaction of his haughty interlocutor, and that the man was well acquainted with Dante's ancestors. Of that we can have our own doubts, but this question will never be resolved.

Some years went by before Dante decided to return to the question of his ancestors and therefore his own nobility, and by that stage he was working on *Paradise*. To argue his nobility, he could assert that he was descended from someone who had established his name long ago. Better still, he could declare that members of his family had been knights in the past. This chivalric status was a delicate matter because Dante himself was not a knight: we have seen that at the field of Campaldino other young men, who were in the same row of *feditori* as he was, were knighted in the morning before the battle; he was not. On the other hand, the popular government in which Dante took an active part before his exile had put down on paper that the families who had knights among their number were enemies of the people, and their members could not hold office in the principal governmental bodies. However, this sanction was managed in a deliberately pragmatic manner: it only affected those who had had knights in their family in the previous twenty years. The

Florentine people were willing to leave in peace families that had been illustrious in the past, but had ceased to be threatening some time ago. Dante, who was not a knight and could not claim that his father, grandfather or great-grandfather were either, decided to tell the story of his great-great-grandfather. According to family tradition, he had been a knight.

When the poet was writing Canto XV of *Paradise*, quite a few years had gone by since *Convivio*, and his life had changed profoundly. He no longer wanted to play the part of the moralist who derides noble blood so admired by ignorant people. Dante has no problem with declaring through the mouth of Cacciaguida that his family is ancient too and has more than a century of history behind it:

Oh, offshoot of mine in which I rejoiced,
albeit awaiting, I was your root
...
... The one from which, it's said, came
your surname and that a hundred years and more
spent in the first circle of the mountain [Purgatory],
he was my son and your great-grandfather.

(*Paradise*, XV, 88–9, 91–4)

In other words, the Alighieris have carried this name for four generations, and the ancestor who provided it has been dead for a hundred years. But this is not all: even further back the father of this great-grandfather, Cacciaguida, was a knight and indeed had been knighted in the most honourable manner possible – directly by the emperor himself in acknowledgement of his acts of valour:

Then I followed the Emperor Conrad,
and he knighted me in his army,
and for good works I came to that rank.

(*Paradise*, XV, 139–41)

Emperor Frederick I's predecessor, Conrad III, took part in the disastrous Second Crusade from 1146 to 1148. Cacciaguida promptly declares that he followed his emperor on that campaign and died fighting the infidels. This aura of martyrdom added the final touch to the idealised portrait of the poet's great-great-grandfather. It would not be surprising if Dante had invented this story, albeit with complete conviction perhaps after having dreamed it. But it is more probable that he heard this story at home when he was a child. Florence had cultivated a legend around another Emperor Conrad – the second of his name – who lived in the eleventh century. According to Villani, he liked to sojourn in the city and had favoured it in many ways: 'many Florentine citizens were knighted by his hand and were in his service.' It would have been strange if there weren't some connection between this civic tradition and the private one of Dante's family.

The fact that these were two very different Conrads was not much of a problem, given that commentators of the time, including Dante's son, often got them muddled up. In any event, the important thing was that the Alighieris also had a knight in the family. Fourteenth-century commentators and later Leonardo Bruni understood this well, and would only refer to Cacciaguida as '*messer* Cacciaguida', stressing that title. It was thanks to that *messer* that Dante could declare his nobility – a claim that would never have entered his head when he was attending the councils of the people's government in Florence but more understandable for someone who lived in Verona as the guest of a chivalric prince like Cangrande della Scala.

There followed one of those extraordinary moments in which Dante observed himself objectively and smiled at his own weakness, because it was a weakness to boast of one's own noble blood, and the author of *Convivio* and admirer of Guinizzelli had not forgotten this. But this was a weakness shared by all men, and therefore something that can make us smile rather than incite our indignation, for this is the way the world works. This, but not this alone, is a weakness that the author indulged in while in Paradise, where nothing can exist which is not both good and just, is no longer a weakness.

> Oh noble blood, such a wretched thing,
> I would never marvel, should people
> boast of it down there
> where affections languish,
> as here where appetite obeys [reason] –
> in Heaven I say, I once did glory in it.*

Having confessed this, Dante allowed himself the luxury of reviving the opinion he'd expressed in the past: not the one in *Convivio*, which was beyond recovery, but the one in *De Monarchia*. He restated the idea that nobility inherited from ancestors would eventually be reduced to nothing if it weren't continuously buttressed with a daily dose of new acts of virtue.

> Truly you're a cloak that quickly shortens [with wear on
>   the lower hem]
> so too does time go around with its scissors [reducing
>   your stature],
> if you don't restore it day by day [with good works].
>   (*Paradise*, XVI, 1–9)

---

*In other words: 'I'm not at all surprised that people down here on earth take such pride in a miserable thing like noble blood, because I took such pride up there in Paradise where there is no place for vain desires.'

CHAPTER THREE

CACCIAGUIDA AND THE OTHERS

This is what Dante apparently knew or thought he knew about the founder of the Alighieri line. But we may know something else: a parchment in the State Archive of Florence states that on 28 April 1131 Gerardo, son of Benzone and his wife Gasdia, daughter of Genesulo, rented out to their nephew Brodario, son of Rodolfo, a house with the surrounding land, next to the Badia of Florence. We can read among the witnesses to the contract the name Cacciaguida, son of Adamo. Is this Dante's great-great-grandfather? The dates do not exclude it. Obviously there's no certainty, but the name is rare enough to incline us to believe it is, although at the time Florentines went a little wild with their names. If true, we would also know that the great-great-grandfather's name was Adamo, something the poet doesn't appear to have known. The Badia district was where the Alighieris would live, which is another argument in favour. It is also interesting to note that Gerardo was the brother of Judge Uberto, the progenitor of the Uberti, who were also rooted in that district: Cacciaguida moved in the upper circles of Florentine society.

There is nothing in the document to suggest that Cacciaguida was a knight, but Dante would not have been concerned as in his imagination his great-great-grandfather was knighted by the emperor during the crusade, which was many years later. This is the moment to reveal that Dante didn't have any idea of what it meant to be noble or a knight in the Florence of Cacciaguida.

He was applying the criteria of his own times: being knighted was a magnificent ritual and an honour restricted to an exclusive elite. Villani wrote that at the time of the clashes between the magnates and the people, and therefore the time of Dante's youth, there were around 300 dubbed knights. Following their induction ceremony they were required to pursue a relentlessly ostentatious lifestyle which came with negative political consequences for the knight and his whole family during the time of popular government. But in twelfth-century Florence the ceremony of knighting was unknown, and all citizens who could equip themselves with arms and horses were considered knights – that is, *milites*. Whether Cacciaguida the son of Adamo was one of them is not something we can infer from the document.

There is no archival source that confirms the family tradition Dante believed in: that Cacciaguida had married a Lombard woman ('my woman came to me from the Po Valley') and that it was through her that the family took the name of Alaghieri, which would become the family surname. Nor is there evidence that Cacciaguida's brothers were called Moronto and Eliseo, as Dante has him tell us in Canto XV of *Paradise*; to be clear, these names did exist in the twelfth century, and the Elisei or Alisei were one of the city's noble families in Dante's times, but we don't have any documentary evidence of this shared descent from a distant past. Everyone can make their decision as to whether to trust this family memory – either being persuaded that some things could never be invented or ignoring them because, as we must surely know, the likelihood of invention over such an extended period was considerable.

The Great-Grandfather Alaghieri

Fifty-eight years pass by before we come across another document concerning Dante's ancestors in the Badia's archive, the richest source for Florentine history in this period. On 9

December 1189 Alaghieri and his brother, sons of the late Cacci-aguida ('Preitenittus et Alaghieri fratres, filii olim Cacciaguide'), promised the rector of the church of San Martino del Vescovo that they would cut down a fig tree on their property which threatened to damage the church wall. This is a few steps away from the abbey and the house that today is presented as Dante's home. Alaghieri was Dante's great-grandfather as well as the ancestor who first bore the family name. As for Preitenitto, it has to be said that if the Florentines had a taste for unusual names, Dante's family were second to none in this. And the fig tree? Disputes between neighbours were a daily occurrence at the time, as perhaps they are in all eras. In the same year the priest Tolomeo, who was the rector at the church of San Martino, was involved in a dispute with the Donatis, who were already a powerful and prestigious family, as well as being residents of the same district. According to Enrico Faini, who has recently been studying these controversies, this is sufficient to demonstrate that Alaghieri must also have enjoyed high social status.

Can we be sure that this is the case? The only other docu-ment in which Alaghieri appears is dated 14 August 1201, and this time it is a public deed that concerns the city-state: two counsellors to the supreme magistrate (the *podestà* in each medi-eval city-state was a professional, often appointed for relatively short periods, who administered justice and commanded the army), *messer* Paganello da Porcari, had agreed a transaction, for purposes unknown to us, with the Republic of Venice in the presence of 'Allagerii, son of Caciaguida, and his son'. The document is a copy carried out fifteen years later, and the notary who copied it was unable to understand the name of Alagh-ieri's son, something that at this stage should not surprise us too much: who knows what name they came up with! However, the fact that Alaghieri was present at this legal process appears to confirm that he was effectively a person of a certain standing. He was not, however, a member of that exclusive aristocracy, consisting of about fifty families, whose members were usually elected consuls and covered all the government positions. Faini, who is undoubtedly the expert on Florence during those years, made every effort to obtain documents shedding some light on the social status of Dante's ancestors, but it is significant that in all his previous detailed analyses of the city's ruling group he never cited a Cacciaguida or an Alaghieri.

A few particularly obscure allusions that Dante puts in the mouth of his great-great-grandfather do allow us to speculate about whether Alaghieri married into one of the powerful families, becoming the son-in-law of one of the most influential figures in Florence at the time: Bellincione di Berta, or 'Bellincion Berti' as Dante calls him. This man was one of the witnesses to the treaty between the Florentines and the Sienese in 1176, and is respectfully recalled by Cacciaguida in Canto XV of *Paradise*. The only son of Alaghieri whose name we know was in fact called Bellincione, and he was Dante's grandfather as well as being the first member of the family for whom we possess a relatively substantial documentation. The name is not rare, and would not on its own be sufficient for any hypothesis, and in the same generation as Alaghieri at least one Donati and one Adimari, exponents of families of the highest level, gave the name Bellincione to their sons, but Dante, through the words of Cacciaguida, implies that they did it because they were both sons-in-law of Bellincione Berti. Elsewhere he casually observes that everyone who took the name of the 'great Bellincione' was of the same family. Did this mean that his grandfather Bellincione took his name for the same reason from his maternal grandfather? The main objection is that if Alaghieri had married a daughter of Bellincione Berti, wouldn't Dante have said this more explicitly, rather than refer to it in such a cryptic manner? His son *messer* Piero, one of the first commentators on the *Comedy*, was convinced that this was the case, but this is not enough to dispel our doubts: he also knew very well that such prestigious relations from the past were something to be proud of.[1]

Grandfather Bellincione and His Sons

Scholars are stunned by the fact that Dante has Cacciaguida say that Alaghieri died more than a hundred years ago while we know that he was still alive in 1201, but their astonishment is out of place: Dante, as was normal, didn't know exactly when his grandfather died. At the time a family's collective memory was not necessarily any more tenacious than our own. The famous preacher Jordan of Pisa, a contemporary of Dante, complained in one of his sermons that people seemed to have little *pietas* towards their dead ancestors: 'Today no one knows who their great-great-great-great-grandfather was; even the great-great-grandfather or the great-grandfather is promptly forgotten.'

In the following generation, that of grandfather Bellincione, the sources start to be more plentiful, although Dante never mentions him once in his writings. Bellincione, son of Alaghieri, is referred to in more than forty legal documents between 1232 and 1270: this figure is very high for a Florentine of his generation and confirms that he was a person of some importance. The fact that he was still alive in 1270 demonstrates that Dante must have known him, although it is difficult to know what memories he retained of him.* Who was this Bellincione?

Two documents show that he was active in the political life of the city-state. On 14 December 1240 'Bellincione Alachieri' was present in the palace of the Abati family when the supreme magistrate of Florence authorised one Alberto, who held a credit

---

* Three of Bellincione's sons appear in contracts as Burnecto Alagherii, Gerardum Alagerii and Bellum Bellincionis; the lack of 'the late' (*olim*) suggests that Bellincione was still alive, but it is strange that the three brothers were using such different conventions.

of 120 pounds (*lire*) owed by some men from San Gimignano, to recoup from any other inhabitant of that locality up to the full reimbursement value, in accordance with the current law of reprisal – a wonderful example of how the Italian city-states defended the financial and commercial interests of their inhabitants. On 10 November 1251, just a year after the establishment of the so-called government of the First People, in which the entrepreneurial and artisanal classes took power from the oldest and richest families, some of whose members had been properly inducted to the status of knighthood, 'Bellincione Allagherii' was taking part in an enlarged council in the cathedral of Santa Reparata which included the whole impressive array of the different bodies governing the city: the Elders of the People, the General and Special Councils of the Republic, the Confidential Council (*consiglio di credenza*, a council of wise men, councillors and *silenziari* who imposed secrecy on the proceedings, which provided legal opinion to the consuls, should they require it), the Council of the Captain of the People, and the standard-bearers (*gonfalonieri*, who also had leading roles in guilds or corporations, although the most important *Gonfaloniere di Giustizia* oversaw the government of six priors) and rectors of the guilds. This came to a total of 206 members. We don't know which of these bodies Bellincione belonged to, although we could infer from the registration of his name among the last of them that he was one of the leading figures in the guilds, which were merchant and artisanal corporations. The assembly had been called to ratify an important alliance with Genoa and Lucca against Pisa. The participation of so many councillors was typical of popular government, and says little about the social status of Bellincione, except that he was economically active and paid his taxes.

The other documents available to us concern Bellincione's business affairs but, although they are numerous, they only give us a partial view of what he was up to, because almost all of them come from the papers of one particular notary in Prato, Iacopo di Pandolfino, who recorded legal documents relating to a single, if highly complicated, business transaction in 1246 and a few other transactions also in Prato, which continued at intervals until 1250. We cannot know how many notarial records in Florence have been lost and how many similar documents they may have contained. In the 1246 transaction Bellincione was acting jointly with his sons – all six of them: Alighiero, Burnetto, Drudolo, Bello or Belluzzo, Gherardo and Donato. At the time sons were subject to their father's legal authority until his father's death unless he emancipated them, which required a contract by deed. Alighiero, who appears here for the first time and will later be Dante's father, declares that he has been emancipated and can act of his own volition even though his father was still alive, and this was probably also true of Burnetto and Drudolo. The three younger sons were still under their father's rule and acted with Bellincione's consent. In accordance with legal requirements, it was certified that Bello and Gherardo were over eighteen years old and that Donato was over fifteen. Calculating on the basis of one son per year, we can infer that Alighiero – in all likelihood the oldest – must have been at least twenty-two years old, but probably quite a bit older, because with six males of adult age statistically there must also have been a few daughters as well as a few children who died in childhood. Thus Alighiero would have been over forty by the time Dante was born in 1265. The poet had an elderly father who soon died and with whom he never had a close relationship. In all his works there is not a single mention of him.[2]

Although we have the records of the notary in Prato, the business affairs of Bellincione and his six sons are far from transparent because the documents were often drawn up, even then, to obscure the reality that lay behind them rather than reveal it accurately. However, we can ascertain that the sums involved were sizeable but not enormous. The main transaction, which is worth describing in detail as it gives us an idea of the financial status of Dante's family, was as follows: on 21 March 1246 Bellincione and his sons sold twenty-five plots of land in the vicinity of Prato, along with its rents in grain paid by the respective tenant farmers, to the knight *messer* Toringo of the late Pugliese for 140 pounds. The total area of land did not exceed ten hectares, because landownership at the time was extremely fragmented. The contract specifies that the tenant farmers had to bring the grain to their master's house in Prato every year. Hence Bellincione and his sons had a house in this city, and every year after the harvest around fifteen peasants came there to pay their rent.

We do not know why the family had these assets in Prato, but the factional struggles that were raging in Florence during that period could be a clue. These were the first struggles between factions that took on the names of Guelphs and Ghibellines, and were the cause of repeated exoduses of Guelph families from the city, driven by violence or threats. This was the first of the two episodes Farinata referred to when speaking about Dante's forebears: 'twice I scattered them.' Did Bellincione and his family move to Prato because the Ghibellines temporarily prevailed in Florence, where they were now *personae non gratae*? This is not impossible, but there is the not insignificant problem that Prato was also governed by Ghibellines. As for the land that Bellincione and his sons sold to *messer* Toringo, this was probably the fruit of their money-lending activities, for which we have proof, and thus confiscated from insolvent debtors: in those times people did not like to sell property inherited from relations whereas they were much more relaxed about selling assets they had recently come into possession of. This suggests that Bellincione and his sons had sold the land in order to have liquidity to reinvest in loans. The demand for cash was always high, but in Prato during those months of 1246 it must have been particularly strong as Frederick of Antioch, the son of Emperor

Frederick II and the Imperial Vicar of Tuscany, had set himself up in Prato and the city was spending vast sums – and therefore increasing taxes – in order to maintain him.

The fact that Bellincione used this opportunity to set up his oldest son, Alighiero, as a money-lender also suggests that this was his principal activity (to avoid confusion, we'll call him Alighiero, although at the time he must have been called Alighieri or Alaghieri, like his grandfather). In fact his father, Bellincione, and his five sons delegated him to collect the payment, and *messer* Toringo paid the first instalment of 100 pounds into Alighiero's hands. The same day he took the sum as a loan from his father and brothers, while undertaking to return it within five years at the interest rate to be fixed by the father. All in the same day, he then lent a sum of 28 pounds and 12 shillings (*soldi*) at very high annual rates of interest, 20 or even 25 per cent. This was a complex business, and we should not delude ourselves that we can understand everything from a parchment, but we can speculate that the time had come for Bellincione to introduce his sons to the family business. The notarial records of Iacopo di Pandolfino, who at the time would not have been short of work, show that a second son, Burnetto, was also in business on his own and lending money, also in Prato. He had lent the small sum of 3 pounds and 10 shillings for six months, and this gave him a return of 10 shillings at an annual interest rate of 28.5 per cent. However, Burnetto was involved in business dealings on a much grander scale and duration, which show him to be a professional money-lender. In Prato during May 1246 he collected the full payment of a debt of 47 pounds, including interest, from *messer* Aldobrandino of the late Pugliese. This debt covered three loans in the past to the payer's father-in-law, *messer* Dagomari of the late *messer* Grazia, and he granted another loan of 16 pounds to *messer* Dagomari. Readers may want to know the value of 1 pound (*lira*) at the time, and it is difficult to calculate it with any certainty, because prices and salaries worked in a very different way from the current ones. Yet we would not be too wide of the mark if we valued it as a few hundred euros or dollars today. The sum Burnetto collected could have been worth between €15,000 or 20,000: neither international bank credits nor the stuff of pawnbrokers.

If we then add that most of these contracts were signed at the business premises of a well-known merchant and money-lender in Prato, Accordo di Segadore, and that Burnetto and Alighiero appear on many occasions as witnesses to loans that he granted, it becomes even clearer that Bellincione's sons were very familiar with the circles in which money was lent out and interest accrued. The world of money-lending was subject to sophisticated regulations, and three contracts in 1249 show Burnetto fulfilling another role, that of guarantor. Money-lenders often demanded that debtors provide surety in the form of guarantors, who undertook to pay the creditor in the event of the debtor proving to be insolvent. This could be done by friends or relations as a favour but also by professionals who obviously counted on a return in exchange for the risk they were taking on. As late as 1270 we find that one of Dante's youngest uncles, Gherardo, was involved in a loan transaction: he was present along with a certain Cambio della Lippa, both acting as guarantors for two creditors of the Republic to certify that the two had been repaid in full and there were no further sums to be recovered. On this occasion, he declared that he had been emancipated by his father, who must therefore have still been alive, and that he was a professional money-changer.

The fundamental question is whether Dante's father, grandfather and uncles were usurers. Technically, at least, there can be no doubt about this, and not only because of the excessive interest rates they demanded. Theologians and jurists were agreed that any loan defined as a contract to lend money against the payment of interest was to be considered usury. In the contracts signed by Bellincione and his sons it is clearly stated that they were granting 'loans' that stipulated an interest payment. But this theoretical position had few social consequences, because during this period of dramatic economic growth experts in canon law were beginning to distinguish between different categories and classified as usurers only those who made their living professionally by lending small sums – in other words, the medieval equivalents of a loan shark. These were isolated individuals, occasionally recent immigrants who owned small, run-down business premises and were despised by their neighbours – a figure that would resurface in other periods of spectacular economic growth, like Scrooge in *A Christmas Carol*.

Money-lending was in great demand and so profitable that it attracted people of the highest social status. Thus the canonists, not without hypocrisy, avoided mention of loans or usury, and preferred to declare that such respectable citizens were contributing to the public interest by increasing the circulation of money. Moreover, they could have put their capital to other uses, so when they chose to lend money to their peers in order to help them with their businesses they were taking on a risk for which they had to be compensated. Bellincione and his sons, who were probably not interested in such refinements and had no problems with using such words as 'loans' and 'interest', were not involved in usury but were instead reputable businessmen who had their fingers in every pie where money was to be made. Of course, money-lending may not have been their principal business activity. It's true that the contracts that have survived demonstrate an evident commitment to dealing in money rather than, say, trading in cloth, but it was in the nature of money-lending to leave behind a substantial body of paperwork which was more carefully looked after than that produced by trading in goods.

In conclusion, Dante's relations were respectable representatives of the 'people' or commoners, as this term was understood in the Italian city-states. They were the kind of people who came to the fore in politics when the popular regime was imposed for the first time in Florence in 1250. So it is not surprising that we find Bellincione taking part in the enlarged council in 1251, just after a genuine revolution in the city. Readers would not be mistaken if they detect a shift in social position between Cacciaguida and Alaghieri on the one hand and Bellincione on the other. In the first half of the thirteenth century many of the families that had been influential under the consular government of the city-state had reinforced their position and were now considered nobles – but not all of them, and it appears that Dante's ancestors were not among them.

The 'Alighieris'

They were respectable without being noble, then, but did they at least have a surname? If we want to find Dante's place in Florentine society at the time, we need to clarify whether he belonged to a family identified with a surname and, if so, for how long. At the time and for quite a few more centuries, a man of the people in Tuscany was known by his own name and the name of his father. In the first contract in which the grandfather Bellincione appears in 1232, Ubaldino the notary, son of the late Guispardo, borrowed 12 pounds from Buonaiuto, son of the late Ponzio, and he had as guarantor Albertino the notary, son of Guida. Such men would obviously have had some brothers, uncles and cousins, but they did not have a surname, and one would have had to have known them personally to know who their relatives were. Then there were the families who had a surname. They wouldn't have called themselves Buonaiuto of the late Ponzio, but Guido Cavalcanti or, at the very least, Guido di *messer* Cavalcante Cavalcanti if you had to distinguish between him and another Guido. In thirteenth-century Florence – before then no one in the city had a surname – having a surname signified belonging to a family, by which I mean an influential and well-known family, which was in turn related to other distinguished families. Having a surname was like having a coat of arms: it wasn't something everyone had, and it denoted high social standing. Those who belonged to a family with a surname were immediately identifiable: they were, above all, people who counted more than any old Buonaiuto of the late Ponzio.

This was, however, an entirely informal procedure, because there was no registry of births and deaths to allocate surnames, which were instead created by custom and usage. The families with a surname were those who people knew because the family counted in Florentine society and acted collectively in the city's political vicissitudes or simply because in a given moment a single man had become important and his descendants took his name. Did they constitute a nobility? No, we couldn't go that far. Possession of a surname did not provide a legal privilege, and anyone who made money could expect their name to become the surname of their descendants, as in the case of the chronicler Giovanni Villani, who was actually called Giovanni of Villano of Stoldo but whose descendants called themselves Villani.

Dante was proud to have a surname that had reached its fourth generation. This is the meaning of Cacciaguida's reference: 'he from whom your lineage took your surname'. In fact, the notary Bencivenni of the late Bencivenni of Borgognone names, in the document from 1240 in which Bellincione appears as the witness for the Florentine government, such people as Piero of the late Ildebrandino and Pegolotto of the late Ardingo, and also people with a surname, like Rainaldo di Giraldo Chiarmontesi. So how are we to interpret the fact that he registers Dante's grandfather as Bellincione Alachieri? Strictly speaking, the Latin version could be translated as 'Bellincione of Alaghieri', but by this date Bellincione's father was undoubtedly dead and so we would expect it to be 'of the late Alaghieri'; as this is not the case, it looks as though the notary believed the Alighieris to be a family, like the Chiarmontesis. But they don't appear to be a well-known family, because when Bellincione's sons appear in documents from 1246 onwards they are not called Alighiero and Burnetto Alighieri but Alighiero son of Bellincione and Burnetto son of Bellincione. It's true that here we are mainly in Prato or Fucecchio, whereas in Florence in 1255 the younger brother Drudolo is recorded as Drudolo of Bellincione Alaghieri. Lastly, the Book of Montaperti of 1260, the codex that binds together the registers of the Florentine army captured by the Sienese at the Battle of Montaperti, refers on one page to a Burnettus de Alagheriis. This is the first irrefutable evidence that in Florence they spoke of the Alighieris (or, to be precise, the Alaghieris). They were not nobility, but they were separating themselves from the mass,[3] and this was five years before Dante's birth.

Chapter Four

THE ALIGHIERI CLAN

The Coat of Arms

Having demonstrated that they were a family, it would not be fanciful to question whether the Alighieris also had a coat of arms. Or rather, it would not be fanciful if we learn to reason as they did, because today the question appears to be wholly irrelevant, and in fact modern biographers usually don't even consider the matter. In part this is due to a healthy scepticism about a later tradition that attributes to the family the canting arms with a golden wing on a dark blue field, which was based on an improbable and supposedly erudite interpretation of the surname: *Aligerii*, bearers of wings. This coat of arms was already in use in the sixteenth century among the descendants of *messer* Piero, and it is still used by heirs of the maternal line, the counts Serego Alighieri – it can be seen on the labels of their bottles of Valpolicella produced on the family vineyard. It is almost certain that no one had come up with this contrivance when Dante was alive, but this does not mean that he didn't consider coats of arms to be important, as can be gleaned from many passages in his works.[1]

Giuseppe Pelli, an early nineteenth-century biographer, claimed to have seen a book of heraldry of 1302 which showed the coat of arms of the Alighieris. Heraldic books were sumptuously illustrated manuscripts in which heralds gathered together the coats of arms of the more prominent families of a city or a region, so that they would be recognisable at tournaments.

The Alighieris' coat of arms was, according to Pelli, 'divided in the middle vertically into one part golden and the other part black, with a white band running across it horizontally'. There is no longer any trace of this book but, because of the manner in which Pelli described it, it seems improbable that this was an invention of his. The fact is that anyone who was rich enough to be required to equip a citizen knight would certainly have had a coat of arms. At the Battle of Campaldino, Dante would have had a shield, and any knight at the time would have painted their family colours on it. In the absence of alternative information we cannot exclude the possibility that these were the colours: gold on the left and black on the right with a horizontal white band.

Alighiero's Family

As we have seen, Dante's father started his business career in 1246, having been emancipated by his own father. The few remaining papers that mention him are also concerned with business. In 1254 he took on the role of legal representative for the monks of San Salvatore di Fucecchio in a dispute between them and two nobles of Pogni, near Certaldo, which was to be judged by the Florentine authorities. It arose from the fact that the monks were in debt to the nobles and risked sequestration unless they came to an agreement with their creditors, and it is very probable that Alighiero not only represented them but also advanced them the money they had to pay out on that occasion. In 1257 Alighiero lent 20 pounds, to be repaid in a year, to the widow of the knight *messer* Ristoro da Montemurlo, and the contract for once did not stipulate the interest rate. After this date, Dante's father isn't mentioned in any document – unless he is the 'domino Adhygerio Adhygerii' who along with his *societas* provided a loan requested by the city-state of Bologna in 1270, together with a large number of other lenders, mostly

Florentines (the notaries of Bologna were generous in applying the title of *dominus* to all their distinguished customers with a casualness that would have been unthinkable in Florence).

The lack of references to Alighiero contrasts with the more abundant information on his brothers, particularly Burnetto. The oldest of Dante's uncles was listed in the Book of Montaperti as one of the infantrymen of the unit which stood guard over the *carroccio* in the contingent of the *sesto* of Porta San Piero (the *carroccio* was a large four-wheeled cart, drawn by oxen, which carried a bell and the standards of a medieval Italian city-state into battle as a symbol of its independence). We should not jump to any conclusions about the social status of Burnetto on the basis of the important task entrusted to his unit here. What matters is that he fought on foot with a spear, like the great majority of the citizens assembled for the military expedition, and was not one of the elite and wealthier citizens who fought on horseback, as would be the case a generation later for his nephew Dante. Slightly more significant is the fact that, when the army set up camp on the Sienese hills, Burnetto was one of the six men charged with marking out and widening the pathway inside the camp. This was not a particularly prestigious task, and the other five were commoners like him, people of no account.

The campaign came to its disastrous outcome, but Burnetto survived. In 1268 Florence was restored to the Guelphs thanks to the victories of Charles of Anjou, and we find him again, this time as the superintendent of the prison at the Pagliazza Tower. It should be emphasised that this was not a state appointment but a private contract for which he was paid. In 1275 the city-state of Prato had to send a notary to Florence 'over the Burnetto Allachieri affair': Dante's uncle (Dante was ten at the time) was demanding repayment of 12 pounds owed by someone in Prato and never paid, so the city-state of Prato had to pay. In 1278 Burnetto (Brunectus de Aligeri) turns out to be a member of two councils, the general one and the Council of the Ninety, which went into a joint session with the Councils of the Consuls of the Major and Minor Guilds to discuss the dispute between the republic and the Francisan friars of the monastery of Ognissanti: it is the last document which demonstrates that one of Dante's uncles was still alive.

As for Alighiero, we cannot even be sure that he was still alive when his wife gave birth to Dante in May 1265 – except that there is evidence that after Dante he had another son, Francesco, by another wife. Readers will quite reasonably ask why we have so far only spoken of men, so much so that we haven't even mentioned the name of Dante's mother. The fact is that the information that has come down to us has all been sourced from documents that concern business and politics, two circles in which only men could move at the time. We would know nothing of Alighiero's two marriages, not even the names of the two women, if marriage at the time hadn't constituted a financial transaction. At the core of the agreement was the dowry, whose return to the assignees could cause protracted legal disputes. Thus we know the name of Dante's mother, *monna* Bella, solely because of the settlement of 1332, when the inheritance was shared out between Dante's sons, Iacopo and *messer* Piero the judge, and their uncle Francesco. The agreement establishes that the two nephews must warrant the part of the family assets allocated to the uncle against any legal claim, even in relation to the dowry of their grandmother, *monna* Bella, who was Alighiero's first wife. We also know that Alighiero had a second wife after her for the same reason – the settlement also mentioned the dowry of *monna* Lapa, Francesco's mother and Alighiero's second wife.*

---

* In Florence all married women were called *monna*, which the notaries Latinised as *domina*, which did not have the same connotations of ranks as the male equivalent. We don't know why some Dante scholars think that the name Bella was a contraction of Gabriella.

There remains the question of which family Bella belonged to. We should point out here that Dante was a contraction of Durante, a fairly common name in Florence but unknown to the Alighieri family, so it has always been thought to originate from his mother's family. There is a theory, based on no hard evidence at all, that she was one of the Abatis, as they did use that forename quite often. In a contract of 1297 which we'll return to again, *messer* Durante the judge of the late *messer* Scolaio degli Abati was one of the guarantors for a large loan that Dante took on, and many have imagined that the maternal grandfather was this same *messer* Durante, who was exiled a few months after Dante in September 1302. This theory, however, cannot be true. The first reference to *messer* Durante of *messer* Scolaio appears in 1289, and during the period immediately before this he was a student in Bologna: it is therefore highly unlikely that he could be Dante's grandfather; furthermore Dante himself was studying in Bologna at the same time! If Bella's father was a Durante degli Abati, the chronology suggests that he was *dominus* Durante Renerii Rustici de Abatibus, one of the Ghibellines who was sent into internal exile in 1268 after the Guelphs returned to power in Florence. He was also the uncle of *messer* Durante of *messer* Scolaio, and therefore the cousin of Dante's wife. But, we repeat, there is nothing to confirm this. On the other hand, we know that Alighiero's second wife was *monna* Lapa, the daughter of Chiarissimo Cialuffi, apparently a merchant of a much more modest social background than the wealthy family of the Abatis which included dubbed knights.

No one knows when Alighiero died. The first document to record that he was deceased is from 1283, and several scholars, unaware of the lack of logic, 'assume' that he died in 1282 or 1283, or even speak of 'his death in 1283'. In reality he must have been dead some years earlier: Bruni tells us that '[Dante's] father died in his childhood', using for 'childhood' the Latin word *pueritia*, which then referred to ages from seven to fourteen, meaning that Alighiero was dead by 1279.[2] Dante, as we know, did not mention him in any of his works, but his friend Forese Donati does refer to him in what for us is a very cryptic and intriguing manner during an exchange of insulting sonnets by which they teased each other. The crudity of these poems has long caused consternation among Dante scholars, but they were nothing more than an amusing literary game. Dante accuses his friend of not keeping his wife warm in bed; Forese responds with a story about having met the ghost of Dante's father, who is also having a hard time:

> and I found Alaghier in the graveyard,
> tied to a knot I know not the name of –
> was it Solomon's or some other sage's?
> So I crossed myself facing east,
> and that fellow said, 'For love of Dante,
> untie me!' I could not see how …

Obviously there are innumerable theories about what such an obscure text could mean. Are the graves just any graveyard or specifically paupers' graves, or the ones for heretics, suicides and usurers outside the city walls, or even those of a prison – perhaps a debtors' prison? The knot that ties the restless soul could be an illicit profit that should be returned, an offence against the family honour or even a suspicion of heresy. This last theory arises from the play on words concerning 'Solomon's knot', which refers to a familiar decorative motif in Christian art but possibly also to the activities of the notorious Dominican inquisitor *fra* Salomone da Lucca between 1281 and 1283, just after Alighiero's death. He held posthumous trials in Florence for heresy which created quite a sensation. But the theory that Forese was referring to the communal graves for usurers is the most credible: perhaps it isn't chance that the usurer Reginaldo degli Scrovegni from Padua, on seeing Dante passing by in Canto XVII of *Inferno*, asks him sharply, 'What are you doing in this graveyard?'

That it was something to do with debts, one way or another, seems plausible given Dante's response, which prophesies that his friend Forese will be the one to end up in prison pursued by injunctions. In the following sonnet Forese responds that, when it comes to poverty, no one can better Dante's family; it is only thanks to his sister and his half-brother, 'Tana and Francesco', that Dante hasn't ended up like Uncle Belluzzo, but in any case it is only to be expected that Dante will end up with just his shirt in a hospice. At this stage Dante comes back very force- fully, declaring that Forese is not his father's son and that people keep an eye on their purses when they see him approaching. The mention of this induces Forese in his final response to have another go at Dante's father, Alighiero: I may not be my father's son, but it is only too clear that you are your father's:

> I know full well you're Alaghieri's son,
> and also take note of vengeance so fine
> and clear-cut you inflicted on a fellow who
> changed him one groat all of two days ago.
> If he'd cut it a quarter, why the haste to
> make up and make peace [with a scoundrel] …

Alighiero is remembered for a money-changing transac- tion in which he was cheated and Dante didn't know how to get revenge on his father's behalf. It is difficult to believe that he is speaking literally of a groat, which was the name given to many coins but all of them silver and therefore of derisory value. It was probably a manner of speaking for a transaction of greater value that went badly wrong. Later Dante inherited the dispute from his dead father and couldn't have been in a greater hurry to come an agreement with the opposite party had he killed someone, running the risk of a blood feud. Critics are unanimous in suggesting that 'two days ago' is a humorous way of saying a long time ago. The only thing that's certain is that, when Forese speaks of Dante's father, the first thing that springs to mind is that he was very good with money!

Adventurous Lives: The Cousins on Bello's Branch of the Family

The portrait of Dante's family would not be complete without introducing the cousins, whose lives provide a magnificent cross-section of the world Dante's family belonged to, split as it was between the matter-of-fact reality of business dealings and aristocratic pretensions. The grandfather Bellincione had a brother, Bello, and this Bello went on to have a son, Gualfreduccio, who by 1237 was an adult, as he took part in a collective oath of allegiance by members of the Guild of Calimala, which gathered together all the most important merchants of the city. These men could have been of the same social standing as the great families of knights and sometimes were in fact members of them. For example, in 1237 Tegghiaio Cavalcanti was one of the consuls and the ceremony took place in the Cavalcanti family tower. More so than in the case of Bellincione and his sons, what we have here is a family involved in business at the most esteemed level and in contact with the highest lineages of the city. The only document in which we can find Great-Uncle Bello, quite a few years later, in 1256, confirms that he was a witness when the abbot of San Miniato rented the Montalto Castle from Guido Caponsacchi, a leading figure in an important and ancient family which had already been renting it for twelve years. We should not be misled by the fact that it was a castle and imagine that there was some kind of 'feudal' context. No, this was strictly business. Caponsacchi had taken on the management of the lands and the monastery's revenues, and this was one of the ways in which the great families of the city made their money. Florentine nobles did not hesitate to get their hands on business dealings.

Another of Bello's sons, Ruggeri, known as Geri, was in Bologna in 1266. We don't have the original document, but only a summary written by a seventeenth-century scholar who translated his name with the pronunciation of Bologna, 'Zerio di Bello Alegheri di Fiorenza'. Undoubtedly Geri had left Florence when the Ghibellines took power after the Battle of Montaperti, confirming Farinata's boast, '... twice I scattered them'. We know this because procedures were put in place to compensate the exiles for damage to their assets when the Guelphs made their final return to the city, and a written record of 1269 acknowledges 25 pounds' worth of damage to a house in the *sesto* of Porta San Piero, parish of San Martino del Vescovo, which belonged to 'Geri of the late *dominus* Belli Alaghieri'.* The family's houses were all in the same parish and next to one another, as was common practice. Geri's house was next to that of his uncle Bellincione, which had not been damaged. There is sufficient evidence to conclude that not all the Alighieris had left or been driven out of Florence during the six years of Ghibelline government. Hence it is not so strange that Dante was born during that period, and very probably in Bellincione's house.

As we have seen in the 1269 document, Bello had the title *dominus*. This formula is interesting because it is the first time that we encounter a blood relation of Dante's who is eligible to hold it, albeit after his death. But the question is from when and why did he have a right to be addressed in this manner. The natural reason would be that it was because he had been knighted, but this would be a little perplexing: we should not forget that he

---

* The papers provide for compensation to 626 people, which amounted to 221 pounds on average; the damage to Geri's house ('considerably destroyed') was therefore fairly limited. Bologna was the place where most of the exiled Guelphs sought refuge.

had a grown-up son in 1237 and at the time was not a *dominus*. Nor was he in 1256, when he must have been close to sixty. That a man of such advanced years would go through the expense of the ceremonial of knighthood would not have been a frequent occurrence. Or would it? One of the Florentine usurers Dante meets in Canto XVII of *Inferno* has been identified with Catello Gianfigliazzi, who had been active as a money-lender in France and returned to Florence in old age, and he too was styled a *dominus* in some documents after his death. In his commentary on the *Comedy* the contemporary Guido da Pisa confirmed that Gianfigliazzi was nearly eighty years old when he was knighted. It may be that obtaining a knighthood was one of the gratifications sought out by those who had made their money in less than reputable ways in order to safeguard their image in old age. However, Umberto Carpi's claim that these spruced-up usurers were the same 'false knights' Dante attacked in his poem 'Poscia ch'amor' is perhaps an overly imaginative intuition.

The title of *dominus* was also attributed to Bello after his death in a contract of 1276 in which Geri of the late *messer* Bello and Bellino of the late Lapo of the parish of San Martino del Vescovo were witnesses at the loan of a stomach plate (part of a suit of armour) valued at 4 pounds (but it may have been security concealing a loan). Lapo must have been another son of *messer* Bello, and therefore Bellino was of the same family and here working with his Uncle Geri. Working as a money-lender dealing in some fairly large sums, Bellino would later move to Ferrara and later still to Bologna, where in 1296 he was a member of a group of foreign money-lenders who officially requested permission to live in the city and engage in the business of loaning money. The statutes in Bologna that governed this procedure allow us to identify him as a professional dealer in money. A third son of *messer* Bello was called Bellincione after his uncle, although in the documents his name always appears in an abbreviated form widely used in Florence: Cione. Having

appeared in documents since 1277, Cione appears in several contracts in the years 1301–2, where he is regularly referred to with
the title *dominus*, which suggests that he too had had himself
knighted in old age.

The fortunes of Great-Uncle Bello and his sons remind us
that the social class in which Dante grew up was accustomed to
violence in a measure that we would struggle to imagine today.
In 1280 the judge of the criminal court of the Republic of Prato
tried nine people for armed assault on the public highway to
Pistoia against one Spigliato known as Balzano, son of the late
Giunta, who was escorting a prisoner of the Republic of Prato.
They had blocked his way, wounded him and thrown him in a
ditch and then took away the prisoner, who was also wounded at
his wrist. The assailants, five men and four women, were Parig-
ino of Calciana with his wife, Diletta, the priest Ubertino of the
parish church of Narnali, Borrisa widow of Giunta (therefore
the mother of the victim and now co-habiting with the priest),
Ghita (her daughter and therefore sister of the victim), Gianna
(another sister, this time with the priest), her husband Piero of
Capezzana, and the brothers Geri and Cione, who were sons of
Bello Alighieri. It is impossible to know what Dante's cousins
were up to in this fine company, but we do know that they were
the only ones who did not respond to the summons. Consequently they were sentenced to be banished from Prato until
they had paid a fine of 300 pounds each.

What is most difficult for us to understand is that people
involved in such sordid affairs as these could continue to live
a very normal life without losing any of their social status,
because recourse to arms, assault, wounding people in the street
and perhaps every now and then killing them was something
that could be carried out not only by people at the margins of
society, as is usually the case today, but also by the most influential citizens. Thus two years later, in 1282, Cione di *messer*
Bello Alighieri was nominated procurator by a Florentine judge

of noble family, *messer* Albizzo of the late *messer* Truffa degli Amidei, in a legal action before the judges of the Florentine court. In 1283 Cione turns up as a member of the Council of the Captain of the People for the *sesto* of Porta San Piero. His money-lending at the highest level continued undeterred: in 1295 Cione del Bello was one of the representatives of the Spini Company, who together with many other companies, including those of the Bardis, the Peruzzis, the Scalis and more than a hundred private citizens, were acting as creditors in the bankruptcy proceedings of the Bonizzi Company; he was clearly involved at the highest level in the lengthy administration of the affair, because in 1298 he would become one of the two auditors charged with the inventory and settlement of the debts in the name of the entire coalition of creditors.

As we have posed the question of whether Dante belonged to a family of usurers, we should emphasise that this cousin of his father's, this banker on a grand scale who was moving around colossal sums of money, did not hesitate to stoop to small loans of the most disagreeable kind. This was the case with four loans of the small sums of 11, 6, 5 and 4 pounds which Cione granted in early March 1299, at a time of year when the poor, having eaten their harvest of the previous year, started to find themselves in difficulty; these loans were to be repaid in kind (i.e., in so many bushels of grain) – by 1 August, after the new harvest. The peasants were obliged to sell their grain when the crops were merely green shoots at a price, as can be imagined, much lower than the market price and often ended up indebting themselves irreversibly. If the person imposing these money-grubbing contracts had been only marginally better off than the peasants, the accusation of usury would certainly have followed, but here the loan shark was an important citizen and no one dared to raise objections.

But being a respectable citizen and conducting a normal life did not exclude the risk of being murdered, and this is what happened to Cione's brother Geri del Bello – as we all know, because his cousin Dante wanted to talk about it in his *Comedy*. On entering the eighth circle of hell (Malebolge), Dante and Virgil meet the sowers of 'scandal and schism', mutilated and covered in blood and sores like survivors of some terrifying battle, and Dante suspects that among their number there's 'a spirit of my blood' suffering his punishment. Virgil confirms this, and a little earlier while Dante was looking elsewhere, he had seen this spirit 'point you out and threaten fiercely with his finger, / and I heard him call out Geri del Bello'. There follows one of those extraordinary passages in which Dante (the character in the poem) openly defends the values of the society he lives in, which conflict with the moral values that Virgil is trying to teach him. While Virgil, in effect, advices him to leave the wretched man alone, Dante earnestly explains that his cousin is right to be angry with him because he died a violent death, and that death hasn't yet been avenged by the family. Dante belongs to the same family and is therefore one of the 'consorts' (*consorti*), a word that was very important in the vocabulary of the time and not in its modern sense but the etymological one of people with a shared destiny: so he should have taken on the task of avenging his cousin. Geri is well within his rights to be angry and leaves without speaking to Dante, who for his part feels he is at fault.[3]

Who killed Geri del Bello? *Messer* Piero of Dante knew that it was one of the Sacchettis, a family of Ghibelline magnates, and the vendetta, which had not yet been perpetrated when Dante was writing, did eventually find its victim: Geri's nephews – and therefore the sons of Cione the banker, and particularly Lapo, who had already been involved in violence – killed one of the Sacchettis.* Dante, if he was in time to know it, would have

---

* Lapo di Cione had been found guilty in 1295 of having taken part in the attack on the palace of the supreme magistrate, and in 1306 he was a mercenary in the service of the Republic of Piacenza. Bambo was another of Cione's sons.

undoubtedly approved. It made no difference that decades had
passed by, as we know that Geri was killed in 1287, as recorded in
the registers of the convent of Santa Maria di Cafaggio, where
he was buried. Dante's teacher, *ser* Brunetto Latini, wrote with
satisfaction that he had seen vengeance for offences whose
memory had almost been lost in time. The obligation to avenge
and its full legal and moral legitimacy never faltered.[4]

It is difficult to know with any certainty whether we have
covered all of Dante's relations. At the time of his grandfather
Bellincione di Alaghieri there also lived a Salvi di Alaghieri,
whose sons – more or less contemporaries of Dante's father and
uncles – appear in many documents until 1295. They probably
weren't his cousins. They lived in another parish, and in 1280,
when Cardinal Latino came to establish peace in Florence, the
only survivor, Caruccio di Salvi Alaghieri, asked for peace with
the Strinati family, with whom they were in dispute, as Neri degli
Strinati asserts in his memoirs, 'because he was a man alone and
feared the worst' – he feared that they would kill him without
anyone lifting a finger to defend him or avenge him. Another
contemporary who was in the councils was Gerardo del Bello,
whom we know nothing about, but he could easily have been
one of Dante's cousins and a brother of Geri or Cione del Bello.

However, we are talking of a smallish kinship group compared with the large memberships of wealthy families. In the list
of Ghibellines banished from Florence in 1268 we find the names
of twenty-six adult males of the Ubriachis, twenty-three of the
Ubertis, fourteen of the Guidis. At the same council meeting in
1278 at which just one Alighieri, Uncle Burnetto, took part, there
were thirteen Adimaris, nine Cavalcantis, seven Della Tosas. In
1293 Corsino Amidei had to produce guarantors for his obedience to the Ordinances of Justice, and fourteen of them were
of the Amidei family. In 1301 the patronate of the church of San
Michele Visdomini (a body responsible for an ecclesiastical benefice) was held jointly by fifty-eight adult men belonging to just

CHAPTER FIVE

INFANCY AND THE DISTRICT

Dante's Birth and Name

Boccaccio wrote in his *Brief Treatise in Praise of Dante* (*Trattatello in Laude di Dante*, referred to as *Trattatello* hereafter): 'This singular Italic splendour was born in our city [...] in the years of the health-giving incarnation of the king of the universe MCCLXV.' How could he have known this? He didn't, but he inferred it from what he was told by 'a gifted man called *ser* Piero di *messer* Giardino da Ravenna, who had been one of Dante's closest friends and servants while he was living in Ravenna'. *Ser* Piero informed Boccaccio that Dante, bedridden with the illness he would die of, had told him that he had reached fifty-six years of age in May. As he died on 14 September 1321, he must have been born in May 1265. His journey to the next world is traditionally supposed to have occurred in 1300, and Dante writes in the first line of his *Comedy* that it was 'in the middle of our life's journey'. Psalm LXXXIX declares that we are destined to live for seventy years: the sums add up. As for the precise day, Dante informs us in *Paradise* that the sun was in Gemini when he was born ('when first I sensed the Tuscan air'), and therefore in the second half of May. More than that we cannot say.[1]

In 1265 the Ghibellines were still in power in Florence, and many Guelphs had been banished, including his cousin Geri del Bello, but clearly Bellincione and his sons, including Alighiero, were not so important or so compromised that they had to leave the city. Dante himself confirms that he was born in Florence in Canto XXIII of *Inferno* ('I was born and grew up / above the beautiful Arno River at that great city'), and in *Convivio* he declares himself to have been 'born and nourished' at its 'sweet breast'. In *De vulgari eloquentia* he asserts that he was 'a native and citizen' of Florence, and had drunk from the Arno before he grew any teeth. In Canto XXV of *Paradise* he calls Florence 'the beautiful sheepfold where I slept as a lamb', and speaks of the 'font of my baptism', meaning that he was baptised, like all Florentines, in the baptistery of San Giovanni, which elsewhere he called 'my lovely San Giovanni'. He was not alone in getting emotional at the thought of that place: Dino Compagni, a prior in the autumn of 1301, summoned 'many good citizens' to San Giovanni in a desperate attempt to stop the city from descending into civil war, and invited them to remember that 'communally you all took the sacred baptism from this font'. He then made them swear peace and concord on the Gospels 'over the sacred font, where you took the holy baptism'. They all took the oath in tears, although those who cried most copiously 'were the first to set about the destruction of the city'. Dino could not forgive himself, believing that by making them take that oath he had damned the souls of every one of them.[2]

The provenance of the name Dante is not clear, but it was not an unusual name, at least in Florence. In his youth Dante exchanged sonnets with his namesake Dante da Maiano. Scholars who sought evidence of a sojourn in Bologna have uncovered half a dozen other people called Dante, all of them Florentine, in the notarial records of that city. In his book on famous Florentines the chronicler Filippo Villani (who died in 1405) states that his Christian name was Durante, but he was called Dante because Florentines liked to use abbreviations. This is certainly true because the city was full of Ulivieris who were called Vieri, just as Raneri became Neri and Bonaccorso became Corso, and there was no shortage of people who were called both Durante and Dante. We have already met some in the Abati family, the one Dante's mother is supposed to have come from.

The poet always signs off his literary works as Dante, and that is what he is called by all his poetic correspondents. In reply to the anonymous poet who sent him the sonnet 'Dante Alleghier, d'ogni senno pregiato' ('Dante Alighieri, gifted with all knowledge'), he responds with the sonnet 'Io Dante a te, che m'hai così chiamato' ('I, Dante, to you who have thus addressed me'). In Canto XXX of *Purgatory*, Beatrice scolds him when she sees him crying at Virgil's departure: 'Dante, cry no more so Virgil can be on his way.' The only exception is *Fiore*, a loose translation into Tuscan of the famous *Roman de la Rose*, where Love at one point declares 'that it would be best that I come to the aid of Durante', and further on a '*ser* Durante' is referred to. Would this be the author? And was the author Dante? Today many think that it was, but it should be noted that *ser* was not a general form of address that could be applied to anyone. In Florence it was strictly attributable only to priests, notaries and schoolteachers, and it seems strange that Dante would attribute it to himself. Even in the documents drawn up during Dante's life the name Durante does not appear a single time. But actually Villani was right: on 9 January 1343 Iacopo of Dante regained possession of a farm that had been confiscated from his father by the Republic of Florence, and in this single contract the poet, for reasons unknown to us, is regularly and in fact insistently referred to as 'Durante, once called Dante'. It is quite possible that the notary, a foreigner from Assisi, was the one who insisted on this precision.

It was not a name used in the family, and it is natural to think that it could have come from his mother's family. This was a widespread custom: Boccaccio in his *Trattatello* uses Cacciaguida's wife to explain the arrival of the name Alighiero in the family and speculates that the woman, having many children, 'liked the idea of reviving the name of her forebears in one of them, since women are in the habit of being eager to do this'.[3] As we've seen, the theory that *monna* Bella was of the Abati family, in which the twin usage Dante/Durante was very common, arose from the same considerations. If so, it is unlikely that Dante was the first son of Alighiero and Bella, but only the first one to survive into adulthood. This would have been entirely normal, and it should be repeated that in all these genealogies we are obliged to ignore the children who died early in life which couples must have had for statistical reasons (this will be equally true of Dante's children when it is the moment to speak of them). Born when his father was already over forty, Dante most probably had survived more than one older brother – who would not have died as new-born babies, because in such cases the name would be recycled to the next boy to be born. They would have died in childhood or adolescence.

Tana and Francesco

Other brothers and sisters survived, and we know about them – although not as much as we would like, especially about the girls. Forese refers to 'Tana and Francesco' in his sonnet. The latter, as we have seen, was a younger brother born to Alighiero's second wife, Lapa Cialuffi. Documented for the first time in 1297, he was still alive in 1342, when in the name of Dante's sons and their wives he signed the peace agreement with the Sacchettis, bringing to a close the feud that had originated with the assassination of Geri del Bello. Documents show that by 1353 he was dead.

Tana married the merchant Lapo Riccomanni and appeared, already a widow, in quite a few documents between 1317 and 1321. With rare exceptions, scholars take for granted that she was a daughter of Alighiero's second marriage, and therefore Dante's half-sister, but the chronology raises various problems. Tana's husband referred to her many times in his book of accounts between 1281 and 1295. Lapo was often away on business, so his wife received and made payments in his name. After a first mention in August 1281 (a hasty 'my wife'), the husband refers to Tana from 1285 onwards, using the nickname Trota or Trotta (or even '*mona* Trotta my wife'). Some wonder whether this really was the same person as the one referred to as 'domina Tana' after his death, but generally we can assume that she was.

Lapo Riccomanni had a daughter, Galizia, who married in July 1295, and a son, Bernardo, who in 1297 was a friar minor who was present as a witness at the will of a benefactress along with other Franciscans of Santa Croce. In other words, Tana was already married and occasionally acted for her husband in 1281. She had a daughter born no later than 1283, but very probably a few years earlier (according to canon law, the minimum age for entering marriage determined by the Church was twelve, but the most frequent age for brides in Dante's Florence was fifteen), and a son who had reached the minimum legal age of fifteen in 1297. If Tana was the daughter of Alighiero's second marriage, we are obliged to believe that the first wife died immediately after Dante's birth (and therefore possibly in childbirth) and Alighiero remarried immediately, because Tana could not have been born after 1266. Of course, we cannot be sure that the mention in August 1281 was definitely of Tana: the hasty reference to 'my wife' could have been to an earlier, first, wife of Lapo, and both Galizia and Bernardo could have been her sons. The decisive argument comes in a deed of sale of 1320, which involved both Tana and Francesco, and speaks of the latter as her brother *of the same father*: the notary would only have introduced this clarification if brother and sister were of the same father but of different mothers. Thus Tana was Dante's sister in every sense: the daughter of Alighiero and Bella, and perhaps even his older sister.

Boccaccio wrote about another sister, and claimed that he was well acquainted with her son, who resembled Dante in a quite surprising manner.

It should be known that Dante had a sister, who was married to a citizen of ours called Leon Poggi, who had children by her. One who was older than the others was called Andrea, whose facial features were marvellously similar to Dante's, and also in his stature and his bearing which was a little hunchbacked, as they say Dante was.

This Leone Poggi was a well-known personality in Florence, because he was the crier for the Captain of the People and a functionary in the Guelph faction. His son Andrea was in fact mentioned in various documents. Around 1260 Leone was married to a woman called Ravenna, who some claim was Dante's sister, but there is an enormous chronological problem, because Ravenna must have been born around 1245, twenty years earlier than her brother. This was not impossible in a world in which women married at fifteen, because those who didn't die could have as many as twenty children, as has been documented for the mother of Catherine of Siena. However, pursuit of such theories only serves to demonstrate how little we know about the marriage of Alighiero and Bella. As for Ravenna, it is much more likely that she was Leone's first wife.

One of the sisters is referred to in *Vita Nuova*, in one of the extremely rare cases in which members of Dante's close family appear in his works. He had been in bed of sickness for nine days and was so weakened 'that he was forced to lie like those who cannot move'. In his fever-induced delirium he imagined the death of himself and Beatrice, the girl he was in love with, and became so agitated that 'a young and gentle woman, who was at my bedside believed that my tears and my words were solely due to the pain of infirmity, and became so fearful that she started to cry', until 'other women in the bedroom' came to see what was happening. No one was ever alone in a house at that time: those women were there not to watch over the patient but to get on with their tasks: they only 'became aware of me and my crying' when the young woman burst into tears. They then took her away and became convinced that he was having a nightmare, so they tried to wake him. Here he mentions almost by chance that the woman 'was a very close blood relation of mine', which could only mean that she was his sister, but whether she was Tana or another of his sisters we cannot say.[4]

Home and the Neighbours

The house where Dante lay in his sick-bed was very roughly the one which today is a museum called Casa di Dante, although alterations, demolitions and woeful renovations during the intervening centuries have rendered the place more or less unrecognisable from what it would have been in his time. Grandfather Alaghieri owned a fig tree (but had had to cut it down) which was beside the wall of the church of San Martino del Vescovo, which faced onto Via di San Martino, today Via Dante Alighieri. In the parish of San Martino del Vescovo the house of Geri del Bello was also to be found. It suffered some damage during the period of the Ghibelline regime, and the owner was reimbursed in 1269, following the Guelphs' return to power. The sources show that it was opposite the church of San Martino, and was next to the houses of the Donatis, the Mardolis and, above all, Bellincione, Dante's grandfather: it is probable that the poet was born in the latter. Just in front, the Castagna Tower loomed up above them, and in the accounts of a bank from 1290 there is a payment to the account of Taddeo Donati made by 'Cione Burnetti degli Alaghieri to his landlord at the Castagna'. Thus a son of Uncle Burnetto was a tenant of a Donati, in the same block. In 1295 Cione del Bello, the son Lapo and the nephew Bellino were the owners of other buildings in the same parish, some adjacent to the Badia and the houses of the Cerchi family.

Membership of a parish was important: in notarial

documents the name of a Florentine was very often followed by an indication of the parish in which they lived. The parish of San Martino del Vescovo was tiny, and the Alighieris and the Donatis were among the most important families in that little group of houses: we have already encountered the legal action of 1277 in which Donato of the late *messer* Ubertino Donati, Burnetto Alighieri and Cione of the late *messer* Bello acted on behalf of neighbours in the parish against the rector of San Martino and the abbey of Santa Maria, which wished to prevent those neighbours from building on an empty plot next to the church. Being close to the abbey was not easy, and relations were nearly always strained: in 1307, when the monks refused to pay the new tax imposed on the clergy by the republic, they barricaded themselves inside the monastery and rang the bells continuously. The parish, incited by 'their powerful neighbours from the great families and from the commoners, who did not love [the monks]', took the Badia of Florence by storm and sacked it, while the republic got its revenge by demolishing the bell tower.

The larger territorial unit that the Alighieri houses belonged to was the *sesto* of Porta San Piero or San Piero Maggiore, one of the six districts the city was divided into. Today we're accustomed to distinguishing between affluent and working-class districts or between central ones and the outskirts, but the *sesti* of Florence were not conceived in that manner: five of the six, which excluded the *sesto d'Oltrarno* (south of the river), divided the city like slices of a cake, starting from the oldest part of the centre. The *sesti* probably didn't have a strong topographical identity; in fact they were abandoned during the fourteenth century in favour of a new subdivision into four districts. However, they had an enormous influence on the everyday life of the city: every nomination or election, whether it was of *feditori* for the front line of battle at Campaldino or of the six priors who were replaced every two months in the government of the city, was carried out through the *sesti*, which therefore became the natural space for political alliances and rivalries: both the Cerchis and the Donatis, future leaders of the White Guelphs and the Black Guelphs, had their houses and towers in the *sesto* of Porta San Piero, a few steps from the Alighieris – which is why Villani called it 'the *sesto* of the scandal'.

While he was in Florence, Dante would certainly have lived in those houses, and at least one of them became his property – probably not Grandfather Bellincione's, where he was born, next to the Castagna Tower, but the adjacent house, which had belonged to his cousin Geri del Bello and was opposite the church of San Martino.* In 1323 a house in the same parish belonging to his cousin Cione di Burnetto was next to the houses of the Mardoli family and another house which was described, using a rather unusual legal phraseology, as the property of Niccolò di Foresino Donati 'or' of one of Dante's sons, Piero. All this suggests that it was the one that had belonged to Dante: all his real estate had been confiscated after his exile, but very probably the brother of his wife, Gemma, the Foresino mentioned above, bought it back, and later the house was open to a claim, at least in part following the death of the exiled poet, from his sons. In 1332 both of Dante's sons, Piero and Iacopo, shared the owner-ship of a house with their uncle Francesco, and all the evidence points to it being the same house in the parish of San Martino del Vescovo, next to the Donatis and the Mardolis. Ownership of this house was assigned to Piero as decided by arbitration in 1341 at the end of the arduous process of dividing up properties between siblings.

---

* Modern scholars believe this, but Bruni asserted that Dante's houses were 'attached to the houses of Geri of *messer* Bello, *his consort* [in the sense of a shared destiny]'.

CHAPTER SIX

LOVE AND FRIENDSHIPS

In the same *sesto* of Porta San Piero and in the parish of Santa
Margherita, which was adjacent to the parish of San Martino del
Vescovo, there was a family who would be of decisive importance in Dante's life: the Portinaris. They were not noblemen
and were active in commerce and money-lending. Their lineage
was probably shorter than the Alighieris, given that they only
appear in documentation at the time of the government of the
First People (1250–60), and initially they were compromised by
their Ghibelline connections but survived the sanctions imposed
by the change of regime.

Folco di Ricovero Portinari was the only one in the family
who was active in the city's political life during Dante's time.
He was clearly a prominent personality, who was married to a
Caponsacchi, a noble in the Ghibelline camp. He was the consul
of the Guild of Calimala on several occasions and was linked
to the Cerchi family, with whom he took the oath of peace
organised by Cardinal Latino in 1280. He was elected once to
the short-lived Magistrature of the Fourteen, and on as many as
three occasions he was one of the Priors of the Second People.[1]
On the authority of the commentators – because Dante was
very careful not to make any mention of him – we know that
he was the father of the little girl Beatrice, whom Dante, also a
child, fell hopelessly in love with.

The meeting between the two is narrated by Dante himself
in *Vita Nuova*. He was nine years old, and she had just turned

eight: this was therefore in the spring of 1274. I said 'narrated', but this is not correct because he doesn't add any details except that Beatrice was dressed in a blood-red frock and he was immediately smitten. Do we have to believe these affirmations, and in particular the age of the two protagonists? Dante presents *Vita Nuova* as a chapter taken from the 'book of my memory', but scholars have rightly wondered whether the author of what is in every sense a work of literature – and, let's face it, a novel in which he introduces himself as a character – was obliged to keep faithfully to the facts that had inspired him. The importance of the number nine in Dantean symbolism could make us suspicious about the ages and therefore the date. We will never know, then, whether Dante invented this first meeting when they were both children.

Boccaccio, who had no doubts about this at all and even claimed to know much more, asserted that the meeting took place on May Day. It was a holiday beloved of the Middle Ages: long before the socialist movement chose it as Labour Day, the first day of May celebrated the start of spring, and banquets and dances were organised in families and neighbourhoods. 'It was the custom of our city, and of men and women, to celebrate in their neighbourhoods, and everyone in distinct companies', Boccaccio wrote in the past tense for no apparent reason.* Thus Folco Portinari, 'on the first day of May had his immediate neighbours gathered in his own house to celebrate', including Alighiero. Dante went along with his father, 'as little boys are in the habit of following their fathers, particularly to places of festivity'. Boccaccio had already made it clear that mothers celebrated with other women, in compliance with the strict segregation in force in Florence, but this didn't apply to small children. At the festivities there were plenty of children, both

---

* This passage suggests that the custom was no longer practised in his own time, but this does not appear to be the case.

boys and girls, who after the first course left the table to play, and so, Boccaccio concludes, Dante met Beatrice, whose father was in the strange habit of calling her by that name, even though, as was clearly the case in Florence, everyone else called her by the abbreviation Bice, just as everyone called a Durante Dante.[2]

And Dante tells us, 'From that time forth, Love governed my soul.' Would it be inappropriate to analyse this infantile love story even through the methodologies of modern psychoanalysis, always supposing it wasn't an invention? Obviously human beings vary from one era to another because they accumulate different information, values and examples, but during childhood that accumulation of experience is a work in progress, and therefore children differ less from one another across various eras than do the adults that they become. Silvia Vegetti Finzi, a specialist in child psychology, writes that the first love usually occurs at 'around eight or nine years, occasionally earlier': it all adds up. It is an emotion linked to the 'latency period, in the early stages of the turmoil of new emotions and sentiments associated with puberty'. This is the point: it is a forewarning, and puberty is still a long way off. These infantile crushes 'are almost always absolutely platonic and idealised. They have nothing to do with sexual curiosity and erotic games.' They are sudden and without motive. The attraction is triggered 'without reason: who knows, perhaps the colour of the eyes, or the way of walking, laughing or jumping' (or perhaps a blood-red frock, we could add).[3]

Between twenty-five and thirty years later Dante would reconstruct this relationship with Beatrice by writing *Vita Nuova* after her death – a relationship that was almost non-existent on any practical level but immensely important for his inner life. He insisted on its absolute continuity throughout the remaining years of what we call childhood and adolescence. He would analyse his own reactions in the light of what was important to his own times, which sought to understand if love, such an evidently irrational force, was a good or a bad thing. This doubt could seem odd to post-romantics like ourselves, who are persuaded that love is the noblest and most important of all things, but men in Dante's time were convinced that behaviour had to be governed by reason and were fearful of the forcefulness with which love takes possession of a person. In the most famous bestseller of the epoch, the *Roman de la Rose*, which everyone had read and which Dante translated in his youth from the *langue d'oïl*, if he actually was the author of *Fiore*,[4] the character Reason has the task of arguing against Love, presenting it as a lunacy man must attempt to defend himself from.

Dante and other poets of his generation would discuss this matter in depth and in terms that are so sophisticated that we cannot possibly go into them here. Significantly, Dante was keen to make clear that there were no contradictions in his own reminiscences of childhood and adolescent love. Love clearly had taken hold of him, and 'commanded me again and again to attempt to see this very young angel, whereby I often went in my childhood to seek her out'. But he was in love with Beatrice, not just anybody, and therefore the object of his love was so noble as to eliminate every trace of the irrational, even in the head of a desperate teenager. Never, Dante assures us, did love take such possession of him that it suffocated the 'loyal advice of reason', and this too demonstrated the sublime nature of the woman he had fallen in love with.

This was platonic love, according to Silvia Vegetti Finzi. Indeed Dante admits that he had been cultivating it for years without ever having exchanged a word with Beatrice. The separation of the sexes was rigorous in Dante's Florence: there more than elsewhere, to judge from some of his comments. It appears that women stayed almost always among other women, and consequently men among other men. They could run into each other in the street and greet each other, but opportunities for the young people of both sexes to stay in each other's company were rare and precious. After the first childhood encounter the young lad often tried to see the young girl but never managed to greet her or make himself known. He probably did not see her for many years: in Tuscan cities parents wouldn't let a girl go out of the house once she was approaching puberty and would segregate her in the home. Then, after exactly nine years – that is, in 1283 – their paths crossed in the street.

Although they were almost of the same age, their positions in society had become very different: at eighteen, Dante was still an adolescent full of unfulfilled desires, while Beatrice, who had just turned seventeen, was a married woman. As such, she could now leave the house, although it would not have been easy to do so on her own, given her husband's rank. He was the knight Simone de' Bardi. That day she was in the company of older gentlewomen, and for the first time she became aware of Dante. Like any other clueless teenager, he was in state of panic and attempted to pass by unseen, but Beatrice caught his eye and greeted him, which sent him to the seventh heaven ('so much so that I felt touched by the outer reaches of beatitude'). This was the first time that he had heard her voice!

At this point the eighteen-year-old ran home and shut himself in his room. Dante had his own bedroom, which sometimes stuns Dante scholars, victims of a stereotypical image of medieval houses as small, overcrowded and lacking specific roles for different rooms. In reality there is absolutely no reason to believe that the house of an affluent family like Dante's would be in any way cramped or poky. We have been assured that Dante had a 'very decent' house by Leonardo Bruni, who had a considerable advantage over us in that he had seen it and showed it to Dante's great-grandson Leonardo Alighieri when he travelled from Verona to visit Florence. As for the matter of having a bedroom for himself, this was something the family of Catherine of Siena prohibited when she was a child in order to discourage her vocation. However, St Catherine went to pray in the bedroom of her brother Stefano, which was empty during the day because he had neither wife nor children. This continued until her father took pity on her and granted her a little room where she could stay on her own away from the others. What was possible for the daughter of a cloth dyer in the house of a numerous family was obviously more than possible in the much richer home of Dante's family.[5]

So the eighteen-year-old shuts himself up in his room to think over his encounter with Beatrice. He dreams about her in the night (it is worth pointing out that in the dream she is naked, although he tells us this with such a light touch that the exegetes usually fail to comment on it), and he wakes up overcome by violent emotions. So far, readers will say, nothing that hasn't happened to us all. But that eighteen-year-old was Dante, and the world he lived in was different from ours. In that world there was a recent development which was causing great excitement among the young – that is to say, youths of sufficiently high social status to know how to read and write, and to have the time to devote to books and debates. Analysing the passion of love, this was the argument of shared interest, and then translating it into poetry – and not into Latin but into their everyday language. That this was a new development is something that Dante explicitly confirms in *Vita Nuova*: 'in the past there were no reciters of love in the vulgar tongue, instead the reciters of love were certain poets in the Latin language.' At the age of eighteen Dante was already proving to be very interested in this matter, and knew by name or by sight several fellow citizens, not much older than him, who were writing love poetry. Thus, having woken from his marvellous dream and given that he had 'already seen for [him]self the art of saying words in rhyme', he decided to write a sonnet to communicate his own experience to other 'famous troubadours' and listen to their opinions.[6]

He sent his sonnet, 'A ciascun'alma presa', anonymously to various addressees. It was a game in which everyone knew the rules: receiving a sonnet was a challenge you had to respond to, and it is no surprise that to this day academics call this kind of poetic exchange a *tenzone* (contest, combat or duel). The other poets responded, sometimes in the same elevated style and sometimes with a brusque and comic lowering of the tone: Dante da Maiano, for example, advised the boy to rinse his testicles in cold water so as to get over that youthful enthusiasm. Naturally everyone was struggling to understand who the new rival was, and one of them was 'someone I call the first among my friends'. To be clear, Dante meant the first in importance and intimacy, not in the chronological sense. He was Guido Cavalcanti, who replied with the sonnet 'Vedesti, al mio parere, onne valore' ('all values, in my opinion, you have intuited'), 'and this was almost the start of the friendship between him and me, when he knew that I was the one who had sent it'. The theme of love was therefore interlinked with that of friendship, and while the love born in childhood continued to obsess the lad in his late teens, it also became an opportunity to discover new friends, the true, unforgettable ones whom he loved more deeply than those of his childhood (whom we know nothing about).

Friends were important for Dante. When he saw some pilgrims in the streets of Florence who were on their way to Rome, and noted how thoughtful they were, he told himself, 'Perhaps they are thinking of their distant friends.' In the language of the time 'friends' could include relatives and people living at home, and this may have been the sentiment that Dante attributed to the pilgrims. But when he empathises with the travellers in Canto VIII of *Purgatory*, who at dusk think back to the day in which they left and feel nostalgia for their 'sweet friends' to whom they said farewell, it is clear that the term has a much more intense significance.[7] In *Vita Nuova* he mentions another young man, whom he considered to be his closest friend after Guido: he must have been one of Beatrice's brothers, one of the five mentioned in their father's will, probably Manetto, who was the oldest.[8] As we know from the exchange of mocking poems, another was undoubtedly Forese Donati, the brother of Corso, the future leader of the Black Guelphs and a ferocious enemy of Dante and Guido (but by that time Forese was already dead, and Dante would meet him in *Purgatory*, where Dante would make him speak ill of his brother).

These friendships introduced him to social circles that were higher than the one into which he was born, even the highest in Florence. The Alighieris weren't magnates, and neither were the Portinaris, who were much richer and more influential than them, while the Donatis and the Cavalcantis were among the most prestigious and powerful families in the city. These were not the acquaintances Dante inherited from his family: suffice it to examine who was in his company on 6 September 1291, when he was the witness along with the notary *ser* Bonaventura of the late Tano at the contract by which one Guiduccio son of Ciampolo appointed a lawyer to manage his legal action against the community and the parish of San Pietro a Petrognano. The lawyer was *ser* Maschio the notary, son of the late Bernardo of the parish of San Piero Maggiore, and therefore from the same *sesto* in which Dante lived: Porta San Piero. It was possibly out of friendship or neighbourliness that Dante agreed to act as a witness for all these people, but it is striking to see him in the company of people who have no surname but just a patronymic, and realise that for the man drawing up the contract he was also one of them: 'Dante of the late Allaghieri'.

When we read *Vita Nuova* we encounter a different Dante, one who is continuously in contact with young men of the highest social standing and with women who are always 'gentlewomen'. The book is a valuable source for getting a picture of how young people in Florence came to meet each other. Such social occasions were frequent if they were of the same sex, but otherwise very rare. In church during the sermon or the Marian devotions Dante would be where he could see Beatrice, and obviously his eyes were constantly looking in that direction, but between him and Beatrice there was another beautiful gentlewoman, who noticed this and thought that Dante was looking at her. Many others who were present came to the same conclusion and commented on it with amusement. Evidently the churchgoers during these rituals were not always listening to the priest.[9]

Another time, 'in the belief that he was doing me a great favour', a friend took Dante to the house of a woman who had got married that very day; there, in a room covered with frescoes, the bride sat at a table in the company of many gentlewomen. Beatrice was among them, and Dante, who didn't expect this, cut a pitiful figure when he suddenly panicked and everyone noticed. His friend had to drag him away. This episode is always described in a cursory manner as a wedding feast, but that isn't really what we mean here. We are at the climax of a complex and symbolic matrimonial procedure: it is the day in which the bridegroom publicly goes to the father-in-law's home and 'leads the bride' – that is to say that he takes her to his own house. It was a rite of passage and as such involved various precautions that underscored its gravity. This was the reason why those women had surrounded the bride, because 'in accordance with custom in the city, it was befitting that they kept her company when for the first time she sat down at the dining table in the abode of the newly wed bridegroom'. Decency required women to keep the company of the bride the first time she dined in that unfamiliar house, before leaving her on her own to her new life of shared intimacy with a man. Dante and the friend had not been invited to the meal but went there 'in order that [the women] should be fittingly served'. The purpose was to honour the bride and her companions in accordance with etiquette, which at the same time emphasised the rigid separation of the sexes and their reciprocal acknowledgement.[10]

There were also the frequent funerals, because many died

young, such as a friend of Beatrice's whom Dante visited to say his last goodbyes, finding her death-bed surrounded by 'many compassionate women who were crying tenderly'. Beatrice's father, Folco Portinari, died on 31 December 1289, and as was the custom at the time – and especially in Florence, according to Dante – women and men participated at the ceremony separately: 'the custom of the aforementioned city' is that 'women meet up with women to grieve over such losses, and men meet up with men for the same purpose'. A passage from the *Decameron* clarifies this: the women went into the dead person's house for the wake and the men waited outside. Thus Dante could only watch and listen to the women as they entered the house to join in Beatrice's tears over her dead father and came out also in tears. When Dante started to cry, he knew that he was transgressing the rule that attributed distinct roles to the two sexes, and he tried to conceal his tears. When the women discovered this, they were stunned and scolded him, 'Leave the crying to us.'[11]

These are just a few of the moments in which Dante mixed with people of this social circle, which had become very much his own, rather than that of his family, whose most frequent encounters must have been with his neighbours in the parish and in the *sesto*. His was an aristocratic circle, in which he met magnates of noble blood, such as the Donatis ('of ancient blood, but not so wealthy', Dino Compagni wrote), those of recent origin, like the Cerchis ('men of low status, but good merchants and very rich'), and the 'fat commoners' (*popolo grasso*, a term for a Florentine class in this period that very roughly approximates to 'wealthy merchants who have not been or don't want to be ennobled'), such as the Portinaris, who owned large houses and towers but didn't seek knighthoods and the associated luxuries, although in many other ways they could no longer be distinguished from the magnates: if all he had been was Alighiero's son, Dante could perhaps have sat among the lowlier guests, but as he had exchanged sonnets with the sons of knights, he could address them with the familiar 'tu' form.[12]

Then there were his musician friends, whom he had also got to know and frequented since he had discovered that he was a poet, because verse could be put to music. Dante presents them to us in the early cantos of *Purgatory*, and it is not surprising that they are the ones he rushes to introduce after the horrors of his journey through hell, in which he met mostly men involved in politics and war, and now that he is getting closer to the kingdom of love. These were friends he lost too soon, because by 1300 they were all dead. Dante is so eager to meet them in the next world that he introduces the first one, Casella, before he enters the walls of Purgatory, and to justify this encounter he has to invent the pretext that some of the souls don't enter that kingdom immediately but wander around for years before being taken in. The musician had been dead for some time, and when 'my Cassella' embraces him with joy, Dante doesn't at first recognise him, and does so only when he hears him speak because it is his voice that has remained impressed in his memory. As soon as he has recognised his friend, he asks him to sing, because 'he placated all my desires' when he was singing love songs back on earth. And of course, Casella starts to sing one of Dante's songs that he had put to music, 'Amor che ne la mente mi ragiona' ('Love that reasons in my mind'). We are in Canto II of *Purgatory*, and in Canto IV Dante meets another friend about whom we know nothing but who for Dante was very important: the lute-maker Belacqua is lazy and witty, and makes Dante laugh, as he did in life. We only know his craft from commentators, and it is probably true, because Dante tells us nothing. Belacqua is a nickname, possibly an ironic one in an era when no one drank water. This passage is light-hearted and amusing, but coming across a friend on the way to Purgatory and therefore on the road to salvation is a way to exorcise the pain of his death: 'Belacqua, I am in pain for you no longer …' This is the same pain that Dante will recall in Canto XXIII of *Purgatory* on meeting another very dear friend, Forese Donati, and once again he recognises him from just his voice. This time it is because gluttons are so skeletal from starvation that they are unrecognisable. While Dante was cheered by seeing Belacqua, now, on seeing Forese in such a state, the pain of his death is renewed:

> Your face, for which I wept upon your death,
> Now has me crying in no less pain.
>
> (*Purgatory*, XXIII, 55–6)

The pain of losing a dear friend or relative too soon was a common experience in Dante's time, and the poet had to swallow this bitter pill on many occasions. Bice di Folco Portinari died at the age of twenty-five on 19 June 1290 – a crucial date in Dante's inner life – and it would take years for him to work through his grief, as we might say today. To achieve this he had to write his *Comedy*, in which he could 'say of her what has never been said of any other woman'.[13] During her short life she had been little more than a pawn in the family's strategies for their advancement. As has already been said, she was a married woman by the time Dante met her in the street when she was seventeen and for the first time she greeted him. Her husband, *messer* Simone de' Bardi, belonged to a great banking family, who were magnates and very close friends of the Donatis, and this meant that they were enemies of the Cerchis and their friends such as the Cavalcantis, the Alighieris and the Portinaris themselves. Beatrice's brother-in-law Cecchino de' Bardi would take part, along with Corso Donati, in a violent brawl in the streets of Florence in which Guido Cavalcanti would be wounded in the hand. Following Beatrice's death, her husband, *messer* Simone, would marry a sister of the 'evil knight' *messer* Musciatto Franzesi, a great financier of the French crown and in particular Charles of Valois, who would destroy the faction led by the Cerchis.[14]

Beatrice's marriage had a clearly political significance and produced a provisional reconciliation between two families belonging to different parties. It had nothing to do with sentiment, which explains why there is not the slightest hint of jealousy in the love story with Beatrice that Dante interweaves into his literary works.

CHAPTER SEVEN

DANTE'S STUDIES

We know almost nothing about Dante's education. Children of his social class obviously went to school. Later, at the time of Giovanni Villani, one gets the impression that almost all children went to school, given that the chronicler speaks of between 8,000 and 10,000 children, both male and female, who learned to read, between 1,000 and 1,200 slightly older children, all boys who studied arithmetic, and lastly between 500 and 600 boys who learned Latin and logic.[1] In the parish of San Martino del Vescovo, a Romano *doctor puerorum* appeared in the registers of 1277, when Dante was ten years old. A few years earlier he might have been Dante's teacher. We should make clear that in this era children were not particularly fond of their primary-school teachers. I remember reading a fourteenth-century ledger kept by the city-state of Turin, in which a notary drew a whip next to the entry for a payment to a schoolteacher.

As a child, Dante learned reading, writing and arithmetic, along with some rudiments of Latin. It was the elementary Latin he derides in *De vulgari eloquentia*, which consisted of constructing such sentences as 'Petrus amat multum dominam Bertam'. This was enough, however, to put him among the elite in the eyes of the great majority of his contemporaries, whose ability to write was strictly limited to the requirements of keeping commercial registers. Latin was the only language taught at school because it was the only one to have a written grammar; indeed *gramatica* in the language of the time was a word for Latin. Dante was persuaded that it was an invented language, the only one that never changed and the one that made it possible to communicate across national borders – a grandiose human invention to remedy in part the disastrous confusion of languages caused by the Tower of Babel.

Dante's knowledge of Latin was indispensable for reading the Bible, of which he had a profound knowledge, as his writings demonstrate, and for reading the classical poets. However, we should not for one moment imagine that his erudition, so clearly evident in all his works, was the product of his schooling. Besides it seems that Florence was not a lively cultural hub at the time; in fact some have spoken of a 'relative cultural backwardness in the city at the end of the thirteenth century'. Dante himself tell us that he was over the age of twenty-five when he started to console himself by reading Boethius and Cicero following the shock of Beatrice's death. He struggled to understand them, because at that stage all he had was 'the art of grammar': in other words, he knew only schoolboy Latin. But he liked the books and wanted to know them better. He also wanted to study philosophy and started 'to go where it existed in its truest form, i.e. in the religious schools and the disputations of philosophers'. He was the master of his own life and lived off unearned income, so he could devote himself to whatever activity he pleased.[2]

From that time on he never stopped studying – so much so that later he would find that his eyesight was fading and that the treatment was to spend long periods of time in a darkened room and bathe his eyes with cold water to avoid further deterioration.[3] There can be no doubt that he studied a great deal and meditated at length on many books, so there was little need for Bruni to write, 'Through the study of philosophy, theology, astrology, arithmetic and geometry, the reading of histories, the turning over of many and varied books, working late into the night and slaving over his studies, he acquired the learning which he could expound in his poetry and use to decorate it.'[4] We do not know exactly which books these were: we still have codices once owned by Petrarch and Boccaccio with glosses in their own handwriting, but we don't have a single volume that belonged to Dante. Attempts to reconstruct Dante's library from quotations in his works or by establishing which codices could have been found in the libraries of the various cities in which he lived do provide some suggestive ideas, but nothing certain. The fact that Dante quotes a particular author doesn't necessarily mean that he has read the original, because in this period a great deal of material circulated in the form of extracts, anthologies and encyclopedias.

Boccaccio at least provides us with a route to learning: having studied the liberal arts as an adolescent – that would be grammar, dialectics (art of reason), rhetoric, astrology, arithmetic, geometry and music – Dante turned to the study of poetry, and in order to understand it better he wanted to study 'histories and moral and natural philosophy' or, to be more precise, 'histories by himself', given that history was not yet an academic subject, 'and the philosophy of various doctors'.[5] It would be wonderful if we could know who those 'doctors' or philosophers were: very probably friars, who taught at the Dominican monastery of Santa Maria Novella or at the Franciscan one of Santa Croce – not exactly places of comfort and tranquillity at the time, given that both churches were major building sites, full of activity.

It is not clear what role Brunetto Latini fulfilled in this educational journey. Dante's encounter with him in Canto XV of *Inferno* demonstrates a very close relationship: the teacher twice calls him 'my son', and Dante responds by evoking his 'dear and kindly paternal image'. But *ser* Brunetto, who had died seven years earlier, in 1293, is in hell among the sodomites: *filthy* with a sin of the utmost gravity, even though Dante treats them with enormous respect – and it is impossible not to notice this. This is true not only of Latini but also of Iacopo Rusticucci and his companions, whom he meets in the next canto. Scholars have long tormented themselves about the motives for this sympathy without arriving at any plausible conclusion other than that Dante may also have been a homosexual. It should be noted that generally modern commentators exaggerate the exceptional nature of his attitude, or even its audacity, because they harbour an anachronistic idea of the disapproval homosexuality aroused in that period, and the gravity with which it would be punished under the law: the truth is that in Dante's times the theoretical guilty verdict for sodomy was not in any way accompanied by ferocious persecution by civil and ecclesiastical authorities.[6]

For the same reason we should not be surprised by the fact that Dante places other sodomites in Canto XXVI of *Purgatory*, and therefore on the path to salvation: no sin is in itself so grave as to condemn someone to hell without a chance of absolution. What we should really be considering is that he could have saved his teacher but he didn't. Evidently he was convinced that Latini practised sodomy in a somehow more sinful manner and, above all, had not repented. The current horror of paedophilia can give rise to the theory that Brunetto Latini was molesting his pupils and that Dante had also suffered this. Boccaccio took it for granted that this often happened, or at least this is what people thought: 'They have young pupils who because of their age are timorous and obedient […] and because of this it is believed that they often indulge in this sin.'[7] But Dante is really surprised to find him there: all commentators are agreed on this interpretation of the way he greets his old teacher ('Are you down here, *ser* Brunetto?'). The rest of the dialogue demonstrates unambiguously that he is fond of his old schoolmaster. If he felt obliged to place him in hell, it was because he knew with absolute certainty of things that would damn him, but it is probable that he didn't know of them when he was his pupil.

There remains another substantial problem: what would

Brunetto have taught young Dante? The poet reminds him in hell, but it is not easy to understand what he meant: 'You taught me how man becomes eternal.' According to Boccaccio, this meant that he taught him philosophy: Dante 'acquired the sublime principles of natural philosophy, as he wanted it to be known through his discussion in this work with *ser* Brunetto Latino, who was reputed to excel in this science' and later 'And thus the author made it clear that *ser* Brunetto had instructed him in philosophy.'[8] In Dante's time philosophy was a new concept that developed the tradition of the liberal arts, conceived up till then as fundamental disciplines of the kind we might call secondary-school level. Philosophy projected them into a new dimension where the study of logic became the analysis of the cognitive abilities of man and the study of astronomy opened the way to the great and unsettling debate about predestination and free will. It was a new way of meditating on the human condition and the purpose of existence along a different path from that of theology. This was why it was called 'natural philosophy', which we would now call science, and it led the way to moral philosophy and ethics. It is therefore possible that, as part of his traditional teaching of the liberal arts, Brunetto, who had experience of Paris, the true home of the new Christian philosophy, had grafted on some mention of these developments. After all, his most ambitious work, *Tresor*, was an attempt at a compilation 'of the marvellous sayings of the authors who discussed philosophy before our times'.

Dante asserts in *Convivio* that he became interested in philosophy and read Boethius and Cicero only 'quite some time' after Beatrice's death, and therefore not earlier than 1291. If Latini had him as a pupil during his adolescence, we're obliged to think that he taught him the art of writing letters and speaking in public: he was primarily a teacher of the *ars dictaminis*, which at that time was not only a technical method but also moral and civil pedagogy, taught to the ruling classes of the city-states through the knowledge of style and rhetoric. This is confirmed by Giovanni Villani's description, according to which Brunetto was the first one 'to teach Florentines to be less coarse and make them aware of proper speech so that they could know how to lead and rule our republic in accordance with [Aristotle's] *Politics*'. In Latini's eyes, this was also part of philosophy, a very broad concept as he defined it in his *Tresor*, and it included universal history, vices and virtues, and the art of government. In his *Rettorica*, in which he popularises and comments on Cicero's *De Inventione*, Brunetto declared that he wanted to instruct his readers on 'how to speak on diplomatic missions and in councils' and 'how to compose a well-dictated letter', but he didn't separate this technical instruction from the ethical dimension ('to give people learning and the path to doing good'). So it is possible that Dante heard him speaking about philosophy and morality before he discovered these things in the books of classical writers, whose arguments were so much more difficult.

In spite of all this, it seems a little excessive to claim that Dante could have learned how to gain immortality through these teachings. Without attempting to exclude such technical and moral instruction, I can't help wondering that Dante may be saying that Brunetto taught him something even more important: that a man can immortalise himself through his literary works. He is certainly leading up to this in the two more explicit affirmations that mirror each other – 'You taught me how a man becomes eternal', which Dante uses to evoke his teacher's skills, and Brunetto's appeal on their taking leave of each other, 'I recommend you my *Tesoro* through which I live on.' Thus Brunetto would certainly have introduced Dante to the idea of philosophy and the secrets of the *ars dictaminis*, but the teaching that was more fully impressed on his pupil's soul was the belief in the possibility of immortalising oneself by writing.

During the 1280s there was almost definitely a period in which Dante was studying in Bologna. We can take for granted that this was an enormous step forward compared with what Brunetto Latini had been teaching him in Florence. He was probably furthering studies he had already started, such as rhetoric in the faculty of arts, rather than commencing other, entirely different subjects. Boccaccio, who provides this information, puts it like this: Dante started his studies 'in his own country and then went to Bologna as it is a more fertile place for that kind of food'.[9] Of this sojourn in Bologna we have confirmation and a date before which he must have moved there, thanks to the habit among notaries in Bologna of filling blank paper in their registers by transcribing poetry or what they called *rime*. In a register in use towards the end of 1287 the notary Enrichetto dalle Quercie transcribed one of Dante's sonnets in which the author speaks of the Garisenda Tower in Bologna, which the poet clearly must have seen in person: he was one of the many notaries working in Bologna who would transcribe Dante's songs or passages from his *Comedy* even before his death, confirming the fame he had already achieved.

The probable trajectory of Dante's studies can then be summarised as follows: a first teacher (a *doctor puerorum*) hired by his family taught him to read and write, and also introduced him to the rudiments of the Latin language, because he read directly in Latin from the Psalter and Donato, to use the jargon of the time. This meant that he first worked on a book of prayers and then moved on to the handbook for grammar erroneously attributed to Aelius Donatus. Subsequently another teacher – a *doctor gramatice* – would have taught him more advanced Latin and some fundamentals of the other liberal arts. During his adolescence Brunetto Latini instructed him in the art of epistolography, which was not a literary recreation but something of crucial importance in politics, where it was necessary to draw up letters and speeches unendingly not just in Latin but also in the vernacular. During the lessons of Brunetto, the commentator on *De Inventione*, Dante must have had his first encounter with

Cicero, the master of eloquence, politics and morality. Then, at around twenty years of age, Dante – having lost his father and consequently now master of his own fate – went to Bologna to improve his knowledge by frequenting the faculty of arts and studying rhetoric more deeply. Thus he would become, as Giovanni Villani would write, 'a perfect rhetorician both in dictating and versifying, and also in delivering a speech': in other words, full command of all the means of expression from poetry to political discourse.[10]

By this time Dante must have been familiar with the classical poets who were most prized in his own time: Ovid, Statius, Lucan and Virgil – the latter conveniently happens to compliment Dante on his perfect knowledge of the *Aeneid* in Canto XX of *Inferno* ('You know it so well that you know every line of it'). Only later would he want to read the philosophical writings of Boethius and Cicero, and discover that he had to struggle. He decided to study at the monastic schools in Florence, which would lead him to the discovery of 'my teacher Aristotle' and his *Ethics* – perhaps the book Dante quotes most often from and with the greatest reverence.[11] This long period of scholarship has its own coherence and explains why Dante gave little importance, taking his works as a whole, to his youthful experiences in Bologna. Even in the *Comedy*, all he remembers is the defamiliarising sensation of looking to the sky while standing below the Garisenda Tower and the movement of clouds which give the impression that the tower is collapsing – essentially the experience of a tourist ...

This does not preclude that, as well as listening to the Franciscan and Dominican teachers 'in the religious schools' in Florence, he was also returning for one or more semesters to Bologna to listen to 'the disputations of the philosophers'. The term 'disputations' (*disputazioni*) was not a vague one but referred to a particular kind of public event that was of crucial importance in the intellectual life of the times. Whereas the

nobles and magnates gave vent to their virility and competitive-
ness in warfare and tournaments, their brothers and cousins
who entered the clergy or at least devoted their lives to study,
enjoyed the same pleasure and release in public debates in which
a teacher put forward an argument and then had to respond
to the objections raised by the audience. Alternatively there
was the 'as-you-please' (*de quolibet*) disputation, in which the
teacher replied to the public's questions on whatever argument
they wanted. Apart from the teachers, who had the right to do
the summing up at the end of debates, students on advanced
courses (*baccellieri*) had the task of sustaining arguments in
favour. Dante compared these highly ritualised trials of intellectual strength to his encounter with St Peter, when in heaven
the apostle started to question him about faith, and an anxious
Dante martialled his arguments in his mind:

> Just as the *baccelliere* arms himself and does not speak
> until the teacher puts forward the question
> for approval and not to do the summing up.
> (Paradise, XXIV, 46–8)

These public debates were also held in the Florentine monasteries, and Dante very probably attended them as well,[12] but
in Bologna there must have been a great deal more on offer:
the faculty of arts and medicine provided teaching with a philosophical bent that was unique in Italy. We're not in a position
to ascertain whether Dante paid to attend the lessons on top of
frequenting the disputations. However, the complete command
of the scholastic method of argument that he demonstrates in
Convivio suggests that there were further university experiences.
This is also true of his repeated polemics against 'Italian men
of letters' who use knowledge solely for work and make it a
source of income, as in the case of 'lawyers, doctors and nearly
all members of religious orders'. His contempt for a culture that

was bought and sold appears to be linked to his attendance of university lessons, which he would not recall as a positive experience. It would not have been the first time that a particularly gifted student was irritated by the mediocrity of lessons, and ultimately concluded that the best way to learn is to read books on one's own.[13]

Philosophy came at a high price for Dante, because it convinced him that the truth is the most important thing of all, and consequently he started 'to hate the followers of error and deceitfulness'. A central concept of Aristotelian philosophy, which was not only a philosophical system as we would understand it today but also a universal interpretive key to the physical and moral world, was the distinction between substance and accident, the inner nature of things and the modifications they underwent. A philosophical education automatically led to an interpretation of the world in these terms, and so in *Vita Nuova* Dante pauses to clarify that 'Love is not at all like substance, but it is an accident in substance' (XXV, 1). By reasoning in this manner, Dante was able to conclude that it was possible to reform those who followed error and mendacity: error was an accident, and it transformed substance, which in itself was not evil, into something worse, so it was necessary to destroy the error and not the person who indulged in it. Dante was convinced that he would have done good work if he fiercely criticised errors in order to correct those in error: 'I abominated and despised people's errors, not because of their innate iniquity and shamefulness, but because of the errors, and I thought that by criticising I would please them.' In short, he believed that by criticising other people's errors, they would become aware of them, abandon them and perhaps be grateful to him for having pointed them out (*Convivio*, IV, I, 4–5).

CHAPTER EIGHT

A MYSTERIOUS MARRIAGE

We've said that Dante, during the years he was staying in Bologna and reading avidly, was an orphan and master of his own destiny, but it is unclear whether he was already married: Dante's marriage to Gemma di Manetto Donati is a tangle of mysteries. Indeed it's surprising that we don't pay more attention to it, not so much because Dante, during the years of his political activism, belonged to the same faction as the Cerchi family, who were bitter enemies of the Donatis, as because of its chronology, which is an unresolved problem.

As in many other cases, we need to look at this backwards if we're to know anything about this wedding, starting with the contract signed in Florence in August 1329, eight years after Dante's death. The practice in Italian city-states of banishing enemies and confiscating their assets was causing complicated legal outcomes, and the city-states had to devote the organisational resources of a special institution to disentangle the mess. The case of Dante and Gemma was a very common situation: the husband had been condemned as a rebel and his property confiscated, but his wife remained in Florence and had not been found guilty of anything. Dante's real estate included the value of the dowry that Manetto had paid the son-in-law at the time of the wedding, and following Dante's death that value should have been restored to the widow. It was not easy to recover the whole sum but, at the very least, widows were entitled to the unearned income produced by those assets, which was often the only income they could rely on: the maintenance of widows through income produced from dowries was one of the most important mainstays of society at the time, so not even a government as violently partisan as the Florentine one could ignore it.

Widows who had a claim to income from their dotal assets had to petition the office that managed the assets of convicted rebels (the Office of Rebel Assets). In 1329 the head of this office was *messer* Guglielmo de' Magnani of Bologna, whose title was *iudex*, which meant that he was a legal expert.* The women had to submit the contract that governed their dowry in order to demonstrate their entitlement, and this is the reason why we know of its existence, even though in the office records the notaries Piero Gucci and Neri Chelli only transcribed the most important details. The contract had been signed on 9 February 1276, of the sixth indiction, by the notary *ser* Uguccione di Baldovino.† However, Gemma did not submit the original but rather an authenticated copy produced later by the notary *ser* Ranaldo of the late Oberto of Baldovino. The agreement valued the dowry at 200 pounds in small florins (a small florin was the equivalent of one *denarus* or penny and was minted in Florence): on this basis, *messer* Guglielmo allocated a yearly income of twenty-six bushels of grain to Dante's widow.

The law stipulated that the grain delivered to the rebels' widows was to be calculated as 18 pounds for each *modius*, and there were 24 bushels to a *modius*. Therefore every bushel was valued at three-quarters of a pound (15 shillings). Gemma had been allocated an annual income of 19½ pounds, almost 10 per cent of the capital. The reason for all these calculations is that

---

* *Messer* Guglielmo was called *de Magnanimis* in the copies of the document, but there is absolutely no trace of a family with this name, whereas Magnani was the name of a well-known aristocratic family in Bologna.

† Indictions were fifteen-year periods, used in medieval notarial documents.

income from capital was usually valued at 5 per cent; in the case of rebel assets, a statute of 1327 stipulated a payment of 8 bushels or 6 pounds for the first 100 pounds of capital, and 6 bushels or 4½ pounds for every subsequent 100 pounds of capital. So Gemma was paid almost twice the percentage required in law, as well as being twice the current market rate, which suggests that the Donati surname still counted for something (or, at such a late date, it could have been Dante's fame, given that the whole of Italy was talking about him).

These are not the 'tangle of mysteries' I referred to at the beginning of this chapter: no one will be surprised that the laws were interpreted with a high degree of discretion and that favouritism affected their implementation. The first real mystery concerns the date of the dowry contract. The notary who transcribed it in the register undoubtedly made a mistake: 1276 was during the fourth indiction, not the sixth. The indiction was a venerable system for calculating the years which medieval notaries had inherited from the administration of the late Roman Empire and continued to be used for no other reason than to parade their knowledge of the more esoteric elements of their trade. They set great store by it, and it was more likely that a notary would get the date wrong rather than the indiction. A further complication is that in Florence the year ended on 24 March, and so what was for them 9 February 1276 would for us be 9 February 1277, unless of course the year of 1276 was the product of an incorrect transcription. But then the truly insoluble problem is that on that date Dante was not yet twelve years old. We don't know how old Gemma was, and usually the wife was much younger than the husband – on average around fifteen years younger, although in this case the difference must have been a great deal less. However Dante's age of eleven is enough to conclude that marriage at that age was illegal, just as it is today, as well as contravening canon law.

The vague idea that in those times anything could happen,

and ignorance about how weddings were celebrated has led some biographers of Dante to minimise the problem, interpreting the contract of 1277 as a preliminary agreement between the families: a promise signed by the parents on behalf of the children which did not involve an actual marriage ceremony and its consummation, in accordance with a widespread practice sanctioned by the Church. Reality was very different. Isabelle Chabot, who has written a very thorough study of these matters, has made it clear that the *instrumentum dotis* (dotal contract) submitted by Gemma was the first stage in a genuine matrimonial procedure, which at the time was celebrated at the bride's home and officiated by the notary – certainly not by a priest in church. The dotal contract was *always* signed on the same day as the wedding: it came after the exchange of rings, and before the bridegroom publicly led his bride to his house. We can rule out the idea of an eleven-year-old boy being the protagonist of such events, or rather it could occur in the extremely rare cases of marriages between children who were a prince and a princess, when political necessity outweighed every other consideration and the required dispensation had been obtained from the ecclesiastical authorities. Equally kings could divorce, but mere mortals could not. The supreme interests of the kingdom – that is to say, the collectivity – took precedence over everything else. With the social standing of Dante and Gemma, or rather of Alighiero degli Alighieri and Manetto Donati, a marriage of two children, after having requested and obtained dispensation, was just as unlikely as it would be today.*

Some biographers take another tack. They fancy that the

---

* Chabot cites the unique example of the marriage of a boy of three or four which was arranged in 1280 to safeguard a colossal inheritance and involved the Counts Guidi and the Pagani da Susinana, both families of princely stature, and she stresses that the contractual language demonstrates that the two families were 'unconcerned about canon law, but entirely aware of the absolute illegality' of the marriage.

family was in a hurry to settle the young orphan's future by placing him in an influential kinship, because they know that marriages were decided on the basis of family strategies and that the Donatis were a powerful and ancient family, and neighbours too. The problem is that such situations were run-of-the-mill: nothing could be more normal than a young lad of good family suddenly losing his parents and two families of close neighbours being keen to become relatives. Gemma's dotal contract, however, would have been a unique and hitherto unknown case in Florence of that period if in that banal situation it had resulted in such an exceptional outcome – not just a promise but an actual marriage between children. Thus there are two possibilities: either Dante and Gemma were really married in 1277 and went through an absolutely astonishing experience that no one else had heard of for reasons we cannot even guess at … or the notaries of *messer* Guglielmo made a mistake in transcribing the year.

This second hypothesis appears to be much more persuasive. Without claiming that it is conclusive evidence, we note that the sixth indiction came round again in 1293, when Dante was twenty-seven, which was a more normal age for a young man to get married, although still lower than the average for that period and that social class.[1] There are no references to Dante's marriage in his writings: not even where we might expect them, such as the *tenzone* with Forese, in which Dante pitilessly takes aim at the sufferings of Forese's wife but his friend doesn't even think of giving him a taste of his own medicine. According to Boccaccio in his *Trattatello*, it was well known that only after Beatrice's death in 1290 did Dante's relations 'discuss among themselves their desire to find him a wife': as usual, academics give very little credence to this information, but everything suggests that Boccaccio knew more than we do.[2] In the same way, we should consider Bruni's observation that Dante 'took a wife in his youth', which doesn't confirm, as some commentators have believe, 'that Dante married very young', because 'youth' in the language of the time came after 'adolescence' and was fully identified with adulthood.[3]

Besides, Manetto Donati himself must have been pretty young in 1277. On 4 March, not even a month after the supposed marriage of Dante and Gemma, his name appeared in the previously mentioned list of neighbours in the parish of San Martino del Vescovo who were quarrelling with the priest over building plans. The representatives of the neighbours included Dante's uncle, Burnetto Alighieri, and his father's cousin, Cione of the late *messer* Bello, and the complainants included another two uncles, Gherardo and Bello, as well as the schoolteacher Romano *doctor puerorum*. That Dante's father wasn't mentioned is powerful evidence that he was no longer alive. But the main point is that the expression 'Mainectum domini Donati' implies that Manetto's father was alive, and was still alive in 1297, when Manetto was called 'dominus Manettus domini Donati de Donatis'. Notaries were very careful to indicate whether the fathers of those who appeared before them were alive or dead, by specifying with a *quondam* or an *olim* the ones who were dead. The reason was that this matter had important legal consequences. This demonstrated that Gemma's grandfather, *messer* Donato, lived at least until 1297 (but proved to have duly joined the *quondam* by 1299). That Manetto, twenty years before his father's death, was already married and father of a girl who entered a precocious marriage is not impossible but adds a further false note. It would be much more logical to think that Gemma was fifteen years younger than her husband, Dante, as was normal at the time, and was born around 1280, and married in the mid-1290s.

A lesser mystery is the perplexity over another curious fact: the low value of the dowry Manetto assigned to Gemma. Those 200 pounds in small florins were much less than the sums usually encountered at that level of society: nearly all widows who submitted a claim to the judge of the rebels' assets had received much larger dowries, which generally exceeded 400 pounds but could sometimes reach the figure of 1,000 pounds or even more.[4] Scholars tend to conclude that Manetto was not rich. It's true that, according to Dino Compagni, the Donatis were not as rich as their sworn enemies, the Cerchis. But the size of dowry did not necessarily correlate to the wealth of the family who had to pay. Of course, providing a daughter with a sumptuous dowry could be one of the forms of conspicuous consumption that signalled the achievement of social status. But not everyone wanted to spend, and we don't know how many other daughters Manetto had to provide with a dowry: on some occasions saving money was an entirely dignified objective even for the rich. Dante himself, in his *tenzone* with Forese Donati, which teases him because he doesn't warm his wife enough in bed and has her suffer a wretched life, imagines the mother-in-law regretting the marriage and saying: 'What a shambles, for a few dried figs I could have had her in with Count Guido!' So the mother-in-law, who had married her daughter into a prestigious family like the Donatis, was kicking herself because she could have arranged a marriage with someone more prestigious for a lower dowry, or rather for nothing: 'for dried figs'. Clearly marrying a daughter and giving her a small dowry was not necessarily proof that the family was in difficulties: it may simply have been a good deal.

Besides, as we've just seen, by comparing the contracts – one of 1277 and the other of 1297 – Manetto Donati at some stage had had himself knighted because in the second document he is called '*dominus* Manettus', and a man who had had himself knighted late in life after his daughter's marriage certainly didn't have financial difficulties. Thus Gemma's small dowry can only mean one thing: it was the Alighieris and not the Donatis who sought after that marriage, and they accepted Gemma without haggling over the money. And of course the Donatis, who had no need to demonstrate their nobility to anyone, were only too

CHAPTER NINE

DANTE'S BUSINESS DEALINGS

Dante was the oldest son of a businessman, who died when Dante was still a teenager or possibly a child, and there was nothing unusual about the fact that he had to look after the business affairs he had inherited from his father when he reached the age of majority. The first document concerning his financial interests is the seventeenth-century summary of a notarial act that has been lost. It was dated 1283 Florentine style (therefore between 25 March 1283 and 24 March 1284). In May of that year Dante reached the age of eighteen, at which point an orphan was freed from his guardianship and could dispose of his property as he wanted. He sold his rights to some assets in the parishes of Santa Maria a Ontignano, near Fiesole, and Sant'Ambrogio a Firenze, which belonged to the merchant Donato di Gherardo del Papa, who had guaranteed a debt of 21 pounds in an agreement with Alighiero. The credit was bought from Dante by the notary Tedaldo Rustichelli, who incidentally would be called on to draw up the will of Beatrice's father, Folco Portinari, five years later, on 15 January 1288.*

The document survived by complete chance: the man of learning Senator Carlo Strozzi wrote that he found it in 1615 while looking through a bundle of documents held in the Florentine monastery of Santa Maria a Montedomini, 'the greater

_____

* The age thresholds that gave young men competence to act legally were varied: it could be first either fifteen or eighteen.

part of which had been ruined and torn by the floods that had afflicted this city (the flood that occurred in 1966 when the Arno broke its banks, which everyone in my generation remembers, was only the latest in a long line of such events). As always, it is good idea to emphasise that we possess only the random wreckage of an immense quantity of documentation, and that it would be a huge misjudgement to believe that Dante's activities – in this case, his business activities – were limited to the deals of which we possess some evidence: we don't know if he ever bought or sold land, and we don't know if he got involved in the administration of the farms he inherited from his father. Of course, the fact that he sold a credit does suggest that he was not too interested in such deals and in trying to extract the maximum profit. As we shall see, he was the owner of considerable assets, and appears to be the first member of the family who could live off unearned income and therefore able to pursue aristocratic pastimes.*

The subsequent evidence of Dante's business dealings all concern loans he took out: an undoubted reversal in relation to his father's habits, which were still being dutifully kept alive by more distant relations such as his cousin Bellino, a professional money-lender in Ferrara and Bologna, not to mention the enormous deals being struck by the other cousin, Cione del Bello. The first debt we come across is dated 11 April 1297, when Dante and his brother Francesco acknowledged that they had been lent 227 gold florins by Andrea di Guido de' Ricci. This information was recorded during the legal action brought by the creditor in 1308 in an attempt to recover his money, and the document

---

* Giuliano Milani has rightly pointed out that Dante was the first member of his family to live off unearned income – like an aristocrat – though he was influenced by the clichés about Dante's poverty and indebtedness, and came to the conclusion that, by doing so, Dante 'got through half of his capital': a clearly groundless assertion, given the considerable property that would be confiscated when he went into exile.

was summarised by yet another seventeenth-century man of learning and recopied in the nineteenth century. We only know about it because of that last copy, which offers little room for comment other than the fact that this was a considerable sum of money, in the order of €100,000 today.

Another even larger debt was taken out by the two brothers on 23 December 1297. It consisted of 480 gold florins loaned by Iacopo of the late Lotto Corbizzi and Pannocchia Riccomanni, the brother of the merchant Lapo di Manno Riccomanni, who married Dante's sister Tana. This contract is significant partly because of the extremely high social status of some of the guarantors: apart from Dante's father-in-law, *messer* Manetto *di messer* Donato dei Donati, the debt was also guaranteed by *messer* Durante of the late *messer* Scolaio degli Abati, Noddo of the late Riccomanno Arnoldi, Alamanno of the late *messer* Boccaccio Adimari and the notary Spigliato of the late Spigliato da Filicaia. These names are very different from those of the acquaintances of Dante's father and uncles: the Donatis, Abatis and Adimaris were three of the most prestigious families. We know that some academics, hypnotised by the nature of the kinship the document reveals, have fantasised that *messer* Durante degli Abati was a relative, perhaps even the poet's maternal grandfather. This theory makes no sense, but on the other hand the Riccomannis were closely related to the Alighieris by marriage. Spigliato da Filicaia was the preferred notary of the Cerchis' bank, and had been the consul of the Guild of Judges and Notaries. All the other guarantors of Dante and Francesco belonged to the city's most exclusive elite.

Scholars from the past, such as Michele Barbi, interpreted such facts as evidence that the Alighieri brothers were in serious financial difficulties, and needed huge amounts of money. Other more recent and subtle scholars have suggested that the debt could be a trick, a legal fiction to create false creditors, who in reality were well disposed to the debtors, and thus put some of their capital in a safe place should real creditors take legal action against them. But if we were to argue, as we usually do, that credit was playing an enormously important role in the Florentine economy at the time, we cannot subsequently think that whoever took out loans was in financial trouble. Cash was an indispensable commodity, but in short supply when the economy was growing. Even the rich had to borrow when they suddenly found that they needed it. There are plenty of reasons why Dante and Francesco might have needed cash, so we cannot infer anything about the state of their finances. In this specific case, the rule is that the rich incur large debts and the poor incur small debts. And only the rich can have the networks and guarantors necessary to take on large-scale debt. The size of the sums in play over these two transactions suggests the two brothers were about to take on some very large undertakings. Clearly they were not supposed to cover everyday living costs. A family like theirs could have lived for ten years on 480 florins!

The larger of the two debts would have outcomes which, though far from clear, confirm the impression of an immense financial and property deal, involving several family groups with adjacent properties. Thirty-five years later, no less, on 3 November 1332, Dante's sons sold Giovanna widow of Litti de' Corbizzi some land inherited from their father for 55 florins. The land was in the parish of San Miniato di Pagnolle, adjacent to the land Litti de' Corbizzi had left to his heirs. The same day and before the same notary, Iacopo di Lotto Corbizzi, the lender back in 1297, having confirmed that the other creditor, Pannocchia Riccomanni, had reached a separate agreement for his part of the credit, to be transferred to Giovanna in exchange of 55 florins, which were his part of the credit, with the proviso that they could only be used for covering any claims for compensation relating to the land she just bought. In practice this meant that if the sale by Dante's sons could be upheld in law and didn't give rise to litigation, Giovanna would have lost that money and that debt would have been cancelled. But what is more extraordinary is that even the remaining sum was cancelled because on the same day Corbizzi credited Francesco and Dante's sons, *ex dono, gratia et amore*, 130 gold florins, which was the balance for the debt incurred thirty-five years earlier. I would be lying if I claimed to understand everything that is going on here, and yet the reader will agree that interpreting the 1297 transaction simply as evidence of Dante and Francesco being in financial difficulty and desperate for money would be a gross simplification.

The two brothers appear to have been involved in money-lending transactions in many other documents and not always in the role of debtors, although the overriding consideration on examining these papers is that we never understand what is going on. Nowhere is there any indication of the most important thing: the motives behind these transfers of money from one person to another. Dante's father-in-law, *messer* Manetto, acted as guarantor to his son-in-law on two other occasions – one for 90 florins lent to Perso Ubaldini and one for 46 florins lent to *messer* Filippo di Lapo Bonaccolti – but we don't know the date of either transaction. On 23 October 1299 Francesco, who was working on his own without Dante's involvement this time, borrowed 53 florins from the well-known money-lender Lotto di Cino Cavolini and undertook to return the sum within six months. The guarantors belonged to the same prestigious families as before, and were Geri of the late Neri dei Donati, Lapo of the late *messer* Scolaio degli Abati and Corso of the late Naddo degli Abati. But five months later, on 14 March 1300, Francesco loaned Dante the sum of 125 florins, and two weeks after that, on 31 March 1300, Francesco borrowed 20 florins from the money-changer Tencino Acerbi and his son Cerbino, who were also professional money-lenders. On 11 June 1300 Francesco lent Dante 90 florins, and on 2 March 1301 it was *messer* Durante, the judge of the late *messer* Scolaio degli Abati, who borrowed 50 florins from Tencino Acerbi and his son, while the guarantors, who must then have been accepted as solvent by the creditor, were Dante and Francesco Alighieri. And on 29 July 1301 Francesco borrowed 13 florins from the ever-present Cerbino.

What conclusions can we draw from this staggering succession of contracts, which have somehow survived where unknown quantities of them have been lost?* Ultimately the only thing they demonstrate is that in Dante's Florence cash was not only an indispensable commodity but also a rare one. Consequently those in need of small sums were continually obliged to take out loans without this telling us very much about their prosperity or indebtedness. But there is something else we have to take into account, and this is that 1300 and 1301 were the years in which Dante held high political office, immediately before being driven into exile. It is not proven that the occasions in which he borrowed money from his brother were directly connected to the requirements of his political ambitions, which he may or may not have owned up to. The last assignment the republic entrusted him with was in the autumn of 1301, and it was both very prestigious and inherently costly. He was the ambassador at the papal court in Rome, and he had quite possibly visited the city on a pilgrimage during the Jubilee Year of 1300 – if the image of the bridge at Castel Sant'Angelo being so crowded that pedestrians had to walk in separate lanes refers to something he actually saw, as is thought to be the case (*Inferno*, XVIII, 28–33). Journeys of this kind were very expensive, and in the case of a diplomatic mission it was obvious that only a rich man could accept such a post. What today we may be in danger of missing is that the need for cash would have obliged even a rich man to take out a loan.

It is not generally accepted that Dante was a rich man, and among scholars the recurrent argument is that he was poor,

---

* Franek Sznura has calculated that only 3 per cent of the registered notaries in Florence in Dante's time produced documents that have survived.

which is mainly due to a naive interpretation of the loans we have mentioned. But Bruni assures us that 'before he was driven out of Florence, Dante, though not a man of very large assets, was nevertheless not a poor one, and had average wealth that allowed him to live honourably', and he also informs us that in one of his letters Dante boasted of having had, before his exile, a rather high domestic standard of living, with 'abundant and costly furniture and furnishings'.[1] In writings going back to the early years of his exile, such as his letter to the Counts Da Romena and the early paragraphs of *Convivio*, Dante insists on the *sudden* poverty into which he was plunged by exile, and the injustice of being punished with 'exile and poverty'. He must have exaggerated, but everyone knew it, and if he had already been poor beforehand he certainly couldn't have invented these grievances. Previously he had been appointed twice to the Council of the Hundred – in 1296 and again in 1301. Only citizens who had an estimated wealth of at least 100 pounds could be appointed to the Council, but this estimate was not an assessment of their wealth, and still less the tax paid, but an abstract coefficient roughly proportional to the presumed income and used from time to time in sharing out positions in the administration of taxes. This is proof that Dante was in the highest stratum of taxpayers, those who 'possessing greater riches carry a higher burden of expenses', as is stated in the charter by which the Council was established.[2]

The mark of affluence for a citizen of that period was the possession of country estates in which, as Villani confirms, they invested more than in their houses in the city: 'There were no citizens – commoners or magnates – who had not constructed or were not constructing extravagant and far bigger buildings than in the city.' It may well be that the chronicler was exaggerating, but of one thing we can be certain: that in his eyes citizens were divided between those who owned properties in the countryside and were therefore rich and could spend money, and those who did not have such properties.[3] We also know that in the case of the Alighieris, the money earned over previous generations of speculation and usury had been invested in land, which allowed Dante and his brother to live off unearned income. This was a lethal mechanism, from the viewpoint of our own era of advanced capitalism, because the idea of reinvesting capital in enterprise had been replaced by hoarding it in what we now call safe-haven assets such as land, but for them it was a decisive step towards achieving financial security and respectable status.[4]

This all confirms Bruni's assessment that Dante lived in considerable affluence before exile, although the only information we have concerns the assets that were confiscated at the time of the verdict, which his heirs would later get their hands on. It emerges from these documents that he owned land at Le Radere in the parish of San Miniato a Pagnolle on the Fiesole Hills (today in the locality of Le Radole or La Radola in the council area of Pontassieve) with: houses 'for a lord', a courtyard, a well, a cottage, an oven, a house 'for a worker', ploughing land, a vineyard, olive groves and trees; other plots of land in the same area and a portion of communal woodland adjacent to the farm; another farm with houses, a courtyard, fields, a vineyard and olive trees in the parish of San Marco al Mugnone, in the area then known as Camerata, a little outside Florence on the road to Fiesole; and an enormous plot of land in Florence in the parish of Sant'Ambrogio and a cottage with a small adjacent plot of land in the same parish. Bruni claimed that Dante's family owned 'properties in Camerata, Piacentina and Piano di Ripoli',[5] and it's clear that he had consulted documents in the archive: the locality called Piagentina was situated in the parish of Sant'Ambrogio. Only the properties in the area of Ripoli do not appear in the documents concerning Dante, but his brother Francesco had considerable interests there, and would set up home there in later life.

It appears that Dante and Francesco held their assets jointly:

the only doubt could arise from the contract of sale of land in Pagnolle in 1311, which mentions only Dante as one of the neighbours, but in 1320 two plots located in different places in the same parish turn out to be next to lands 'of Dante and Francesco Alighieri', and in 1343 Dante's son Iacopo, on redeeming confiscated properties in Pagnolle, declared that at the time of the deed of sequestration they were jointly owned by Dante and Francesco. Everything leads us to believe that the two brothers never split their inheritance, a decision that was very common at the time and which must have caused serious administrative complications for officials in the city-state when it came to confiscating properties, given that it was probably only directed against Dante.[6]

Some documents, which must however be interpreted with care, offer some idea of the value of these properties. In 1341 the division of the properties between Dante's sons, *messer* Piero and Iacopo, did not create two halves of equal value, and it was decided that Iacopo would have to pay his brother 159 gold florins and pay him the proceeds of his canonry near Verona for three years to make up for the difference. Six years later, in 1347, Iacopo had not paid the 159 florins, and arbitration transferred half of the farm at San Miniato a Pagnolle and four other plots in the same area by way of compensation. This implies that together the various properties in Pagnolle were valued at around 320 florins. A document in the Portinari family viewed by a descendant in the early eighteenth century is supposed to have declared that Dante's other farm in Camerata, which was purchased by the Portinari, had been sold in 1347 for 1,050 florins. The figure appears to be exorbitant, and one wonders whether the eighteenth-century man of learning made a mistake. If it had been pounds in small florins instead of gold florins, it would have been much less improbable and much closer to the other figure: 336 gold florins.[7]

In 1350, following Iacopo di Dante's death, possibly caused

by the Black Death, the brother of Iacopa di Biliotto Alfani, whose engagement to Dante's son had been broken, took legal action against the heirs for damages. Given that the heirs were nowhere to be found, the complainant had the estate valued and the judge awarded him the farm at San Miniato a Pagnolle and another plot in the same area, which together were valued at 110 florins. This is much lower than the valuation in the agreements between the two brothers in 1341 and 1347, but it should be remembered here that the price of land fluctuated dramatically according to the circumstances in which it was calculated, such as whether the context was friendly or litigious, or whether relations were involved. In the absence of anyone with a claim on the property, it was easy for the complainants to keep the valuation low.[8]

Finally we have some information on the value of the real estate in Sant'Ambrogio. In 1312 Francesco sold a cottage and a small piece of land in that area to the Peruzzi brothers for 59 pounds and 10 shillings 'in florins'. The fact that his mother, Lapa, took part in the sale leads us to believe that these assets belonged to her dowry, but in 1332, when Francesco and Dante shared out their properties, the cottage and its annexes were still included as part of their shared ownership. Evidently the sale was only security for a loan granted by the Peruzzi bank. In the separation of the assets, half of the cottage was assigned to Francesco and half to the grandsons. The other plot of land in Sant'Ambrogio was to be wholly owned by Francesco until Piero and Iacopo paid off the loan of 215 florins he had granted Dante in 1300. It would be jumping to conclusions to assert that the plot in Sant'Ambrogio had been valued at exactly 430 florins, but it would be reasonable to believe that it was a very large area of land of high value, comparable to that of a farm.

We also have figures relating to the income from these properties, but in this case they have to be viewed with even greater caution. In 1336 the properties in Camerata were still technically under judicial attachment, and the Portinaris, who had bought them, paid a rent of 48 bushels to the Office of Rebel Assets every year. In 1339 the inhabitants of San Marco al Mugnone were questioned about the possible income from Dante's assets in Camerata. The response was that they could be rented out for 60 bushels. In 1343 Iacopo, on recovering the assets in Pagnolle, declared that following the confiscation they had been rented out by the republic for 24 bushels (or 1 *modius*) per annum. Twenty-four bushels per annum was also the rent a tenant farmer paid in 1336 to the Office of Rebel Assets for Dante's property in Sant'Ambrogio. The office then transferred the rent to the rebels' wives and widows and valued 24 bushels of grain at 18 pounds, so it appears that properties confiscated from Dante could provide an income of around 80 pounds a year, which in 1302 would have been the equivalent of 25 to 30 florins: more than the salary of a professor at the University of Bologna – enough to maintain a respectable lifestyle and a little less than the threshold for being eligible for the Council of the Hundred, which represented the major taxpayers in the city.

But we must be careful: these figures refer to rents demanded by the Office of Rebel Assets, which were famously much lower than the market price, as always happens when a public body rents out confiscated property through a network of friendships and vested interests, as we can well imagine. If managed by the owners or even just rented out by them, those farms would have provided an income two or even three times higher.[9] Moreover, at the moment of the verdict against Dante, the farms would have been laid waste, and the rents were subsequent to the devastation: it was the custom to cut down vines and olive trees when it came to ruining an enemy's property. It would have taken years for them to bear fruit again.

If, as seems probable, only Dante's part was confiscated and rented out by the republic but not Francesco's, the rents we've mentioned would only have been for half of the overall

CHAPTER TEN

POLITICS: THE MAGNATES
AND THE PEOPLE

Dante's lack of involvement in business was in part due to his studies, which he threw himself into with a passion, and later, at around the age of thirty, his active participation in the political life of the city. The Republic of Florence was governed by a popular regime, which meant that participation in the decision-making bodies embraced a large section of the economically productive population. The actual government was made up of the six priors of the guilds, which represented the entrepreneurial and artisanal community, and the *Gonfaloniere di Giustizia*, whose task it was to ensure compliance with the Ordinances of Justice that defended the commoners from the violence of the magnates. They were called the *Signori* (the Lords), and only remained in post for two months, to avoid any concentration of power in the hands of the few. Beneath them, the decision-making process involved no fewer than five councils: the Council of the Hundred, the Special and General Councils of the Captain of the People and the Special and General Councils of the Republic (or of the Supreme Magistrate).

In all there were 676 citizens sitting on these councils, and their members were renewed every six months. But the Captaincies of the Guilds – that is to say, the boards of consuls that managed each of the twenty-one corporations – were also politically active and they were often called on to participate and vote in council meetings. Whereas the supreme magistrate who held a large part of the executive and judicial power was a professional who came from another city and was subject to an inquiry on termination of his annual contract, the government posts were entrusted not to professional politicians but to an enormous number of people taking turns, who didn't abandon their normal activities. Consequently the term 'political career', with the professional implications it implies in our modern parlance, would be quite misleading: in Florence, at the time, practically all taxpayers could expect to be co-opted onto one of the councils. Even if we examine the more restricted number of those who sat more frequently on those councils, we should never confuse them with a political caste.

Dante's participation in Florentine politics is evidenced by many documents over a period of six years from 1295 to 1301, but it definitely began earlier than that. He declared in *Vita Nuova* that in 1290, on the death of Beatrice, 'Still crying in that desolate city, I wrote to the princes of the land a great deal about its condition, taking as my starting point what the prophet Jeremiah said, "How lonely lies the city" (*Lamentations*, 1: 1).'

The passage starts with the powerful image of Florence abandoned and desolate after the passing of Beatrice, and it is frustrating that we don't have any idea of what Dante had written to the 'princes of the land', an expression that we have to interpret as the *Signori* of the city. We can exclude the possibility of his having explained to them why Beatrice's death was a tragedy for Florence: it is more likely that he took advantage of the moment to denounce in general terms the woeful conditions of the city. In other words, there is a considerable temptation to see in that lost text the first of his political epistles, already loaded with the prophetic language which would characterise the manifestos published from the start of the reign of Emperor Henry VII. The same quote from Jeremiah opens the letter Dante sent to the Italian cardinals in 1314 – this time it referred to Rome, which had just lost its pope. However, Marco

Santagata has noted that among the priors who took office on 15 June 1290 there was a cousin of Beatrice's husband, so the letter could have referred to the recent bereavement. In any event, this was, as far as we know, Dante's first foray into public life.[1]

The next evidence of Dante's political involvement takes us to 1294, and this too was provided by him, without any documentary confirmation. In March of that year Charles Martel of Anjou, son of the king of Naples and pretender to the Hungarian crown, stayed for some weeks in Florence, where he was greeted by the Guelph republic with triumphal festivities. On that occasion he met Dante, who was six years older than him and was possibly in one of the delegations the republic appointed to entertain the count fittingly. The two immediately struck up a close relationship, which would not come to much as Charles died unexpectedly the following year. The source for all this is Canto VIII of *Paradise*, in which Charles Martel of Anjou comes towards Dante with joy and after revealing his identity, because he is enveloped in light and therefore unrecognisable, he reminds Dante among other things that:

> you love me so much, and with good reason;
> so if I had remained there, I would have shown
> you my love well beyond the foliage.
>
> (*Paradise*, VIII, 55–7)

The fact that, immediately before revealing himself, Charles was reciting the first verse of one of Dante's songs, 'Voi che 'ntendendo il terzo ciel movete', has triggered speculations on the young prince's probable interests in poetry, which would have provided common ground sufficient to overcome the distance between them in terms of social status. But we cannot exclude the possibility of a meeting in very different circumstances, when the lector at the Dominican faculty of Santa Maria Novella, the famous preacher Remigio del Chiaro Girolami, gave a sermon in honour of Charles in which he commented on the biblical verse, 'Deliver me in Thy righteousness, and cause me to escape; incline Thine ear unto me, and save me' (Psalms 71: 2).

We have referred to two cases in which Dante mentions early involvement in the city's politics. We'll add the theory, which Dante scholars are divided over, that he was part of a diplomatic mission sent to Naples in October of 1294 to pay homage to the new pope, Celestine V, whom Dante, having placed him in hell, claims not only to have seen but also to have met – always supposing that Celestine really is the anonymous damned soul 'who out of cowardice made that terrible refusal'.[2] In reality, everything we can find out about the youthful formation of his intellect and poetry suggests, as Giuliano Milani has written,

> the image of a Dante who, even before he was thirty, was no stranger to political reflections. Quite the contrary, as a poet and intellectual he proved to be fully aware of the close-knit fabric of ideas relating to urban society, its conflicts and his government, and within this complex and layered debate he had marked out his route through existing positions.

It is not at all surprising, then, that at some stage Dante, like thousands of his fellow citizens, started to participate in the councils, which day after day decided the policies of the Florentine republic. It is striking, however, that his first documented intervention in the councils took place in a particularly dramatic moment, when crucial decisions were taken for the survival of the popular regime.

On 5 July 1295 Florence was on the brink of civil war. The magnates, powerful families which the Ordinances of Justice, promulgated two years before, had excluded from the principal government bodies in the city, had armed themselves and gathered in the squares along with peasants from their lands and private guards (*masnadieri* in the language of the time, or mercenaries hired by feudal lords or, in this case, a magnate). They had occupied Piazza San Giovanni, Mercato Nuovo and access to Ponte Vecchio. They demanded that the priors modify the Ordinances of Justice by removing the more restrictive clauses. The people, by which we mean the merchants and artisans, organised in local militias, had immediately taken to the streets as well, forming a defensive shield around the Palace of the Supreme Magistrate and the Castagna Tower, in which the priors resided with a permanent escort. For the whole day they stared each other in the face under a July sun, nervously expecting something to happen, while leading citizens and friars ran back and forth between them in attempt to find a peaceful solution. Eventually the magnates agreed to return home and empty the squares, but only if there was a promise that the Ordinances would be amended as they had requested.

The next day, 6 July, a resolution reflecting the agreed compromise was duly put to the vote. Knights continued to be banned from standing for the post of prior, and the obligation to sign up to membership of a guild, namely a professional corporation, remained an obligation, but it was no longer necessary to actually carry out that profession. Now the post of prior was open to citizens 'who exercised a trade full-time, or who are registered in the book or register of a guild in the city of Florence, as long as they are not knights'. In short, it was enough to be registered, and no one was denied registration, because in Florence – more than in other cities – the guilds were hybrid organisations that combined the roles of a sectorial confederation, an industrial–financial lobby and a religious confraternity. They did not correspond rigidly to real distinctions in the way the economy worked. The other aspect of the Ordinances which the government of the people agreed to amend was the fearful punishments that could be inflicted on magnates who offended commoners. Those punishments were slightly mitigated, primarily because they wanted to accommodate those who were inclined to support the popular government, even though they were magnates. It was therefore established that, excluding the seventy families listed as magnates in the Ordinances, no other family would be penalised unless they had had more than two members knighted in the last twenty years, which was considered to be a sufficient display of wealth, power and belligerence to define them as a manifest and brazen enemy of the people.[3]

Putting a resolution to a vote was easier said than done: the institutional mechanisms of a medieval city-state became more complicated as the population grew, and Florence was an enormous metropolis. Initially the Council of the Hundred met, and it represented the interests of those paying the most tax. One of the priors, the judge *messer* Palmieri Altoviti, put the reform to the vote. The notary, *ser* Bene del Vaglia, spoke in favour, and the resolution was approved by eighty-nine votes to one. Then the Special Council of the Captain of the People met along with the captaincies of the twelve major guilds; Lottieri di Benincasa spoke in favour, and the resolution passed unanimously with seventy-six votes. Then the Special Council went into a joint session with the General Council of the Captain of the People, Cambio Guidalotti spoke in favour and the vote was almost unanimously in favour. Armed with all these votes, *messer* Palmieri Altoviti took the resolution to the General Council of the Republic. Someone, whose name is not legible in the minutes but ends with -*herii*, spoke in favour and the reform of the Ordinances was definitively approved, 'almost' unanimously once again.

This somebody whose name ended with -*herii* was none other than Dante Alighieri, in the almost unanimous opinion of academics. The missing letters correspond exactly to the illegible space, and in the minutes for that year there are no other speakers with surnames that could correspond to those final letters. Here we will proceed on the basis that this theory is correct, even though we cannot be absolutely sure. Thus Dante was one of the 300 members of the General Council of the Republic in 1295. The oft-repeated assertion that the poet 'went into politics in 1295' has no foundation: we don't possess the complete lists of the members of the councils, only at best the names of people who spoke, and therefore it is perfectly possible that Dante had been a member of the Council or some other body in the city-state in the preceding years.

In spite of the emergency facing the city-state, the rigidly codified procedure was followed to the letter on 6 July: when there was a desire to get a resolution passed and people were fairly sure of the majority, there would be only one speaker in each council and he would speak in favour of the motion. Then they would proceed with the vote, which could be by a show of hands, in accordance with the circumstances.* This meant that, during the frenzied hours before voting, leaders of the popular regime had to identify the four councillors who could speak in favour of the resolution. It follows then that Dante, like the other three, was considered someone they had absolute confidence in. The priors who put through the 1295 reform represented the moderate wing of the regime, which a few months earlier had gained the upper hand and driven out of the city Giano della Bella, who had devised the Ordinances of Justice. The moderate wing also persecuted his followers. It was a government of 'the more powerful fat commoners', as Villani wrote, as he was hostile to the extremism of the little people and open to a more conciliatory attitude to the magnates, as long as they renounced their violent behaviour; all the evidence points to this being Dante's position too.[4]

---

* Piero Gualtieri has demonstrated that the trend towards council debates in which the priors presented stereotypical speeches in favour of a motion was already present in the 1290s, though it was increasingly accentuated in the first decade of the next century.

What exactly did they mean when the spoke of 'magnates' and the 'commoners'? Florentine society was stratified, complex and characterised by a high degree of social mobility: clearly the historians who have been studying it for a long time struggle to give precise definitions. Even contemporaries risked getting tied up in knots when it came to formulating explicit definitions, but it is also clear that in everyday life they knew exactly what they were talking about when they used these terms. The magnates were those who belonged to important, wealthy and well-known families with a great number of members. They lived in palaces with towers, owned land, received unearned income, had retainers and mercenaries, and regularly trained for combat on horseback. In a violent society they were inevitably the ones who instilled fear. The great majority of them were nobles, or rather *gentili*, as they were called in the vernacular, and this meant that they belonged to families who flaunted their chivalric lifestyle and had already been participating in the government of the city for several generations. A few others were new men – bankers and businessmen who had recently enriched themselves, and perhaps even immigrants from the countryside – and these *nouveaux riches* backgrounds were things that people noted and remembered. However, the lack of illustrious ancestors did not prevent them from becoming magnates, if such men also took up the custom of arming knights or having their own sons knighted, and of parading the superior social status guaranteed by their acquired chivalric condition.

The people, on the other hand, worked, traded in workshops or business premises, engaged in financial deals and sold goods, and were known for this (many of the magnates were also involved in financial dealings, tenders and money, and the large banking companies on which Florence's international clout had been built were mainly in their hands, though they didn't get their own hands dirty). The people were highly diversified within their own ranks: there was a gulf between the wealth and prestige of the entrepreneur who imported wool in bulk from England and put it out to a multitude of workers in a cottage industry and the poverty and low status of the cobbler in his miserable roadside workshop. Hence that entrepreneur could have had more in common with a knight than an artisan. Yet as long as he didn't take those final steps and arm his son as a knight, give over the management of his business to others and adopt an aristocratic lifestyle, the entrepreneur was, as far as politics was concerned, still in the same party as the cobbler except, we should be clear, when he attempted to steer that party in a more moderate direction. Anyone can see that these definitions leave room for an infinite number of intermediate positions, but this is typical of any open society where there are no hereditary castes. This should not prevent us from clearly seeing what Florentines in those times meant when they contrasted the magnates and the people.

Thus Dante was typical of those intermediate positions. He claimed to be noble, because he had ancestors, or rather he would start to claim this later in life, but the evidence suggests that the name of Alighieri did not evoke a great deal of respect among his fellow citizens (the claim to nobility did not bother anyone, as he had few relatives and was not surrounded by armed followers, so there was no reason to mark him down as an enemy of the people). Personally, he was in contact with many magnates: his wife, Gemma di *messer* Manetto Donati, came from a family of magnates, as did his best friends, Guido Cavalcanti and Forese Donati. His great-uncle Bello had been a knight, which according to the stricter interpretation would have been enough to have made a magnate of Dante: a statute of 1286, which was voted through to dispel all doubts over who was a magnate, defined a magnate as anyone who had had a knight in the family in the last twenty years. But of course Bello was already 'the late' in 1269, so the twenty-year limit had expired. In any event the amendments introduced in 1295 altered the situation: a family needed to have had more than two knights to be defined as a family of magnates. Indeed, no members of the Alighieri family appear in any of the lists of magnates drawn up during those years, and Dante held a seat in the council under a popular regime, which in all likelihood he had held since before that 6 July when the decision was taken to mitigate the Ordinances against the magnates. Politically he was a man of the people, albeit a moderate one inclined to a compromise with the magnates and horrified by the dictatorship of worthless people. He did share something with the people, and that something was the official ideology, which was interested not so much in extending the participation of the lower ranks of society in the business of government as establishing the supremacy of the law and peaceful procedures that defended social harmony and the common good rather than the violence that continually tempted the magnates.

At this stage it would be interesting to examine the others who were called on to speak that day. *Ser* Bene del Vaglia, notary, had had a seat in the council for years and had spoken in favour of the proposed resolution on some previous occasions. He was evidently a man of authority, but without a surname – a classic advocate of the people. Lottieri di Benincasa was also an expert and had served as prior in 1284 and 1291. Someone of the same name had been registered in the Guild of Calimala since 1244, and this namesake was the son of a Benincasa dei Balsami, a family of leading Ghibellines, who had been banished on successive occasions. It's difficult to know if they were the same person, but the onomastics suggest that they were at least of the same family. These Benincasas, who often appear in documentation of this period, were important partners in the company of the Scalis and belonged to a large contingent of nobles who had decided to support the popular party, and weren't classified as magnates. Lottieri was definitely one of these, because in accordance with the Ordinances of Justice a magnate could not hold a seat in the Councils of the Captain of the People. On the other hand, the Guidalottis were magnates and a very numerous family some of whose branches were Guelphs and some Ghibellines, but in this case many of them had espoused the cause of the people, because Cambio Guidalotti sat on the General Council of the Captain of the People, and in the following year, 1296, Cante Guidalotti would be the *Gonfaloniere di Giustizia*, another position that was expressly denied to magnates.

The fourth was Dante, and this quartet starts to acquire some significance, as it embodies quite well the socially composite nature of the popular elite while it was in power: fairly rich, open to dialogue with persons of aristocratic origin and not very willing to follow the less well-off commoners in their indiscriminate hostility towards the magnates. It was an elite clearly well represented by the proponent of the resolution, *messer* Palmieri Altoviti: a protagonist of the change towards a more moderate policy shortly before Giano della Bella was sent into exile, and a member of a family that had always been classified as commoners – indeed Giovanni Villani declared that he was one of the most influential people in the 'new popular state'. In reality he came from the branch of an ancient family of magnates who had specialised in legal careers and yet had retained many of the social characteristics of magnates, such as the ownership of towers. Although governing on behalf of a people's regime, he and the other priors in office were actually, as the chronicler Marchionne di Coppo Stefani would write a century later, 'people who favoured the magnates'.[5]

However moderate Dante may have been, his friend Guido Cavalcanti was not happy that he was supporting the popular government. Guido was a great poet, but he was a magnate through and through – indeed one of the most haughty and violent, who was regularly involved in clashes, occasionally physical, between factions of the nobility. Now Dante had decided to align himself with a party that wanted to impose pacification at all costs, and which had gone so far as to prohibit Guido and people like him from the most sensitive positions of power. Guido had known a different Dante, one who was keen to fraternise with gangs of noble youths and wrote poetry that celebrated an aristocratic culture and lifestyle, but he no longer recognised him. This, at least, is a possible explanation for the sonnet, 'I' vegno 'l giorno a te infinite volte' ('I think daily of you infinite times'), in which he accuses Dante of 'despicable thoughts' and of joining a herd of mediocrities, 'annoying people' who left their little businesses to sit on the councils of the people's regime. Who would have thought it, given that he detested the crowd ('Many people incurred your displeasure')! Dante had definitely changed, and Guido at least wasn't happy with it. He did not know then that in a few years Dante, as one of the priors, would be one of those responsible for sending him into internal exile in Maremma, along with the most dangerous of the magnates.

Confirmation of how he had clearly positioned himself politically came little more than three months after the vote on 6 July, when Dante was appointed as one of the thirty-six members of the Special Council of the Captain of the People for a term of office that ran from 1 November 1295 to 30 April 1296. 'Dante Alagherii' is registered in the list, which has survived by sheer chance, as one of the six members from the *sesto* of Porta San Piero. As we would expect, the thirty-six councillors were enthusiastic advocates of the people: only two of them carried the title of *messere* or its Latin equivalent, *dominus*, and both of them were legal experts and not knights. Many were supporters of important families, but still indisputably members of the people: Albizi, Bacherelli, Raffacani, Altoviti, Acciaiuoli, Beccanugi, Canigiani and Ricci. Most of them were little-known figures who championed the middle-ranking people, and identified more than all the other social groups with the government of the people. Five were notaries, distinguished by their title *ser*.

One was Bonaccorso, son of *ser* Brunetto Latini, and another the previously mentioned Gerardo del Bello. The list was used for noting down absences at the meetings of the council, which were punishable with a fine unless there was some justification. Next to Dante's name there are six letters, of which five have been rubbed out, which is usually interpreted as meaning that out of six absences Dante managed to find an excuse for five of them. We don't know how often the council met, but it is reckoned that there were between six and nine sessions each month, so six absences in six months would not have been excessive. We should remember that Dante, like anyone else, would have had many other matters he had to see to, and we know nothing about what they were.[6]

But the most important point is that, according to the regulations, Dante had to be registered in a corporation before he could be co-opted on to that council. In fact, he had been registered with the Guild of Physicians, Apothecaries and Haberdashers. We know this because in 1447 the consuls of the guild decided to copy out in a single register in alphabetical order the names of everyone who had been enrolled on existing records. The guild's archive had conserved seven successive registers in chronological order; the oldest one covered the years from 1297 to 1301, and all the preceding ones had been lost. Today we have lost them all, but we have the transcription of 1447, and there we find the name of 'Dante d'Aldighieri degli Aldighieri, Florentine poet', which had been taken from the oldest register. Dante was famous among fifteenth-century Tuscans, and we can be certain that the added detail of 'Florentine poet' was not in the original register. It is undeniable that Dante was registered in the list of persons enrolled in the art compiled between 1297 and 1301, but this does not preclude his registration from an earlier date, because registrations could be repeated for one reason or another, and the registration would have been a renewal.

His choice of guild has sparked off the strangest of

interpretations by men of letters. As Bruni asserted that Dante knew how to draw, there are some who had assumed that he enrolled in that guild because it was also a corporation of painters – something which is less surprising if we remember that apothecaries sold colouring agents and more generally the raw materials painters used for making paints. No less bizarrely, Barbi thinks that Dante was able to enrol in that guild because of the 'fame he enjoyed as an expert in philosophy', as medical science at the time had a robust foundation in philosophy. All these fantasies fall away once you reflect that the guild, which is still called the Guild of Physicians and Apothecaries, in practice included traders and dealers in widest possible variety of goods, from nails to paper, and it was precisely for this reason that printers would enrol in this guild towards the end of the fifteenth century. Stationers were also enrolled, by which we mean retailers and resellers of vellum, paper and manuscripts: we may as well decide that Dante chose this guild because it was involved in books! The point is that anyone could enrol themselves in the 'matricula artis, collegii et universitatis medicorum, aromatariorum et merciariorum Porte Sancte Marie civitatis Florentie', as the 1447 register was pompously entitled, because that guild was a vast and heterogeneous container of professionals and entrepreneurs of all kinds, and as clearly stated in the Ordinance of Justice, engaging in a trade was not a necessary condition for being registered.

Dante's second speech in a debate, and the first of which we are absolutely certain, was on 14 December 1295, and took place not in the Special Council of the Captain of the People, which he was a member of at the time, but in the Council of the Captaincies of the Twelve Major Guilds, which represented the most important financial and mercantile groups. On that day the council, which had been enlarged with a group of wise men nominated by the outgoing priors, discussed the voting procedure for electing the next priors, who had to be elected the following day in the same council. The Republic of Florence operated through extraordinarily flexible procedures which were continuously amended: the priors were replaced every two months, and there was no set procedure for electing them, but procedures were discussed every time on the day before the end of the term of office. That day, as many as eleven of those present stood up and each one proposed a different procedure for selecting the candidates. One of them was 'Dante Alagherii'.

As the register is mouldy and largely illegible, we cannot understand exactly what each proposal was suggesting, but they were mainly concerned with establishing whether the leaders of guilds in each *sesto* had to choose the candidates together with the wise men appointed by the outgoing priors or whether separate proposals should be submitted. There was also the question of whether they should select two, three or more candidates. The ubiquitous *ser* Bene del Vaglia proposed quite bizarrely that the leaders of each *sesto* should appoint the candidates not for their own district but for the adjacent one (the proposal did not go down well and met with no support). And Dante? According to his proposal, the captaincies and the wise men had to choose candidates by common agreement, but Lando Albizi's proposal would prevail, whereby each group should decide separately on its candidates.

This may all seem pointlessly complicated, but by patiently analysing the circumstances we can understand that there was a great deal at stake. It was a matter of deciding between a procedure that would have produced a single list of candidates, obliging the management of the guilds to come to an agreement with the outgoing priors while guaranteeing an election guided without risks of divisions, and one that would have led to a possible confrontation between different lists while giving the corporations full autonomy over the choice of their own candidates. Compared with the proposal that was approved, Dante's undoubtedly went in the direction of greater continuity with the outgoing government and reduced the importance of the final vote, because they would have voted on a single agreed list of candidates for each *sesto*, instead of contrasting and potentially divisive lists. The procedure that was adopted was the one generally used during the revolutionary years of Giano della Bella, which guaranteed autonomy for the consuls of the guilds in the choice of candidates and had in the past often favoured the election of new men: Dante's opposition was entirely in line with what we know of his approach to the problems dividing the city at the time.*

Thus, having taken the floor in July at the General Council of the Republic and having been appointed in October to the Special Council of the Captain of the People, Dante spoke in December in this other perhaps still more important council, that of the Captaincies of the Twelve Major Guilds, which was about to elect the priors. It is almost certain that he was not a full member, which would have meant some position within the management of the guild – something of which there is no evidence – and so he must have been one of the 'wise men' invited for the occasion at the request of the outgoing priors. This is very significant, because it means that the current priors had put their trust in him during a period when there was still a great deal of tension in the city and when, following the amendments mitigating the Ordinances of Justice, some people were talking of betrayal by the wealthy or the 'fat commoners' (*popolo grasso*), as they were called at the time, and there was even talk of the magnates preparing a coup. This appears to confirm that Dante was hand in glove with a party that was willing to run considerable risks to impose a more restrictive and elitist mould

---

*John Najemy has analysed the debates before the election of priors from 1293 to 1303, and has demonstrated that the autonomy given to the consuls of the guilds in proposing candidates was directly proportional to the drive for greater popular participation, and was regularly challenged by the more powerful families with a propensity for oligarchy.

on a government that was still officially defined as belonging to the people.

The third occasion on which Dante rose to his feet to speak was in a session on 5 June 1296. Little more than a month after his term of office on the Special Council of the Captain of the People, we now find him back in the Council of the Hundred. Appointed directly by the priors for six-monthly terms, this council had originally been set up to approve exceptional expenditure, and precisely for this reason its oversight often involved political issues that were highly controversial. The criteria on which it had been established seven years earlier are extremely instructive, and it is strange that they are given so little consideration when it comes to placing Dante in Florentine society at the time. The idea was to have public expenditure controlled by the citizens who were most affected – that is to say, those who were paying the most taxes. Therefore only registered citizens could be appointed to the council – to be precise, those who were registered taxpayers for a sum of at least 100 pounds. Of course they still had to be members of the people, and the appointment of nobles and magnates was expressly denied; the Hundred had to be 'the best and most trustworthy of craftsmen and other commoners'. Dante was a member of the Hundred because he was one of those who were making the largest contributions to the public purse. He may not have been a craftsman (*artifex*), but he was a commoner (*plebeius*) and in any event someone trusted by the regime – a 'best and most trustworthy person'.

The agenda for that session is indicative of the vast range of competences assigned to the Hundred. The Captain of the People requested authorisation to: move a hospital out of Piazza di San Giovanni; prohibit entrance to Florentine territory by exiles from the Republic of Pistoia, currently a loyal ally of Florence, and exempt citizens of Pistoia who own property in the Florentine countryside from taxation for a period of five years; increase the powers of the priors and the *Gonfaloniere* of

Justice to punish magnates who insult the people; amend the legal procedures for appeals; and respond to the petitions of tax collectors and notaries of a tax while it was being collected (it appears that they were requesting a salary increase) and of the overseer of the prison for magnates (we do not know what he was asking for). Quite a mishmash of subjects, but then the assemblies voted docilely in accordance with instructions from the majority party, just as they do today. Only one councillor raised specific observations on two points in the debate. Three others spoke in favour of all the proposals, 'Dante Alagherii' being one of them. The council approved all matters with an overwhelming majority. The greatest number of noes – seven against sixty-eight in favour – were for the vote on the increased powers of reprisal against the magnates, but Dante voted in favour: however much he was in favour of a more conciliatory policy, he was still an exponent of a regime whose principal purpose was to defend the people against the violence of the magnates.

CHAPTER ELEVEN

POLITICS: THE WHITE GUELPHS
AND THE BLACK GUELPHS

At the end of these eleven months in which we have so much information on Dante's political activities we suddenly have nothing more until 1300. Obviously we shouldn't jump to the conclusion that during this lengthy interval Dante didn't take part in any councils; the opposite is much more probable, but during those years much is missing from the minutes of the meetings.* This is a great pity, because it was a period of high drama. The republic continued to be governed – badly or 'with little justice', in the opinion of Dino Compagni[1] – by the moderate regime of the people to which Dante belonged, but another fracture was forcefully emerging in the political life of the city, which the Ordinances of Justice were not sufficient to heal. The Guelph magnates were divided into two factions, the White Guelphs and the Black Guelphs, led by two families that lived in Porta San Piero and whose houses were adjacent to those of the Alighieris: the Cerchis and the Donatis. As a consequence of this rift, which was just as savage as the one between Guelphs and Ghibellines, Dante's political life would end in the catastrophe of exile.

The two families appeared to embody the profound differences that existed within the magnate class, as all the chroniclers emphasised. Villani wrote,

---

* An erudite but no longer verifiable note testified that Dante spoke at a council in 1297.

Messer Vieri de' Cerchi was the head of the Cerchi family, and he and others in the family were powerful men dealing in big business and linked by marriage to many other families; they were extremely rich merchants whose company was one of the largest in the world. The men were docile and innocent, savage and ungrateful, as happens with people who in a short period of time have come to positions of great power.

They weren't nobles, in other words, and this was clear because they had not learned to maintain their place in the world. They were not made of the right stuff to be anyone's enemy ('docile and innocent'), nor were they capable of making friends, as is the custom in politics, along with the game of reciprocal favours ('savage and ungrateful'). All this, however, did not prevent them from becoming magnates.

The leader of the Donatis was Corso Donati, 'and he and others in his family were gentlemen and warriors, and not excessively rich, but were known as the *Malefami*'. We do not know whether this means 'Of evil fame' or even 'Do me evil', but it certainly wasn't a reassuring nickname.[2] Dante's father-in-law, Manetto Donati, was a distant cousin of Corso Donati, and Corso's brother Forese was a friend of Dante's youth. However, none of this drew Dante over to the Donatis' side. Marriages meant very little in these matters, because they were sometimes arranged with enemy families in moments when they were negotiating a truce. Corso Donati himself had taken a young woman of the Cerchi family as his first wife (the rumour was that he poisoned her).

Everything suggests that Dante was closer to the Cerchis, who reduced their commitment to that pro-magnate organisation that was the Guelph party, believing that this would strengthen their position, and they sought out the support of commoners in government, 'who looked on them favourably', according to Dino Compagni. Many other magnate families took the side of the Cerchis, such as the Abatis, whom Dante was very close to and who were possibly the family of his mother, and the Cavalcantis, the family of his 'first friend' Guido, who was a personal enemy of Corso Donati to the point that the latter tried to have him assassinated while on a pilgrimage to Santiago. On his return and having been informed of the matter, Guido tried to kill *messer* Corso, and was wounded in the brawl along with others in his band. We have no information about whether Dante participated in such clashes in the street, in which deaths could easily occur. Of course, it would not have been strange if he had, given that such a refined intellectual as Guido was involved.

Even though the Ordinances of Justice excluded magnates from all the more important positions in the republic, they continued to exercise enormous influence over Florentine politics, simply because of their number, their wealth, their networks and their military strength. It was no surprise, then, that they managed to influence the election and conduct of the priors. By the end of 1299 the Cerchis' rapprochement with the people resulted in the priorship being mainly composed of persons agreeable to the White Guelphs – so much so that Villani would write that 'because of the Cerchis' huge following, the government of the city was almost all in their power'.[3] For the Donatis, the temptation of recourse to violence was increasingly hard to resist, and the enmity between the two factions accelerated dramatically on May Day 1300. In the evening of that holiday, a 'brigade', as they called a company of young men – in this case friends and relatives of the Donatis who had been dining together – attacked a similar company of young friends and relatives of the Cerchis, who were celebrating nearby in the same district. In the scuffle one of the young Cerchis had his nose cut, and then everyone ran off and shut themselves in their houses. The Cerchis, who knew who was responsible, threatened to 'take revenge on a grand scale'.[4]

The government of the people found itself having to manage a highly dangerous situation. For as long the magnates were fighting among themselves it was impossible to invoke the Ordinances of Justice and put an end to the violence, but the hatred between the Cerchis and the Donatis was no longer an internal matter between magnate families, because many of the 'fat commoners', who were almost as rich and powerful as the magnates, had allowed themselves to get involved. The clash between the two factions revealed and ignited all the unresolved problems in the politics of the city. One was the rancour of the Ghibellines, who had been excluded from any participation in government and, above all, hated the most bellicose and arrogant Guelph magnates, such as the Donatis. Consequently, Compagni argues, 'all the Ghibellines sided with the Cerchis, because they hoped that the Cerchis would mistreat them less.' Another cause of complaint was the dissatisfaction of those who had supported Giano della Bella and disapproved of the moderate policy of the popular regime. According to Compagni, these too sided with the Cerchis, who had given the impression of opposing Giano's exile.

The government's position was made even more difficult by the fact that a division within the Guelph party in Florence could not be managed as a purely internal matter. Florence was at the head of a regional alliance, the Taglia di Tuscia (Tuscia Alliance), which united all the cities governed by Guelphs, and the party also had an international reference point, which was the papacy, whose wishes could not be ignored. Now the wish of the pope, who at the time was the formidable Boniface VIII, was primarily that the party should not split, but if it did, everyone knew that the pope would side with the Donatis, because his bankers, the Spinis, were of the same faction. The pope was strong enough to make sure that whoever he supported would win. In Compagni's words, 'he guided the Church in his own manner, and he humbled whoever did not agree with him.'[5] The

Florentine government even feared that the city's liberty was at stake, and on 18 April 1300, shortly before the May Day brawl, it had imposed a colossal fine on three Florentine residents in Rome, including the agent of the Spinis, accused of conspiring to deliver Florence into the hands of Pope Boniface. The pope reacted by threatening excommunication.

In such a dangerous situation the government decided to convene a meeting of the Tuscia Alliance to elect a new captain: i.e., the military commander of all the Guelph forces in Tuscany. It was an ordinary administrative procedure, but in these circumstances it acquired a particular importance because the pope, then in conflict with the Counts Aldobrandeschi of Maremma, had let it be known that he would be in need of military support. Immediately after May Day, ambassadors were sent to all the cities inviting them to a meeting. Dante was sent to San Gimignano, and he spoke at a General Council of the city on 7 May. The council's minutes notify us of his presence and call him 'nobleman Dante Alighieri, ambassador of the Republic of Florence'. We know enough about the terminology of nobility not to attach too much importance to this form of courtesy, but it is clear that this was not an insignificant mission, and that Dante enjoyed the full trust of the six priors in office in the two-monthly term from 15 April to 14 June, although it should be said that others were sent to the more important cities of Siena, Lucca and Pistoia.

From that moment on, events developed at a frenetic pace. The pope, displaying an untypical benevolence, sent Cardinal Matteo d'Acquasparta to Florence with the task of making peace between the two factions. The cardinal, whose credentials are dated 23 May 1300, must have been in the city for very little time when the new priors took office, summoned to govern from 15 June to 14 August. We don't know what method was used to elect them, but they must have been people the regime was fairly trustful of, if they transferred power to them in such dramatic circumstances. They were Noffo Guidi for the *sesto* of Oltrarno (south of the river), Neri of *messer* Iacopo del Giudice for the *sesto* of San Pier Scheraggio, Nello of Arrighetto Doni for the *sesto* of Borgo, Bindo of Donato Bilenchi for the *sesto* of San Pancrazio, Ricco Falconetti the sword-maker for the *sesto* of Porta Duomo and 'Dante Alagherii' for the *sesto* of Porta San Piero, with Fazio da Micciole as the *Gonfaloniere di Giustizia*. After a few years in which the White Guelphs had the lion's share, one has the clear impression that in setting up this priorship they attempted to balance the factions: while the last two were White Guelphs and the first two are Black Guelphs, the third and fourth are of unknown party affiliation. On the very day they took office – 15 June – the *Gonfaloniere* and the priors came to know all the confidential papers, including the guilty sentences passed on the three Florentines resident in Rome.*

Dante had the most important appointment in his political life, and it came at an extraordinarily difficult moment. The arrival of Cardinal d'Acquasparta, who stayed in Florence throughout the summer, did not calm down the hotheads. It was a matter not just of victory going to one or other of the factions but of the very survival of the government of the people, because some magnates saw a civil war as the opportunity for a coup. On 23 June, the eve of St John's Day, the feast of the patron saint of Florence, and therefore of great symbolic importance for the citizenry, the consuls of the Guilds, who were going in procession to the baptistery to offer gifts to the saint, were attacked and beaten by some magnates. The aggressors openly declared that they would not tolerate a government that excluded them. 'We are the ones who were victorious at Campaldino,' they shouted, 'and you have removed us from office

---

* The fact that Noffo Guidi and Neri di *messer* Iacopo Alberti del Giudice were again elected as priors (in 1315 and 1323 respectively) after the White Guelphs had been banished confirms that they must have been Black Guelphs.

and honours in our own city.' The priors, including Dante, were 'outraged' at what had happened, according to Dino Compagni, and after taking advice from many citizens they condemned dozens of magnates from both factions to internal exile. After all, Dante had also fought at Campaldino and was very proud of it: no one had a history more likely to make him react harshly to the boasting of the magnates.

But whether the government had sufficient grasp on power to have the sentence carried out was another matter. The Cerchis, who were to be exiled to Serrazzano in Maremma, departed, but the Donatis, who had to go to Castello della Pieve, did not make a move. The priors either had to eat humble pie or enforce the punishment with force, which risked triggering a civil war. It was known that the Donatis had requested assistance from the Guelph government in Lucca, and that an army was preparing to leave Lucca to come to their aid. The priors wrote to the authorities in Lucca warning them not to enter Florentine territory, ordered rural communities to guard the passes and tried to convince the condemned Donatis to accept their sentence. Eventually the Donatis did not have the courage to attempt an insurrection, and they left the city. Immediately afterwards, the priors allowed the White Guelphs to return to Florence from exile, while the Black Guelphs stayed outside the city. One could say that the impartiality of the priors, including Dante, was far from guaranteed.

Meanwhile the cardinal continued to negotiate in public and in private. He claimed that he wanted to settle the conflict in the interests of the city and the Guelph party, but the Florentines realised that his true mission was to support the Donatis and ruin the Cerchis. The anger in the city was considerable, and there was even 'someone of not great wisdom' who shot a crossbow arrow at the window of the Bishop's Palace, where the cardinal was living. The distressed priors sent a present of 2,000 newly minted florins to the cardinal: close to a million euros in modern terms. It was the maximum they could give him without the authorisation of the councils. Anxious to placate him, they asked him not to disdain such a small gift. 'He said that he held it dear, and stared at it for a long time, but he did not take it.'[6]

Two months in government may not seem very much, but no one could deny that the bimestrial term in which Dante held the position of prior was full of events, which came at a breathtaking pace. We don't know what position Dante took in the events we have outlined: the punishment of the aggressors on the eve of St John's Day by exiling exponents of both factions (including his friend Guido Cavalcanti), the authorisation for the White Guelphs to return shortly afterwards, the warning to their allies in Lucca not to interfere in the internal affairs of Florence and the attempt to appease the furious cardinal. Witnesses to these events never mention any splits among the priors. In any case, the decisions that he and the others had to take were sufficiently dramatic to justify Dante's bitter comment in one of the letters seen by Leonardo Bruni, according to which 'all the evils and mishaps that afflicted me had their cause and commencement in the inauspicious meetings of my priorship'.[7]

On this point it would be appropriate to remind ourselves that the months immediately before Dante's priorship were the ones during which, in the fiction of his *Comedy*, he declares himself to have been led astray into 'a dark wood'. No doubt about the essentially moral implications of this image, which introduces the reader to a vision of the next world, but equally no doubt about its autobiographical truth: in the second canto of *Purgatory* Virgil would say with fearful candour that, in this moment of corruption, Dante 'because of his folly' had come close to damning his soul. Given that Dante was scrupulously attentive to ensuring that the chronological arithmetic added up, by disseminating clues that allow us to identify the exact days on which the actions in the poem took place, it would perhaps be useful to ask what the poet was actually doing on those days. Dante reached 'the middle of our life's journey' in the second half of May 1300 (and we should take note that the idea of placing his journey to the next world must have been suggested not only by the Jubilee Year taking place in 1300, but also by the memory of Isaiah 38: 10: 'I said: half-way through my days, I shall go to the gates of hell'). However, the start of the poem was set a little earlier, because in Canto XXI of *Inferno* Dante declares, with attention to detail that extends to the time of day, that his journey came exactly 1,266 years after the death of Christ, and so we are immediately after 25 March, the day on which Jesus died according to one particular patristic tradition. Moreover, in Canto II of *Purgatory* we discover that three months have passed since the beginning of the Jubilee, which Boniface VIII declared on 22 February 1300, back-dated to 25 December 1299.[8] So what could Dante have been doing during those days in late March of 1300 in which, according to himself, he was close to losing his soul? The answer is that he was up to his neck in political activity which shortly afterwards would have him tried and condemned for embezzlement, aiding and abetting, and corruption – rightly or wrongly, as we will examine later.*

Bruni emphasises that the decisions taken by the priors during those two months caused fierce criticism of Dante, and public opinion started to identify him as a partisan of the White Guelphs, although he denied this in his letters ('and however much he excused his behaviour as that of a man without faction, he was nevertheless reputed to be inclined to the White Guelphs'). Like every politician, Dante had his own unique method of recording and assessing his own actions: accused of having wanted, along with the other priors, the return of the exiled White Guelphs, he retorted that at the time 'he did

---

* Strangely there has been little investigation of the relationship between the plot of the *Comedy* and Dante's political activities over the same period.

not hold the office of prior', and yet the only chronicler to date that event places it in July. Dante added that in any case they had returned because the air in Serrazzano was unhealthy and Guido Cavalcanti had got sick and died. This additional justification, when the first alone should have been sufficient, weakens rather than strengthens his defence.[9]

As God willed, the two months came to an end, and on Assumption Day the new priors took office, but the situation did not improve partly because the balance in the previous priorship was not maintained. The White Guelphs returned to dominance in the government. All the causes of the conflict remained unresolved following the failure of Cardinal d'Acquasparta's mission and his departure from Florence at the end of September, not without passing an interdict. Corso Donati was in Rome and hoped to convince the pope that, if the Cerchis and their friends continued to rule Florence, there was even the risk that the Ghibellines would return to power.[10] Each faction was meeting in secret and sharpening its swords, while the government of the people continued to play it by ear, changing its priors every two months and imposing ineffective sentences on those magnates who compromised themselves more than others, without having the slightest idea of how to get out of the crisis. On 14 April 1301 Dante spoke at the Council of the Captaincies of the Twelve Major Guilds and the 'wise men', on the occasion of the customary and inescapable two-monthly meeting on how to elect the new priors, and he came out in favour of the prevailing motion, which tended to limit the autonomy of the guilds by obliging the consuls to propose candidates in agreement with the 'wise men' nominated by the outgoing priors. On the same day Dante presented a single motion on how to elect the next *Gonfaloniere* to a more select council, in which there were the captaincies and only two 'wise men' from each *sesto*, and spoke in its favour. It was passed unanimously. Clearly he continued to be a leading exponent of a regime that was a sinking ship.

Before the end of April, Dante had a new and apparently banal position. Among the many commissions that administered the Republic of Florence, there was one consisting of six officials charged with building and repairing roads. A large and expensive undertaking to build a road called the San Procolo Way was already in progress. The road ran from the city walls to the small village of Piagentina and from there to the Africo stream, and the first section had been completed. However the final section was still winding and impassable, and to straighten it they needed to expropriate land, cut trees and demolish houses. Dante was appointed overseer of the works, charged with organising the expropriation, road-building and paving, with full powers to tax the inhabitants of the area who would benefit from the road.

Scholars are divided between those who are surprised that Dante would get involved in such humdrum affairs at such a dramatic time and those who argue that the commission was in fact a very delicate one, given that the resolution emphasises how indispensable the road was for the people of the rural district, who had turned to the priors and the *Gonfaloniere* for assistance. The road would have allowed them to get to the city without being observed by the magnates, who may have made things difficult for them. But the fact is that the current Government of the Second People was *largo* (which we can translate as 'relatively inclusive') and was expected to assign innumerable commissions of this kind, all of which had political implications (as well as economic ones). Those who engaged in the city's politics always had to be ready to accept whatever was put their way, and we should add that Dante owned land in this very area, which refutes the idea that it was in some way exceptional for this work to be awarded to him. This should also remind us that the city in which Dante lived was full of building sites. The republic and the Church were spending huge sums and giving work to armies of labourers so as to create the Florence we know today. But Dante never saw it completed. Building work at Santa Maria Novella commenced in 1279, at the Badia Fiorentina in 1284, at the church of Santa Croce in 1295, at Santa Maria del Fiore in 1296 and at the Palazzo Vecchio (which would become the seat of government) in 1299. Like modern London and New York, Florence pulsated with life and money, and changed its look without regrets or concerns for the past.

About two months later, on 19 June 1301, Dante had to confront an extremely compromising situation. On that day the Council of the Hundred, which once again he was part of, met in a joint session with the General and Special Councils of the Captain of the People and the Council of the Captaincies of the Twelve Major Guilds to vote on two requests. The first was from Pope Boniface VIII, who had asked the Republic of Florence to send 100 knights to be deployed in Maremma against the Counts Aldobrandeschi. The second was from the Republic of Colle Val d'Elsa, and we don't know its content, but we think that it was a request to send a Florentine to act as their supreme magistrate, in accordance with usual practice between allied cities. First to stand up to speak was *ser* Ruggero of Ugo Albizi the notary, and he advised the councils to accept both requests. Then Dante took the floor and said that as far as the request from Colle Val d'Elsa was concerned he had no objections, but they were not to send the knights requested by the pope. After his speech, *messer* Guidotto Canigiani the judge stood up and spoke in favour of both requests. The atmosphere was becoming tense: for once they were discussing not resolutions that had already been agreed but a decision that was truly divisive. Indeed something happened which so often happens when a government finds itself in difficulty: *messer* Albizzo Corbinelli the judge proposed that the vote on the pope's request should be postponed. And this is what they did, and then they unanimously decided to accept the request from Colle Val d'Elsa by a show of hands.

It is difficult to know whether, on being informed of this session, Boniface VIII marked down Dante's name in his black book, but evidently this was a moment when passions were running high and Dante had put himself at quite some risk of being isolated. As though this was not enough, it has been noted that there are two oddities in the minutes of the session. The notary had prepared the register for the minutes of the meeting of the Council of the Hundred, at which the most delicate questions would be discussed and voted on by secret ballot, but at the last moment he added between the lines the names of the other councils convened along with the Hundred, who could vote by a show of hands. There's enough here to speculate on some kind of underhand deal, possibly to favour approval of the motion or possibly even to sabotage it. To say much more than this would be difficult, but clearly everything was very tense. The challenge would have created difficulties for seasoned politicians, but these more amateurish ones were replaced every two months: they had to keep together a popular government disliked by magnates of both factions without alienating the powerful families among the 'fat commoners', who increasingly found themselves in agreement with the magnates, cultivate good relations with the White Guelphs, who were inclined to compromise (and precisely for this reason more attractive to the Ghibellines), and keep the leaders of the Black Guelphs in exile; but because of their influence with the court of Rome, there was the risk of being accused of betraying the Guelph party and the Church.

On that same 19 June the councils went back into session, but this time separately. In the Council of the Hundred the Captain of the People resubmitted the request for 100 knights in the service of the pope with the addition of new details: the commander of the contingent would be *messer* Neri de' Giandonati and his secretary *ser* Torello de' Bronci, and the expedition would not continue beyond 1 September. The Captain of the

People was Atto da Cornalto, who had carried out the same duties in Lucca during the period 1299–1300, which was also the period in which Corso Donati had secured the military support of Lucca in the event of a final reckoning with the rival faction. We can speculate that he and those who had nominated him had made up their minds to get the pope's request approved, and the fact that they had already nominated the commander shows that the executive expected it to be approved. The Captain of the People then added another proposal, the allocation of 3,000 *lire* to pay the wages of the foot soldiers recruited in the countryside. *Messer* Guidotto Canigiani spoke in favour of both proposals in a detailed manner. Then Dante stood up and spoke against the first proposal but accepted the second one. The secret ballot resulted in forty-nine votes in favour of the first proposal and thirty-two against, and eighty votes in favour of the second proposal and one against. The rift in the city caused by Boniface's policies and shameless support of the Donatis could not have been clearer.[11]

Dante's next speech was on 13 September 1301. Once again it was a plenary meeting. Indeed it was the most inclusive of all the others mentioned so far: along with the Council of the Hundred there were the General and Special Councils of the Captain of the People, the General Council of the Republic, the Council of the Captaincies of All the Twenty-One Guilds, and other 'good men' invited to participate, so that no one of note in the city was missing. The matter at stake was evidently the fundamental point: a discussion and a decision on what to do about 'the preservation of the Ordinances of Justice and the Statutes of the People'. Such a generic and yet onerous agenda proposed to such a large assembly reveals just how dramatic the situation was: in effect it was an admission that the regime was in danger. The relationship with the pope was a festering wound and increasingly looked incurable: Charles of Valois, the brother of the king of France, had come to Italy at the head of a French army, having been called by Boniface VIII to assist Charles II of Naples in his war against the Aragonese in Sicily, and everyone expected that the pope, with such a military force at his disposal, would make use of it to settle a score with Florence.

Dante was the first to stand up and speak: the notary who kept the minutes for the session wrote his name and left a blank space for a summary of his speech, but he never wrote it down, which feels like a bad omen. We don't know what Dante said, but certainly something different from what the next speaker said after him, which was minuted. As one would expect, it was *messer* Guidotto Canigiani, who proposed that full powers in managing the crisis should be granted to the supreme magistrate, the Captain of the People (who was still Atto da Cornalto), the priors and the *Gonfaloniere*, along with the councillors who would eventually be chosen. We do not know, however, if anything was actually decided.

In September the council meetings came one after another, and with them Dante's speeches. On 20 September in a joint session of the Council of the Hundred, the General and Special Councils of the Captain of the People and the Captaincies of the Twenty-One Guilds, ambassadors from the Republic of Bologna requested permission to transport through Florentine territory the grain they had bought abroad and had shipped to Pisa. The fact that on that date, shortly after the harvest, the authorities in Bologna had gone to such lengths to purchase grain tell us that 1301 must have had a bad harvest which promised famine – certainly not an encouraging sign for a city on the brink of a coup. But Bologna was a friendly city: *messer* Lapo Saltarelli the judge, one of the principal advocates of the White Guelphs, spoke in favour, and then Dante spoke and also supported the proposal, which was approved almost unanimously.

A week later, on 28 September, the Council of the Hundred discussed a long list of measures, some of little importance and others alarming. As always in such cases, it is difficult to know whether the apparently chaotic range of resolutions is a sign of mental confusion or the product of a well-thought-out plan. The priors started by requesting permission to spend the small sum of 25 pounds, not having exceeded the monthly spending limit; then they proposed the purchase of a missal for their chapel which cost as much as 63 pounds – so far, ordinary administrative matters. Then, however, they asked for the power to appoint all the officials they wanted to, in any capacity, and set the salaries at the level they preferred, for powers to be granted to the supreme magistrate to judge false complaints, false witness and acts of violence committed since the middle of September, for powers to grant pardon to the son of Gherardino Diodati, who had been found guilty of murder (Gherardino had been a prior for the two-month period before Dante's and was therefore one of those who had proposed his candidature), and for the 100 soldiers (*masnadieri*) recruited for the protection of the government building to be paid for another six months starting from 1 October.

It is difficult not to frown on an executive that at such a delicate moment requests authorisation to appoint all the functionaries it wants and to decide on their salaries quite freely. Even the reference to the punishment of false accusations and acts of violence from such a specific time – the middle of September, just two weeks earlier – cannot fail to set alarm bells ringing. But *messer* Albizzo Corbinelli the judge, the same one that three months earlier postponed the vote on the pope's request, spoke in favour of approving all the proposals, and immediately afterwards Dante stood up and spoke in the same vein. All the proposals were passed with just a few votes against or none. Dante could not have known, but this was the last time that he would stand up to speak in any of councils of the Republic of Florence.

Chapter Twelve

BANISHMENT

At the beginning of November 1301, Charles of Valois entered Florence with 1,200 knights. The Black Guelphs had never ceased sending ambassadors beseeching him not to trust the Ghibellines, who they said were governing the city. Presenting the government of the Cerchis as Ghibelline was something of an exaggeration, but the French did not understand the complications of Italian politics and you could get away with telling them this and much more. The White Guelphs fooled themselves that the brother of the king of France really was coming to bring peace and harmony, but the Black Guelphs knew very well that the pope had sent him to destroy their enemies. When they eventually understood the truth, the Cerchis' supporters took fright and each one tried to save himself by distinguishing his own position from that of the condemned faction. 'Bandino Falconieri, a cowardly man, was saying: "My lords, I am well pleased, because I was not sleeping safe in my bed,"' Compagni wrote in disgust. The priors, one of whom in that particular two-month period was Dino Compagni himself, negotiated with the pope and desperately tried to placate him, but the Black Guelphs lost their patience and started to carry out acts of violence and aggression. On the advice of a holy man, the priors organised a procession to implore divine mercy, 'and many mocked us and said that we would do better to sharpen our swords'.[1]

Ultimately Charles of Valois threw off his disguise and had the leaders of the White Guelphs arrested, while Corso Donati and the other exiles returned to the city with impunity. For five or six days the Black Guelphs killed, tortured, plundered and destroyed by fire just as they wished. Dante's properties were also laid waste, as Bruni recalled: 'they rushed to his house, and stole everything, and devastated his properties.' When Villani wrote of those days of terror, he was very specific: 'They started to steal from the warehouses and shops, and the houses of those who had supported the White Guelphs', and then the Black Guelphs proceeded with systematic punitive expeditions against their rival faction's properties in the countryside. The devastation 'continued in the countryside, forays in search of plunder, and stealing and setting fire to houses for more than eight days, whereby a great number of beautiful and expensive possessions were ruined or burned'. One document recorded as late as 1343 that one farm once belonging to Dante turned out to have houses that had been 'burned and not burned', confirming the absolute truth of what Bruni had recorded.[2]

The new masters of the city illegally forced the supreme magistrate and the priors to resign, and they set up a new government of 'appalling commoners' – appalling in that they betrayed their own kind in the inevitable opinion of Dino Compagni. Once *messer* Cante de' Gabrielli da Gubbio had been appointed to the position of supreme magistrate, the anarchic violence was replaced by legal violence: the victors started to make false accusations and prepare legal cases against their adversaries.

Many were accused, and forced to confess to conspiracy even though they had not done this, and then each was fined a thousand florins. Whoever did not defend themselves was accused and sentenced *in absentia* against their property and their person. Whoever obeyed and paid was then accused of other crimes and mercilessly driven out of Florence.

In the first few months of 1302 the exiles numbered more than 600, according to Compagni, who listed by name about forty of the most important ones, either individuals or entire families, and one of them was 'Dante Allighieri who was an ambassador to Rome'.[3]

Doubts have frequently been expressed about his ambassadorship. After having recorded the arrival of Charles of Valois in Rome, Compagni had previously written that 'the White Guelphs had ambassadors at the Court of Rome', but he did not mention any names. This must have been in October 1301, but later he mentions two of the ambassadors, Maso di *messer* Ruggerino Minerbetti and Corazza da Signa, whom the pope sent back to Florence with his proposals while keeping the others in Rome. Dante must have been one of these. It has been noted that the phrase 'who was an ambassador to Rome' has the look of an interpolation – an addition which copiers inserted in a manuscript when they had more information than the author in order to enrich the text. We have already seen that in the list of members of a guild, the fifteenth-century copyist inserted 'Florentine poet' after the entry for Dante, and it was undoubtedly the case that Dante's name was most likely to give rise to such temptations. As we have no documentary evidence of this diplomatic mission, the doubt is perhaps permissible, if only because it surely wouldn't have been wise to send Pope Boniface a man who had made his own views very clear in public, only to have his request rejected. But the White Guelphs, as the chroniclers bear witness, were not known for their cunning.[4]

On the other hand, we are very well informed about Dante's trial and the accusations of extortion which forced him into exile. When the supreme magistrate imposed by the Black Guelphs took office, he brought with him a team of judges and policemen, as was the custom. The separation of powers between executive power and judicial power had not yet been invented. One of those judges, *messer* Paolo da Gubbio, was appointed to deal with barratry, which in its original medieval usage meant the illicit trade in Church or state appointments, and was the term generically used to indicate corruption, extortion and embezzlement of public funds. Barratry was a nightmare in Italian political life in the Middle Ages, and Dante denounces it furiously in *Inferno*, where he reserves a *bolgia* for barrators and obliges them to swim in boiling tar.* In January 1302, however, he was the one on trial. Following the orders of his superiors, *messer* Paolo prepared a series of trials against the priors who had been in office since the end of 1299, and in one of these preliminary investigations he targeted five people, all *in absentia*. The first, Gherardino Diodati, was accused of having accepted 72 gold florins for freeing a magnate who had been detained for serious crimes, and was convicted separately. The others were *messer* Palmieri Altoviti, 'Dante Alaghieri', Lippo di Becca and Orlanduccio Orlandi.

To give an idea of the prevailing climate in these trials, we should mention that one evening Orlanduccio Orlandi, 'a valiant commoner' according to Compagni and therefore a loyal supporter of the government of the people, was attacked and left for dead in the street by members of the Medici family during the tense days that preceded the coup. It goes without saying that the aggression went unpunished, and here the Medicis appeared in a chronicle for the first time. They weren't magnates but 'powerful commoners', the ones that by now were in agreement with the magnates and behaved just like them, but they could not be prosecuted under the Ordinances of Justice, while the ordinary judicial processes were subject to politics and impotent in cases such as this.[5]

The day after the coup, justice revealed its most intransigent

---

* *Bolgia* (plural: *bolge*): each of the concentric ditches in the Eighth Circle of Hell (*Malebolge*, meaning 'Evil Ditches'), according to the architecture of Dante's *Inferno*.

side. The judge proceeded against the four defendants (including the one who was moribund) in his own capacity, given the absence of any complainants, with accusations of barratry and extortion, or more specifically of their having accepted bribes for the election of the next priors and other high officials in the republic, and of having approved measures and the allocation of funds that benefited friends. He also accused them of having accepted, approved and spent public funds greater than the permitted level and having used them in a fraudulent manner to the detriment of the pope and Charles of Valois and to prevent his arrival, which was against the interests of the city and the Guelph party, but also to divide the city of Pistoia and have the Black Guelphs, who were loyal to the Church, expelled from that city.

The trials of 1302 were a turning point in the political life of Florence. From that point on it was no longer the custom simply to drive defeated adversaries out of the city, using executive measures without any pretext required, and the preference was now for regular judicial procedures; but, in spite of the façade of a formally correct trial for barratry, no one tried to conceal the fact that the accusations against the defendants were purely political. Was it an unfair trial? Without doubt: the new regime was taking revenge on its enemies. Yet regular preliminary investigations were carried out, and unlike Stalinist trials, where convictions were based on confessions extorted through torture, here no defendant was forced to confess: they were tried *in absentia*. Above all, the purges were selective: the majority of the priors in office during those years were left in peace. The inevitable conclusion is that they wanted to take legal action mainly against those who could be convicted with at least some degree of credibility. Was Dante a corrupt politician, embezzling for private financial gain? Certainly not, but what of a Dante who in a governmental position agrees to exert some pressure in the interests of the party or faction, to make sure that a particular office does not go to the wrong person or to guarantee funding goes to some friends? This, to be frank, is quite possible.

As none of the accused appeared in court, all four of them were deemed self-confessed criminals and sentenced to a colossal fine of 5,000 pounds each, on top of the return of the extorted sums, always supposing that someone would put in a claim for restitution. *Messer* Cante de' Gabrielli published the sentence on 27 January 1302: if the condemned men did not pay within three days, all their property was to be confiscated and their houses demolished. On the other hand, if they did pay, they were still condemned to exile outside Tuscany for two years. Their names would be transcribed in the city statutes as a reminder of the fact that 'as fraudsters and barrators' they were excluded in perpetuity from holding any office in the republic.[6]

Yet this was not enough for the new regime. On 10 March 1302 the supreme magistrate pronounced a new sentence against the fifteen men found guilty of barratry during the trials of the preceding months, nearly all ex-priors from the years 1299–1301. None of them had appeared before the court or paid the fine. The supreme magistrate, who quoted the statutes and the Ordinances of Justice while in reality acting in an arbitrary manner, declared that they would be burned at the stake, should they ever fall into the hands of the Republic of Florence. The fifteen included Dante and his four co-defendants.

The Black Guelphs' coup held together various interests and produced various outcomes: it had sanctioned the triumph of one of the factions of magnates and 'fat commoners' over the opposing faction, but it had weakened the popular regime, which while accepting compromises still attempted to stay loyal to the spirit of the Ordinances of Justice, which excluded the magnates from government. As Iacomo della Lana, a citizen of Bologna, wrote in his commentary on the *Comedy*, the 'angry Guelph families' were now in power, 'and they humiliated the commoners who had been in power, drove out some of them and killed others. Some of these commoners remained in the land, but they had to be as vigilant as a mouse in flour.' In other words, those who weren't killed or driven out had to keep quiet and not draw too much attention to themselves. Dante was too compromised to rejoin such people: ultimately, as Villani wrote, he had become one 'of the leading governors of our city' – that is to say, one of the most influential politicians. And this must have been the case, if we consider that none of the other five priors in office with him were put on trial during those months. The new regime could not forgive him. 'Among those driven into exile was Dante, who was one of the middle-class people who had been governing the city.'[7]

Chapter Thirteen

AN EXILE'S FAMILY

What did Dante's exile mean for his family? If he had not yet returned from Rome when the banishment was announced, his decision to face his future on his own without requesting his wife to join him would have been much easier. Boccaccio confirmed that Gemma did not accompany Dante into exile: he abandoned Florence, 'having left his wife there along with the rest of the family ill-equipped for flight due to their tender age, while she was safe because of her close blood relationship to one of the leaders of the other faction'. In other words, the children were too small and therefore Dante preferred them not to follow him and he was relaxed about Gemma's personal safety as she was a relation of Corso Donati.

This portrait, in which the dominant theme is his concern for his family, jars with what Boccaccio had just written in a famous passage in which he criticised Dante for having got married and thus subjected himself to all those irritations and demands that women inflict on their husbands. This was a popular theme in the Middle Ages and engendered a flourishing literary genre, which was both moralistic and humorous. However, Boccaccio took it very seriously. Dante, he asserted, was so unhappy with Gemma that he took advantage of his exile to never see her again: 'once he had left her [...] he never wanted to go where she was, nor could he suffer her ever to come to where he was.'[1] It is impossible to reconcile the two versions: either Boccaccio was speaking the truth, and therefore the marriage between

Dante and Gemma was a failure, or he was indulging in idle gossip.

Gemma's continued residence in Florence was confirmed by an account given to Boccaccio many years later by Dante's nephew Andrea di Leone Poggi: after the verdict, fearing that her husband's house would be plundered, 'Dante's wife, who was called Gemma, following the advice of friends and relations, had several strongboxes containing various objects of value and Dante's writing removed from the house and put in a safe place', which would have been a monastery, as Boccaccio also pointed out. During moments of political crisis the reflex action for wealthy Florentines was to ensure the safety of their most precious possessions by entrusting them to friars and monks. A few years later the wives of exiles were permitted to claim back the properties that came with their dowries, and Gemma needed documents contained in those strongboxes, which she had never removed from their hiding place, so she sent her nephew Andrea to get them, accompanied by an attorney and in possession of the keys to open them.

This little story is somewhat undermined by the fact that Boccaccio had a conversation with another person, a *ser* Dino Perini, who claimed to have been a close friend of Dante (there were many of them!) and told him his own version of the same episode. Apparently Gemma had sent him and not Andrea to open the strongbox. It is further undermined by both witnesses claiming to have found the original manuscript of the first seven cantos of *Inferno*, circumstances that were a little too much even for Boccaccio.[2] But the very fact that legend was circulating among friends of the family confirms that Gemma did stay on in Florence, and it was equally true that at some stage she contacted the authorities to request the restitution of the properties covered by her dowry. Apart from this, we know very little about her after that fateful 1302. Her mother, *monna* Maria, died in 1315 (her father, *messer* Manetto, was already dead), and she left her daughter 300 pounds, as long as Dante freed other Donati heirs from any obligation resulting from the famous guarantees signed off by *messer* Manetto in favour of his son-in-law. Subsequent documents in which Gemma appears all refer to the period of her widowhood. She died in 1343.

Necessarily Dante's children were born before 1302, when their father left Florence for good. The fact that in the sentences of that year there is no mention of them confirms that they were minors, and suggests that they really were living with their mother in the city.* The first to appear in documents after that date is the one we know least about, so much so that some scholars have questioned whether he really was Dante's son. On 21 October 1308 in Lucca, 'Giovanni son of Dante Alighieri from Florence' appears among the witnesses to a business deal between merchants of Lucca and the Florentine company of the Maccis, who were White Guelphs, Dante's fellow comrades in exile. It has been inferred that perhaps Dante himself was living in Lucca at the time. An adult son in 1308 is possible for a marriage that started in the early 1290s at the latest, given that the age of fifteen was sufficient to act as a witness. We have already made clear that the marriage contract between Dante and Gemma could well have been carried out on 9 February 1293, though it had been erroneously dated 9 February 1276 (which for us is 1277). So there is still a very narrow margin for speculation that Giovanni Alighieri had just turned fifteen or was considered to be fifteen on 21 October 1308, but we risk entering the realm of fiction. In short, if Giovanni was a legitimate son, it is more likely that Dante and Gemma were married earlier. His presence in Lucca would imply that he had followed his father into exile. However, he reappears in 1314 as 'Giovanni son of Dante Alighieri', a witness at the election of the mayor of

---

* Iacopo had died by 1349, and Piero died in 1364.

San Miniato a Pagnolle, where the family had a farm.* By that date, then, Giovanni had returned to Florence and no longer lived with his father. We have no further news of him after that date, and we assume that he died without leaving heirs.

Dante's other sons were mentioned for the first time in a new verdict issued against him in 1315 by the viceroy of King Robert of Naples, to whom the Republic of Florence had ceded the government of the city two years earlier. Like many other rebels, Dante had rejected the chance of an amnesty to those who were willing to subjugate themselves, pay a surety and spend a period in internal exile. On 15 October 1315 it was announced that the term for acceptance of the amnesty had expired, and all the exiles who hadn't appeared before the court by the following day would be condemned to decapitation. (Dante had already been condemned to be burned at the stake, but no one was very fussy when it came to these collective sentences.) On 6 November a verdict was recorded against three families in the *sesto* of Porta San Piero, or rather against all male members between the ages of fifteen and seventy, except those who had paid the surety. They were all the Portinaris, Beatrice's family, except the fifteen who had paid, all but two of the Giochis and, lastly, 'Dante Alighieri and his sons'. We don't know whether Giovanni was still among those anonymous sons on that date, but if so, he would have had to leave Florentine territory where he had been living the year before. The second son, Piero, was certainly one of them, as was the third son, Iacopo, about whom we have no information until the very end of Dante's life, when he was living with his father in Ravenna, as we shall see in the last chapter.

Giorgio Petrocchi pointed out that the three names of

---

* This presence in Pagnolle decisively strengthens the argument that Giovanni was Dante's son and not one of those namesakes of whom there was no shortage.

Dante's sons – John, Peter and James – are those of three apostles, the same ones that the poet will meet in *Paradise*. They are certainly not names used in the family: Dante had not 'redone' (*rifatto*, to use the term of the time) his father's name, Alighiero, or his grandfather's, Bellincione, and this was unusual: there is enough evidence to speculate – without fear of fictionalising the past – about whether these decisions were an act of rebellion or at least an individualistic indifference to male forebears. Nor is it easy to explain the name of Antonia, Dante's first daughter we know of, because he doesn't appear to have been a devotee of either St Anthony the Great, whose order he mentions disparagingly in Canto XXIX of *Paradise*, or St Anthony of Padua, who never gets a mention. Antonia appears along with her mother in a contract of 1332, when her consent is requested for the sale of some land by her brothers Piero and Iacopo.

Very significant is the name he chose for another daughter: Beatrice (one wonders what Gemma thought about this!). The woman was mentioned in a document of 1350 which was seen by various eighteenth- and nineteenth-century scholars and then mysteriously disappeared, in which Boccaccio, no less, was charged by the Confraternity of Orsanmichele with delivering 10 gold florins to 'Sister Beatrice, nun at the convent of San Stefano dell'Uliva in Ravenna, who is the daughter of Dante Alleghieri'. Dante scholars assume that this Beatrice, whom Dante himself must have placed in the Ravenna convent and who was recorded as deceased in a document in 1371, was the same woman as Antonia, because in the contract of 1332 they requested only the consent of Gemma and Antonia for the sale of the farm in Pagnolle, and therefore it is believed that there could be no other daughter of Dante's still living. However, this reasoning is mistaken. If Beatrice was a nun, she had renounced all her hereditary rights and obviously would not have been convened for the contract in 1332; and if we suppose that she entered the convent when her father was still alive and living in Ravenna, then the contract itself demonstrates that Beatrice and Antonia must have been two different people.

There is the question of whether Dante's half-brother, Francesco, shared his guilty verdict. On 13 May 1304 Francesco Alighieri of Florence found himself in Arezzo, where the majority of exiles lived at that time, and there he took out a loan of 12 florins with a guarantor who was a Lamberti, one of a Ghibelline family that had long been in exile. It seems fairly evident that Francesco had also been obliged to leave Florence, and in fact an administrative document of 14 August 1305 refers to real estate belonging to the two brothers and confiscated when both were declared rebels. But Francesco's absence did not last long, because in 1309 we find him as a witness to a contract signed in Pieve a Ripoli, close to Fucecchio, in Florentine territory. He is referred to in a curious manner: 'Francischo Allagherii, called *ser* Geri', but we have been able to cross-check it, and it is definitely him. He may well have been pardoned: there was no shortage of ways to come out of exile for those who were willing to accept compromises. However, everything points to the notary who drew up the contract in 1305 having got a little confused, and suggests that the assets he wrote of were, it's true, owned in common, but only the half that would have been Dante's share was confiscated. We should not forget that Dante had been condemned on the basis of specific accusations relating to his term in the office of prior, which his brother had nothing to do with. Dante's name appears in many official lists of exiles, whereas Francesco's name never does. After Dante's death, contracts for property deals that concern Francesco and his nephews often refer to the past confiscation of Dante's property, but there is not one reference to the confiscation of Francesco's. The most likely conclusion is that Francesco was never convicted or banished from the city, even though the confiscation of half the jointly owned property must have brought with it many complications and abuses.[3]

After his return to Florence, Francesco appears in many documents – if only we had half this number on his brother! Thus we discover that he was married to *monna* Pera of the late Donato Brunacci, continued to live in the parish of San Martino del Vescovo but at some stage moved his residence to the parish of Pieve a Ripoli, which was where his maternal family, the Cialuffis, came from. We also discover that he was turning over large amounts of cash in buying and selling farms, which further disproves the myths about his poverty and Dante's. His business transactions were regularly supported by his blood relations and those acquired through marriage, such as his aunt *monna* Bice, who was the sister of his mother, Lapa, and widow of Scorcia Lupicini, her nephew Goccia of the late Lippo Lupicini, his half-sister Tana, who was the widow of the late Lapo Riccomanni, his cousin Niccolò of the late Foresino Donati, and his nephew Iacopo di Dante. Family ties and those of the neighbourhood constructed an incredibly tight network around each individual, which is often impossible for us to decipher. However, it is clear that Francesco was a businessman of some importance, and the catastrophe that struck his brother did not lead to his ruin. At this stage we have to ask ourselves what exactly happened to Dante's property.

CHAPTER FOURTEEN

THE FATE OF DANTE'S WEALTH

On 14 August 1305 two messengers of the republic, accompanied by two guards, made their way to San Miniato a Pagnolle on the Fiesole hills to notify the mayor and the inhabitants of the locality of the order to deliver a certain quantity of grain. They were sent by one Vezzo Vezzosi, at his expense, as he had been allocated that payment in grain to be collected out of the revenue from the land confiscated from Dante (and Francesco, but we know that almost certainly he had made a mistake about the brother). The amount paid to Vezzo corresponded to the salary of a citizen knight, and thus compensated him for the costs of maintaining a warhorse on behalf of the republic, which was one of the normal ways of allocating the revenues from confiscated properties. If the community of San Miniato a Pagnolle was responsible for the payment, this meant that no tenant farmer had been found for Dante's land, and the local community was obliged to farm it and pay the revenue to the Republic of Florence.

We might naively think that, once they were confiscated, Dante's assets were no longer his, but that was not the way of things. During the following years many deeds of sale in Pagnolle mentioned Dante as one of the owners of adjacent land without any mention of the confiscation. The fact is that sequestrated land was administered by the republic and the exile had no rights over how it was used, but it was still registered in his name. Property, along with the rights of the wives and the heirs, was a serious matter and could not be obliterated so easily.* The family of the condemned man had many ways to get their hands on the confiscated assets and stop them from being lost for ever. The wife could assert the rights of her dowry, as Gemma had done, which Boccaccio pointed out: 'A part of his possessions were defended by his wife with great effort from the choleric city by asserting the rights of her dowry, whose revenues meagrely supported her and her little children.'[1]

Other clues, as we have seen in the case of Dante's house in San Martino del Vescovo, suggest that Gemma's brother Foresino Donati and his son Niccolò managed to recover some of the confiscated properties by buying them from the republic when they were put on sale. In these cases people with well-established connections could get extremely good value for money, and who would try to obstruct the Donatis by competing with them to buy those houses?† One should also remember that the exiles could be pardoned, and one of the reasons why the properties continued to be registered in their names was precisely this: if they were pardoned, then they had the right to recover their property. In Dante's case, the question was further complicated by the fact that Francesco's part had not been confiscated, if ours is the correct interpretation. We can imagine how difficult it was for the Office of Rebel Assets to confiscate and manage separately half of each farm when the other half continued to belong to its legitimate owner. It now becomes clear why the revenues that the republic managed to collect by renting out

---

* Giuliano Milani has ascertained that in Bologna 'the name of the owner is never missing from the lists of assets' and concluded that 'respect for property clearly prevailed over the need to persecute political enemies in the scale of shared values'.

† Milani demonstrates how in Bologna, following the confiscation of the exiled Ghibellines' assets in 1277, 'the republic started immediately after the registration [...] to return lots of confiscated assets to returned exiles, their relations or citizens capable of proving their rights'.

confiscated lands or, still worse, forcing local communities to farm them when no tenant could be found were very low and undoubtedly lower than what the legitimate owners would previously have been earning.

Given this state of affairs, it is hardly surprising that after Dante's death, one way or another, access to his property was restored to his heirs. In May 1332 arbitration led to the division of the property – which confirms that up to that moment it had been jointly owned – between the uncle Francesco on one side and Dante's two surviving sons on the other: Piero, who had now become *messer* Piero the judge, resident in Verona and represented by his maternal cousin Niccolò di Foresino Donati, and Iacopo, who was still living in Florence, where he had returned after paying the fine stipulated by the amnesty of 1325. The assets jointly owned until then, half of which were due to Francesco and half to his nephews, were those we already know about, and whose configuration we have been able to reconstruct from these documents: the house in Florence in the parish of San Martino del Vescovo, the farm at Camerata, the farm at San Miniato a Pagnolle and other plots in the area, and the cottage with plot of land in the parish of Sant'Ambrogio.[2]

Not all the properties at that time were accessible to Dante's heirs. The arbitrator chosen by the uncle and nephews, the notary Lorenzo da Villamagna, had ascertained that the property in Camerata had just been sold by Francesco to the sons of Manetto Portinari without the nephews collecting their half of the proceeds. The house in San Martino del Vescovo had been sold by common agreement of the three joint owners and in their shared interests, but it was once again a transaction covering the guarantee for a financial transaction: in other words, it was security on a loan. Indeed the contract specified that the owners intended to redeem it. The arbitrator decided that Francesco would keep the sum paid by the Portinaris for the farm in Camerata, the plot of land in Sant'Ambrogio and half of the cottage with land in the same place, while *messer* Piero and Iacopo would take the farm and the other lands in Pagnolle and the house in San Martino del Vescovo, once it had been redeemed, as well as half of the cottage in Sant'Ambrogio.[3]

The best of it is that all these transactions took place while the properties concerned were still sequestrated. Francesco had sold the farm in Camerata to the Portinari brothers (who were Beatrice's nephews and probably the sons of a close friend of Dante), even though they were still listed as properties that had been confiscated from the rebels – or rather a 50 per cent share of the properties, we assume. Until the republic removed the farm from that list, the purchasers would be forced to pay rent to the republic, and Francesco had to reimburse them. Because this charge was paid out of his share, his nephews had to shoulder their half of it and pay him 30 bushels of grain every year.[4] The share-out of properties in 1332 did not mention the farm at Pagnolle, but nine years later, in 1341, when Dante's sons decided to split their properties, the arbitrator, Paolo di Litti de' Corbizzi, who was their neighbour in Pagnolle, allocated the farm to Iacopo but added that in the event of further sums due to the Republic of Florence to redeem it, Iacopo would have to pay 15 florins to his brother or cede half of the property redeemed in this manner. It seems that even they didn't know whether or not the farm was entirely in their hands, and we can only guess at what the Office of Rebel Assets thought. The fact is that two years afterwards Iacopo paid exactly 15 gold florins into the treasury of the Republic of Florence for the definitive cancellation of the farm from the list of confiscated properties.[5]

But at the time of the division of assets between Francesco and his nephews, Dante's half of the property in Sant'Ambrogio was still administered by the Office of Rebel Assets, but this did not mean that it had escaped the family's notice: in 1336 it was rented by Goccia di Lippo Lupicini, the nephew of Francesco's aunt Bice, as well as the future heir of his wife, Pera. It becomes clear that the network of family solidarity was interfering with the procedures of confiscating and renting out rebel assets, and making it possible to avoid complete loss of control over sequestrated assets.[6] This also confirms that for these people landownership was also a matter of affection and identity, so one farm was not interchangeable with another, and they would do everything they could to maintain their ownership of houses and land inherited from their forebears, to such an extent that they were able to hang onto them for almost half a century in spite of sentences of the court and confiscations. When we think of Dante, we should remember that the names of Pagnolle, Camerata and Piagentina very probably touched his heartstrings.

Chapter Fifteen

KEEPING COMPANY WITH THE WICKED

Sudden and violent expulsion from one's own city was not an unusual event for anyone involved in Italian politics. The ferocity of the clashes inside the republics had for some time entailed the delegitimisation of adversaries, perceived not as an opposition but public enemies and delinquents to be annihilated. This is partly why the Guelphs and the Ghibellines had taken on the role of some kind of transversal community that offered refuge and assistance to exiles. Consequently it was possible not only for individuals but also for entire family clans to continue to live and prosper in exile. This was true of the Ubertis, the leaders of Florentine Ghibellinism, who at that time had been exiles for more than thirty years. Dino Compagni described them as 'always living abroad in a state of grandeur, and never did they diminish their honour, and they were the guests of kings and lords, and they devoted themselves to great achievements'.[1]

Predictably the White Guelphs who had been driven out of Florence sought the assistance of the Ghibellines, who had been in exile for so long, and as there were so many of them, they hoped to retake the city by force. In the spring and summer of 1302 the White Guelphs and the Ghibellines formed a coalition, and with the support of the Ubaldinis, lords of the mountains of Mugello, persuaded many castles to rebel against the Republic of Florence and 'fought a full-scale war in Valdarno'. Dante, Bruni wrote, heard of his sentence as he was returning from Rome and was already in Siena when, being better informed, he realised that it would not be wise to return to Florence. Immediately afterwards he joined the rebels for a meeting in Gargonza, a castle of the Ubertinis between Siena and Arezzo.[2]

Dante was at war once more but this time against Florence, and it was a real war. Florentine tribunals during those months issued a torrent of verdicts against exiles, both Ghibelline and White Guelph, who were fighting against their city, and they contained a dramatic list of attacks, raids and plunder, castles taken through underhand methods, houses and churches destroyed or burned down, kidnapping with torture and extortion, rustling, and people wounded and killed. For the Florentine judges, the guilty were both enemies of the people and common delinquents, 'desperate Ghibellines and private mercenaries and men of evil disposition and fame'. The sentences all claimed to be those for common criminals, but they always emphasised the political intentions of the accused, repeating that their crimes were carried out to cries in Latin of 'May they always die; let the Guelphs die!'

Dante was at war, and there would be nothing surprising if he were dressed in chain mail and had a sword in hand as he rode under the white insignia of his party: shortly afterwards he would write in an official letter of 'our' spotless white flags and 'our' swords red with blood, and it is not at all clear that this was only metaphor. One document implies that during those months Dante was not only a member but also one of the most prominent leaders of the rebel coalition. It has been damaged by damp and is therefore difficult to read. It appears to have been dated 8 June 1302. At San Godenzo, in the castle of the Counts Guidi in the mountains between Mugello and Casentino, eighteen Florentine exiles promised the Ubaldinis, an extremely powerful family in the region, to reimburse them for damages that they might suffer because of the war against Florence. The eighteen include Ghibelline magnates, four Ubertis, four Ubertinis, two Scolaris, one Pazzi and the leaders of the White

Guelph exiles, *messer* Torrigiano, Carbone and *messer* Vieri de' Cerchi, *messer* Andrea Gherardini and Dante Alighieri, who was undoubtedly the one with the lowest social status, and therefore surely present at the meeting because of his personal prestige.[3]

In short, the White Guelphs in exile, who a few months earlier had governed a proudly Guelph city, were quite willing to make common cause with the Ghibellines and go into battle to the cry, 'Kill the Guelphs!' This surprising fact cannot be challenged, just as there can be no doubt that during the early years of exile Dante exalted such illustrious heroes as Emperor Frederick II and his son King Manfredi of Sicily in his *De vulgari eloquentia* – writings that appear to be those of a fervent Ghibelline. In other words, it seems that the Black Guelph Guido Orlandi was right when he wrote a spiteful sonnet against the White Guelphs accusing them of having switched sides: 'Because they were Guelphs and now they're Ghibellines / let them be called rebels from this day forth, / enemies of the republic like the Ubertis.' Was it possible that they had all become Ghibellines, and done so in such great haste? Could they have already been crypto-Ghibellines, as their enemies had whispered in the ear of Boniface VIII? Dante scholars have trawled through his works, which unfortunately can only be dated speculatively, in order to establish if, when and for how long Dante ceased to be a Guelph and became a Ghibelline. Perhaps we should accept the idea that, in the situation the exiles found themselves in, there was little room for ideological loyalty. The parties had become transversal groupings in which all positions could be found, so you could easily have a Guelph who enthused over Emperor Frederick and King Manfredi, just as there were Ghibelline cardinals at the top of the Holy Mother Church. These alignments were held together by the expediency of the moment and not support for any particular belief.

During the summer of 1302 the campaign turned against the exiles, who lost, one after another, the castles that had allowed them to sustain their guerrilla warfare in Valdarno. They decided at this stage to entrust command of their forces to someone with military expertise, and they chose Scarpetta degli Ordelaffi, a leading figure in a family that had been ruling over Forlì for a few years. The historian and papal secretary Biondo Flavio, who wrote in that pretentious and elusive Latin used by some humanists in the fifteenth century, suggested that Dante was sent to Forlì to negotiate with Scarpetta and other Ghibelline lords in the north, one of whom was Cangrande della Scala, the ruler of Verona. Biondo claimed that he got all this information from the letters of Pellegrino Calvi, a native of Forlì who had been Scarpetta's chancellor. These letters often mentioned Dante and indeed had occasionally been dictated by him. As Biondo was from Forlì, it is plausible that he had access to those documents, but the mention of Cangrande raises some doubts as the future ruler of Verona was only eleven years old at the time, and the ruler of the city was his brother Bartolomeo. Leaving aside the information provided by Biondo, which at the very least was somewhat confused, it is likely that Dante was in Forlì during that period, because Dino Compagni recorded that the White Guelphs sought refuge in Arezzo, but Supreme Magistrate Uguccione della Faggiola, at the behest of Pope Boniface VIII, was most unwelcoming, and 'most of them departed for Forlì'.[4]

The achievements of the new alliance turned out to be disappointing. In March 1303 the exile army marched through Mugello in high hopes under the leadership of Ordelaffi, but they put up a shameful fight and were routed close to Pulicciano Castle.[5] The Florentine army was led by Supreme Magistrate Fulcieri da Calboli, a leading figure in another Forlì family which was a rival of Ordelaffi's, whom Dante would cruelly portray in Canto XIV of *Purgatory*. The exiles finally had a change of fortune six months later, when the most powerful of their enemies, Pope Boniface, was arrested in Anagni by the king of France's envoy,

Guillaume de Nogaret, supported by the Colonnas, a powerful Roman family who were sworn enemies of the pope. The bitter feuding in Florence between magnates and commoners and between factions in the nobility continued even after the expulsion of the White Guelphs, which Villani simplified to a single cause: 'because *messer* Corso Donati didn't feel that he held the suitably high office he desired'. They continued with such ferocity that in early 1304 the new pope, Benedict XI, unamused by the behaviour of the Black Guelphs' government, sent yet another papal envoy to Florence to impose a peace agreement. For this task he chose one of his closest aides, Niccolò da Prato, a Dominican like himself, who had just been appointed cardinal and enjoyed a reputation for favouring the Ghibellines – demonstrating once more the transversal nature of party loyalties.[6]

The first surviving letter from Dante is from this period, and it speaks of Guelph banners and swords covered in blood. It is Dante's, because that is what tradition demands, even though it was written in the name of the Council and the whole membership of the White party of Florence and its captain, whose name began with 'A' and at that time was almost certainly Count Aghinolfo dei Guidi da Romena. It was sent to Cardinal Da Prato, informing him that the exiles were ready to obey his orders and accept his peace conditions. The letter was not dated, but it presents itself as the White Guelphs' first, belated response to the letters the cardinal had sent them. It was probably sent after the peacemaker's arrival in Florence in March 1304. Of all Dante's writings, this is perhaps the one that most strongly represents the language of Florentine factionalism: the certitude that the White Guelphs, unlike their enemies, are the ones who truly love Florence, defiantly claiming responsibility for having fought a civil war in defence of their liberty. Dante assured the cardinal that his efforts to bring peace were all the White Guelphs desired and all that they had been fighting for: 'What else were our unblemished white banners requesting, and why else were our swords red, if not from forcing those who had arrogantly broken off civic co-existence to submit to the law and bring peace to the country?'

When he entered the city, Cardinal Da Prato was greeted enthusiastically by the people, who had lost all patience with the infighting among the magnates, and after re-establishing the popular government and carried away by his successes, he went so far as to invite the return of the exiles, both White Guelphs and Ghibellines, in the hope of pacifying the enemies. The rebels, it goes without saying, agreed and sent two representatives to the city, one of whom was *ser* Petracco of *ser* Parenzo dell'Incisa, who was Petrarch's father. On 26 April 1304, before the people gathered in Piazza di Santa Maria Novella, the representatives of the 'outside party' and the two of the 'inside party', namely the Black Guelphs in government, 'kissed each other on the mouth to make peace', after which the cardinal 'had twelve representatives of the exiles come to Florence – two for each *sesto*, one of whom was a White Guelph and one a Ghibelline' to negotiate the details of the agreement. Once again it became clear that hugging and kissing each other on the mouth was not sufficient to reconcile the parties. It all went badly wrong. The Guelph magnates decided to sabotage the cardinal's efforts by persuading the people that his real intention was to restore the Ghibellines. There were increasing tensions in the city, and eventually the twelve representatives abandoned Florence and took refuge in Arezzo. At the beginning of June 1304 the exasperated cardinal also left the city, passing an interdict and excommunication on the city.[7]

Bruni confirmed that the exiles in that period gathered in Arezzo, where 'there were twelve councillors, of whom Dante was one of their number'. (There were always twelve, like the apostles, and we cannot help thinking that Dante may have been one of the twelve who temporarily returned to Florence, but from the few names we have it seems unlikely).[8] Between

January and August 1304 the draft contracts of a notary in Arezzo registered a loan taken out by Scarpetta degli Ordelaffi from Pellegrino da Forlì, who was the Pellegrino Calvi referred to by Biondo, and other loans to leading figures in the Ghibelline and White Guelph faction in exile, including the son of Farinata degli Uberti. The same notary recorded a loan of 12 florins contracted on 13 May by Dante's brother Francesco. Clearly members of what Dante defined in his letter to the cardinal as the 'fraternity' or 'consortium' of White Guelphs were indeed in Arezzo in the fateful year of 1304, which was, as Villani recorded, a famine year in Tuscany, following two or three bad harvests,[9] even though Dante probably only stayed there for a short while.

The failure of Cardinal Da Prato's mission did not discourage the exiles. They had many supporters in the city, who were fomenting a climate in which civil war seemed imminent. They counted a great deal on the support of the commoners, who were terrified by the violence of the magnates in the Black Guelph party. A few days after the cardinal's departure the situation deteriorated so dramatically that they could not think of a better way to prevent the White Guelphs' from retaking the city than burning down their enemies' houses. The flames, fuelled by the wind, caused a terrifying fire throughout the centre of the city, causing incalculable financial damage. On reading the cardinal's report, the papal court was increasingly outraged at the government's actions. Since the new pope had been elected, relations between Rome and the Florentine banks had changed. Benedict XI preferred to use the Cerchis' bank rather than the banks connected to the Black Guelphs, such as the Spinis' bank, which his predecessor had favoured.[10]

So the exiles nurtured this hope of retaking the city by force, taking advantage of the dismay and division among the citizens. They secretly called on their friends in Tuscany and Romagna, and crossed the Apennines with 1,600 knights and 9,000 foot soldiers on their way to Florence, which was unaware of these manoeuvres. When they arrived at Lastra, above Montughi, they stopped for two days to wait for their allies from Pistoia. Then, on 20 July 1304, they moved on the city, which by now was in a state of alarm. They entered the suburb of San Gallo without resistance ('at the time the new walls around the city did not exist, nor did the ditches, and the old walls were open and broken in parts', Villani wrote). The army deployed next to San Marco in what was then a kind of park, the Cafaggio del Vescovo. They stood there in the sun and without water for hours while they waited for the many supporters they believed would assist them to start the insurrection. Then, as nothing was happening, they took control of one of the gates in the old walls and entered the old city as far as Piazza di San Giovanni, where they clashed with the defenders. They were pushed back and, suddenly discouraged, they fled.

The disastrous outcome of what came to be known as the Battle of Lastra was so inexplicable that every chronicler attempts to rationalise it in some way. According to Dino Compagni, the rebels went into the city too soon, when the allies they were expecting were not yet ready, and during the day, when their friends wouldn't have had the courage to show their faces, rather than waiting for night. Conversely Giovanni Villani felt that the mistake was to stay for an extra day at Lastra rather than go down into the city immediately, because they would have undoubtedly taken the city. Such an unpredictable outcome, the chronicler concludes, 'appears to have been the work and the will of God'. Whatever the case, the exiles had played their last card, particularly as Pope Benedict XI, who seemed to favour the White Guelph and Ghibelline party, died and thus ended his papacy, which only lasted eight months. Shortly afterwards, 'the White Guelph and Ghibelline party was crushed and defeated in nearly all parts of Tuscany.'[11]

If we are to believe Bruni, Dante was still with the White

Guelphs at the time of this disaster, indeed he was one of the twelve 'councillors' leading the party, and only after the Battle of Lastra did he decide that there was no more hope. He went in search of hospitality in Verona, where he was courteously received by the Lords Della Scala, and stayed with them for some time.[12] Dante tells the story differently in Canto XVII of *Paradise*, when Cacciaguida describes his future: he will have to leave Florence, where people are already plotting against him – in 1300! His enemies were about to obtain the support of the court of Rome, 'where Christ is bought and sold every day' (many years later Dante was convinced of this, and this too is of interest). He will be exiled along with others, and finding himself associated with their destiny will be an extra burden:

> And weighing most greatly on your shoulders
> shall be the wicked, foolish company
> with whom you'll fall into that valley.
>
> (*Paradise*, XVII, 61–3)

'Foolish': there can be no doubt that anyone would have judged this true of the Battle of Lastra, but the same could have been said of Scarpetta degli Ordelaffi's abortive campaign in Mugello. Dante declares that he quickly arrived at this judgement, argued with the other exiles and was in disgrace – all things that Cacciaguida foretold in the most unequivocal manner: the company 'all ungrateful, all mad and evil / shall turn against you'. At this point, his great-grandfather announces, you shall go your own way, and not you but they will be the ones banging heads against the wall and paying the price for their stupidity and ingratitude:

> … but, shortly afterwards,
> they, not you, shall have livid temples.
> Their behaviours shall be the proof

of their bestiality; so it shall stand well
with you having made your own party.

(Paradise, XVII, 65–9)

The rift with the White Guelphs must have been nasty. In *Inferno*, written when the memory was fresher, Brunetto Latini even prophesies that both the White and the Black Guelphs will be thirsty for Dante's blood, although fortunately he will escape their clutches.[13] Why were they so angry with him? One of the first fourteenth-century commentators, Ottimo, comes up with the bizarre story that Dante argued in the party council for the call to arms for their allies to be postponed and thus they didn't come at all, which led to accusations of treachery. It remains a mystery how this anonymous writer knew this and why only he knew it.

On the question of this rift, we should remember the cryptic prophecy that Dante puts in Farinata's mouth in Canto X of *Inferno*:

Before the face of the woman who here governs
has been relit but fifty times, you'll know
what heavy burden that art can be.

(Inferno, X, 79–81)

The art the Ghibelline leader refers to is that of returning to one's native city once you have been banished. In the fiction of the *Comedy* we are at the end of March 1300, and he tells Dante that before fifty months have passed he will realise that returning to Florence will not be as easy as he hopes. He is certainly alluding to the moment in which Dante breaks with the White Guelphs, on whose imminent victory all his hopes were pinned. Fifty months take him to March 1304, two months before the disastrous Battle of Lastra. Some people believe that, as Farinata is talking about the moon, it must be a question of lunar months, and in this case the period would only have been three years and ten months, which means that the break would have been in January 1304. But we know that in March Dante was full of hope and self-confidence when he wrote to Cardinal Da Prato in the name of the White Guelph party. So Farinata's months must be calendar ones, and the moment Dante realised that his return to Florence would not be so easy was at the end of May 1304, when the representatives of the exiles left the city and it became very clear that the cardinal's mission had failed.

Following the rift with the White Guelphs, the sequence of events outlined by Cacciaguida coincides with the one reported later by Bruni. Dante went to Verona, where he was the guest of the city's ruler, one of the Della Scalas:

> Your first refuge and first dwelling
> shall be the courtesy of the great Lombard
> who in a stairway carries the holy bird.
>
> (*Paradise*, XVII, 70–73)

The 'holy bird' is the imperial eagle which the Della Scalas, imperial vicars, displayed at the top of their coat of arms above a stair (from which they took their name) at the time Dante wrote the above lines.

CHAPTER SIXTEEN

THE MYSTERIES OF VERONA

Dante lived the last twenty years of his life in exile. These are years we know very little about, much less than what we have been able to establish so far. There are practically no archival sources that refer to him. The autobiographical references in his works become increasingly cryptic and can be interpreted in many different ways. While Dante scholars have reached a broad agreement on the stages through which the *Comedy* was written and they argue over the dating of *Convivio* and *De vulgari eloquentia*, they are in complete disagreement about the period in which *De Monarchia* was written. Of the superficial facts in Dante's life, the most important would be where he was living, which would allow us to know who was maintaining him, but in this area too all attempts to bring the pieces in the puzzle together and establish a coherent story have varied quite stunningly. What for one academic is a virtual certainty is an absurdity not even worthy of discussion for another.

In this situation where questions abound and reliable facts are remarkably absent, it is consoling to know that Dante himself provides us with information on the break with the White Guelphs and his transformation from a leading figure in the party to a solitary one embarking on a new life in Verona in search of a refuge. He does this in an autograph version he puts into the mouth of Cacciaguida. But the consolation is only apparent, because as soon as we try to anchor this narrative to some chronological fixed point we can rely on, we discover that

Dante's version is more than suspect. We are obliged to conclude that when he wrote those cantos – everyone agrees that he wrote them in Verona as a guest of Cangrande della Scala – either he had forgotten the exact sequence of events or he had a reason for obfuscation.

While asserting that leaving the 'wicked and foolish company' who shortly would be banging their heads against a wall or would at least be ashamed of themselves (because both interpretations exist), Dante on the face of it is saying that he abandoned the other exiles before they revealed all their ineptitude in the wretched venture of Lastra, and the first to give him refuge was one of the Della Scalas, whom he calls 'the great Lombard'. It seems reasonable to give credence to him rather than Bruni, according to whom Dante went to Verona *after* the failure of 'so many hopes'. So Dante arrived in Verona earlier than July 1304, but how much earlier? We have seen that Farinata's prophecy could suggest two possible dates for the break with the White Guelphs: January or May. Or rather we could say *by* January or *by* May, and of the two the second is decidedly more likely, because that much argued-over letter to Cardinal Da Prato was written in the name of the White Guelph party in which Dante was still a leading figure, very probably in March. In short, the break from his comrades must have occurred in April or May.

It follows that the 'great Lombard' was Alboino della Scala, who had just replaced his brother Bartolomeo as the ruler of Verona, following the latter's death in March 1304 (the third brother, Cangrande, was still an adolescent). In truth, the ruler of Verona at the end of March 1300, when the journey in the *Comedy* is supposed to have taken place, was still Alberto della Scala, who was the father of the three brothers. Indeed Boccaccio believed that he was the courteous host who took Dante in.[1] Why then should we not believe him? Dante was always so careful to adjust all direct speech so that it corresponded to what was actually happening in the world in that particular moment! But all the early commentators, including his son *messer* Piero, know that this was impossible because Alberto died in 1301. The problem is that they all agree that it was Bartolomeo and not Alboino who was the host Dante treasured so greatly, and nearly all today's academics are of the same opinion for the good reason that Dante comes out with a rather unpleasant and even gratuitous comment about Alboino in *Convivio*. In Book IV of the work Dante discusses genuine nobility and declares that you would have to be crazy to believe that *nobilis* ('nobility') derives from *nosco* ('to know' or 'to acquire knowledge') and therefore means the quality of being well known (unfortunately this is precisely the etymology from which the adjective derives!). He then proceeds to provide examples: if it were all about being well known, 'Alboino della Scala would be nobler than Guido da Castello di Reggio', which, he exclaims, would be 'completely mistaken'.[2] Because of this, most people think that Alboino could not have been the 'great Lombard', even though around twelve years had passed between the time when Dante was disparaging him in *Convivio* and the time when he was writing the cantos in which Cacciaguida extols the unnamed lord of Verona.

But here is the main problem: if the 'great Lombard' was not Alboino but his older brother Bartolomeo della Scala, who died in March 1304, shortly before Dante wrote to Cardinal Da Prato as the official spokesperson for the White Guelph party, it is no longer possible to accept the assertion fictionally expressed by Cacciaguida, namely that Verona's ruler would have Dante as his guest *after* the break with the 'wicked and foolish company'. Attempts to resolve this contradiction have led to some fanciful theories. Perhaps Dante had sought refuge in Verona after having quarrelled *a first time* with the other rebels, when Bartolomeo was still alive, for instance after the unsuccessful military expedition in Mugello in the spring of 1303: this is supposed to be confirmed by a document recording the loan taken out by the White Guelphs in Bologna on 18 June 1303, in which as many as 131 leading figures in the party appear along with Scarpetta degli Ordelaffi, but Dante does not. He is then supposed to have left Verona in the spring of 1304 to return and rejoin the rebels gathered in Arezzo in the climate of expectations prompted by Cardinal Da Prato's mission.

Are we to believe that Dante would have had Cacciaguida produce such a false version of events? We should bear in mind that, according to his fictionalised ancestor, he is supposed to have had to put up with the 'wicked and foolish company', then to have argued with them and decided to form a party consisting of himself, to have sought refuge with the 'great Lombard' and finally to have seen the wisdom of his decision to break away confirmed by their spectacular failure. But according to this new version, he rejoined the White Guelphs after having enjoyed the hospitality of the Della Scalas, and far from setting up on his own, he agreed to become one of their councillors and write to the cardinal in the name of the party! At the very least, this would have meant that in his *Paradise* Dante rewrote his past in a decidedly biased manner, and attempted to obscure the vacillations and inconsistencies that preceded his definitive break with the White Guelphs.

Perhaps this evolved in a different manner. Dante could have gone to Verona at the time of Bartolomeo della Scala not as an exile in flight, but rather as an ambassador of the coalition. This theory would be a bizarre notion unworthy of further discussion, if it weren't yet again for a scrap of information we can use as a source: it is Biondo's obscure record that, during his ambassadorship in Forlì, Dante travelled on to Verona to ask for the assistance of the ruling Della Scala at the time. We'll gloss over the fact that Biondo believed that it would have been Cangrande della Scala, the only member of the family who had any prominence in the memory of later generations. There has been speculation on a journey of this kind, which would have been compatible with the brief period of Bartolomeo's rule, possibly at the end of 1302 in preparation for the coalition led by Scarpetta degli Ordelaffi, or again in 1303 following the disappointing performance in Mugello and with a view to the military operations the White Guelphs were planning to resume in the summer. At this point, however, Cacciaguida's prophecy loses all its ties with the facts and presents a radical reinvention, not to say mystification, of the past: having taken advantage of the 'courtesy of the great Lombard' in the capacity of official representative of the 'wicked and foolish company', Dante turns up some years later seeking hospitality in Verona as a consequence of having broken with that same company. To accept this interpretation, you have to concede that the version of events expressed through Cacciaguida's prophecy completely overturns both the meaning and the chronology of that first sojourn at the court of the Della Scalas. Of course, this is not at all impossible: anyone who writes a biography of Dante today cannot ignore that Dante 'changed his mind quite often about the general plot and details of his life'.

A final possible version is that Dante described what happened accurately: he broke away from the company of the White Guelphs and the Ghibellines after they had gathered in Arezzo in the spring of 1304 and he had written to Cardinal Da Prato, deciding to leave for Verona not long before the disaster at Lastra. But rather than salvaging the credibility of his autobiographical account using Cacciaguida as his mouthpiece, this version creates even more problems. By writing those lines at the court of Cangrande, the poet gives the impression of recalling with affection or even strong emotion the hospitality received from Cangrande's brother, who at this stage must have been Alboino, while previously he saw things in a very different manner. There was that unfortunate comparison in *Convivio*, which could not have been pleasant for Alboino or indeed his family. Clearly Dante didn't feel any particular gratitude to the

Della Scalas when he was writing that treatise, which according to one scholar was during his first sojourn in Verona. But even later his feelings remained unchanged, because in Canto XVIII of *Purgatory* an anonymous abbot at San Zeno in Verona expressed extremely offensive views about Alberto della Scala, the father of Bartolomeo, Alboino and Cangrande, prophesying his damnation for having put his disabled, illegitimate son in charge of that powerful monastery:

> Already he's placed one foot in the grave,
> so soon he'll agonise over that abbey, and
> unhappy he will be for having had such power;
> because he replaced its true pastor
> with his son, sick in his body and mind,
> still worse, for he was born ill-formed.
>
> (*Purgatory*, XVIII, 121–6)

Dante's hatred for this abbot, who was called Giuseppe and who would die in 1313, must have derived from personal acquaintance, and strengthens the argument that his first visit to Verona did not make a good impression on him. Thus we have to ask whether the image in *Paradise* of the 'great Lombard' and the courteous hospitality of the Della Scalas wasn't forcefully influenced by the fact that, when he was writing these cantos, Dante was once more a guest in Verona, this time with Cangrande, and he was obliged to change his opinion of a family for whom he had previously felt no liking.

Immediately after his reference to the 'great Lombard', Cacciaguida prophesies that Dante will meet a boy in Verona who in 1300 is only nine years old but has been born under an extraordinarily auspicious star and will achieve great things. As Dante, however much he was struck by Cangrande's precociousness, certainly did not return from that first stay in Verona convinced that an exceptional future awaited the youngster, it is clear that the prophecy after the event was entirely the result of Cangrande's cumbersome presence. He now looked back on the court of the Della Scalas during his first stay as the most courteous of refuges – either that or he felt obliged to describe it as such. We shouldn't be surprised if Dante cool-headedly decided to please the ruler of Verona by speaking nicely of his brother while he was writing the Cacciaguida canto. Later we'll find that he was to go much to greater lengths to ingratiate himself to his host.

Leaving aside all attempts to mythologise the 'great Lombard', who, it's now plain, could easily have been Alboino, it is firmly established that Dante remembered the city of the Della Scalas as the place where many years earlier he had found himself alone in search of refuge and without any support. It is of little importance that later he would again share experiences with White Guelphs and Ghibellines exiled from Florence, so that Cacciaguida's prophecy is also dramatising his break with those groups retrospectively; what matters is that Verona was the first place in which Dante felt that he was there not as a leading figure in a party but as a 'pilgrim, almost begging', as he wrote in his *Convivio*.[3]

And this was not only his opinion, as his time in Verona coincided with Cecco Angiolieri's sonnet, in which the Sienese poet ridiculed him for ending up with the same fate that Cecco was already accustomed to, that of being dependent on other people's charity:

Dante Alighier, if I'm a harmless buffoon,
you hold your lance at my kidneys [i.e., you've followed
    me]
if I dine with others, you similarly take your supper;
if I chew some fat, you suck on a lump of lard …
if I've become a Roman, you've become a Lombard.

The sonnet is evidently a response to an equally mocking one sent by Dante, which is now lost. Even in exile, Dante continued to keep in touch with his correspondents – but this exchange demonstrates that he must have been a fairly famous writer if many people were following his movements, which made the impotence and solitude in which he now found himself all the harder to bear.

He confesses this with extreme sincerity right at the beginning of *Convivio*. Having described the disorientation of someone who is suddenly drifting without any resources ('Truly I am a ship without a sail and without a helm, carried to ports, estuaries and shorelines by the dry wind of painful poverty'), he immediately admits that what hurts most is being seen in poverty by those who once had admired him: 'and this is how I must look in the eyes of many people who perhaps because of some measure of fame would have imagined me in a different way, and now that they see me so humiliated, they will have little respect for my works, both past and future ones.'

In other words, Dante was ashamed, and the life we now have to examine is the life of an exile obliged to seek hospitality in the courts of lesser Italian princes. For as long as he was in a party, the problem would not have been difficult to resolve as to some extent the assistance of friends could be found everywhere. This was the importance of Dante declaring proudly that he had set up a party for himself: it meant that he had to manage on his own without the help of the factional network. The fact that he was a political figure of some fame, and above all a poet and orator of considerable fame, certainly helped him to find hospitality. There can be no doubt that at least on some occasions he was employed in the chancelleries of the lords with whom he resided: some of the letters that manuscript tradition attributes to him were written in the name of the host he was staying with at the time, and recently philologists have been identifying Dante's stylistic features in more and more letters and peace treaties produced in chancelleries of minor rulers. Dante was also a consummate professional in political communication, whose services were sought out and could be remunerated.

In Verona, Dante would have discovered a world that in some ways was less different than we might think. Of course, the vernacular spoken there would have been very different from Florentine. A few generations earlier, when the Franciscans decided to send missionaries from their original centres in central Italy, they entrusted the mission to Friar Barnaba, who was an excellent preacher 'in Lombardic and German', as though these were both foreign languages. But in Dante's times, and particularly for someone who had his ear for languages, this was no longer the case. He would comment that the language spoken in that part of Veneto was coarse and uncouth, but it was still in the land of *sì* (the territory where *sì* was used to mean 'yes'). Moreover Verona was a great city not that different from Florence in terms of its economic activity: its strategic position on the road to Brennero made it an obligatory stopping place for all trade between Venice, the Po Valley and Germany, and its hotels and fairs were full of foreign merchants. It had one of the most important horse markets in Europe, was an important hub in the timber trade, which came down along the River Adige from the forests of Trentino, and was the centre of a rich textile industry, with many mills that used water power to mechanise the fulling process in the production of textiles. Like Florence, it was a city where mercantile and popular organisations had developed so much that they influenced the city's politics, and the great noble families had been marginalised or banished.

There the similarities ended. Unlike Florence, the commoners in Verona had aligned with the Ghibellines, as was perhaps inevitable in a city whose prosperity relied on trade with the empire (this meant that Dante found many other Florentine exiles there, who had found hospitality in the city long before him, such as the Ubriachis, a large family of Ghibelline bankers and magnates, who had a significant role in the local money-lending business). Another difference was that in Verona the people had ceded power to a strong man, rather than govern the city directly or struggle to do so, in accordance with a model that was spreading through most of northern Italy. This model was that of an overlord who guaranteed peace within the city, an end to factional struggles and the regular promotion of 'new men' (merchants, artisans and notaries) to government positions. This is what Dante has Cacciaguida say in Canto XVII of *Paradise*, a sure sign that Cangrande attributed considerable importance to this acceleration of social mobility under his rule, and wanted it to be known:

> many people will have their lives changed by him,
> between situations of poverty and wealth.
>
> (*Paradise*, XVII, 89–90)

The first of the Della Scalas to concentrate in his own hands the powers of the Captain of the Trades and the People and the Supreme Magistrate of the Merchants was Cangrande's uncle, Mastino della Scala, before Dante was born. He was assassinated in 1277, when Dante was twelve, and the powers were transferred to his brother Alberto, the father of Bartolomeo, Alboino and Cangrande, as well as Abbot Giuseppe, whom Dante so detested. Like many of the families who passed for nobles in the Italian city-states of the time, the Della Scalas descended from citizens who had been judges and occasionally consuls in the twelfth-century republic, and had no links with the rural aristocracy. But when Dante happened to go to Verona for the first time, their style had started to change. For a few years these rulers had got into the habit of celebrating family weddings, as well as rites of knighthood for their sons and nephews, with grand public ceremony, called 'courts', which combined aristocratic pomp, courtly sophistication and chivalric ostentation. This dimension to social life existed in Florence on the margins of politics and was cultivated by the magnate families that the people had distanced from high office. Here, on the other hand, the celebrations of knighthood and courtly behaviour were becoming the very heart of political life, and brought with them public ostentation that in Florence would have been unthinkable.[4]

Dante was a believer in courtly behaviour seen as a supreme form of sophistication, including intellectual sophistication. It is not by chance that the first word with which he described the welcome of the 'great Lombard' is 'courtesy'. Never mind that the openly political meaning that courtly culture was taking on in that part of Italy was hardly reconcilable with the values that a good supporter of Florentine popular government should have been defending. Exile was changing many of the ideas of this former trailblazer for the popular regime. In Verona, Dante was a petitioner, as Cecco Angiolieri had cruelly reminded him. To save his dignity, it served his purpose to recall that in the tradition of princely courts courtesy was an obligation for the lord, and therefore there was nothing humiliating in receiving his gifts and in return celebrating his generosity. Even in Cacciaguida's prophesy there remains a slight indication of the fact that for a citizen of a free and very powerful republic there still was something humiliating in this situation. It comes when Dante, having just introduced the 'great Lombard', loses no time in asserting that he had never had to ask him for anything because the host was courteous and loved him so much that he anticipated all Dante's desires. The time he spent in Verona was truly the moment in which Dante came to know:

> ... how salty
> is another man's bread, and how harsh a path
> coming down and going up another man's stairs.
>
> (*Paradise*, XVII, 58–60)

CHAPTER SEVENTEEN

TURNCOAT

While Dante's stay in Verona is surrounded with uncertainties, the years that came afterwards are immersed in darkness. So far, the chronology has been structured out of the relatively well-documented events involving White Guelphs and Ghibellines, who initially were still capable of acting as an organised party and undertaking important military campaigns, albeit disastrous ones. But later the party's initiatives became less frequent, though they never completely ceased, and after Dante lost his hopes of returning to Florence as a victor alongside the other exiles, our frightful ignorance of his movements is revealed with all its undeniable forcefulness. The only thing we can be certain of is that Dante never stayed anywhere for long. He was an exile and could say, as he asserted not without pride in *De vulgari eloquentia*, 'My country is the world, as fishes have the sea' (I, vi, 3).

What was his itinerary? Boccaccio claimed that, 'having come back from Verona', Dante lived for quite a few years as a guest of various nobles in the Apennines: the Counts Guidi, the Marquises Malaspina, the Lords della Faggiola; 'then he went to Bologna, where having stayed a short while, he went to Padua, and then he returned to Verona.' Finally he went to study in Paris, and then returned to Italy in 1310, when Emperor Henry VII crossed the Alps and suddenly rekindled his hopes (and not only his). Bruni, on the other hand, believed that Dante remained in Verona until Henry VII came to Italy, and only after the emperor's death did he roam 'stopping in various places in

Lombardy, Tuscany and Romagna reliant on the beneficence of various lords'.[1] We have some corroboration for many of the moves suggested by Boccaccio, but they refer to a slightly later phase. There are absolutely no documents for the period between the middle of 1304 and the autumn of 1306. Of the various possibilities, two have had greater fortune than the others, and many scholars present them as certainties, even though it is not certain that they could both be right.

The first theory is that Dante spent his longest and most important stay during the early years of exile in Bologna: perhaps for as long as a year and a half, up till February 1306. Bologna was still the great university city that Dante had known in his youth, possibly even more bustling in those early years of the fourteenth century, when medieval Europe reached its maximum demographic growth. It was a city so large that the residents of Borgo San Felice spoke a different dialect from those of Strada Maggiore, as the stunned Dante pointed out in *De vulgari eloquentia* (I, ix, 4). It was also a city full of foreign students, workshops in which books were copied for payment, booksellers capable of sourcing books from far away on request, but also merchants, many of whom came from Florence or its surrounding countryside, who had almost exclusive use of particular hotels and warehouses concentrated in the area around the two towers and mainly managed by Florentine landlords. Of all the Italian cities, Bologna was the most similar to Florence because of its political regime, the people in power, the wealthy families partly in opposition or exile and an unfaltering loyalty to Guelph orthodoxy.

When the Florentine Guelphs split, Bologna took the side of the White Guelphs, and its knights took part in military operations against the Black regime, even though the repeated failure of these enterprises was costly and humiliating for its citizens and put their friendship with the exiles under considerable strain. Nevertheless sources demonstrate that there was a large contingent of White Guelphs still living in Bologna in 1305. Dante could therefore have been among them. This theory is supported by many academics, including one of the more recent editors of *De vulgari eloquentia*, Mirko Tavoni, who is convinced that Dante wrote that work in Bologna and also most of *Convivio*, which he had started shortly before in Verona. Tavoni also believes that both works are characterised by the same political and pedagogical intentions generally aimed at the ruling groups in Italy, but with Bologna particularly in mind. It was, after all, a large city ruled by a popular Guelph regime, but also the seat of the largest and most prestigious university south of the Alps. There Dante would have wanted to build his future as an orator, politician and 'lay philosopher'; thus *De vulgari eloquentia* would have been written not only *in* Bologna but also *for* Bologna.

Of the arguments used to back up this theory, which are as fascinating as they are unverifiable, the least convincing is that the vast Aristotelian and scholastic bibliography that Dante used in the two treatises could only have been available in a university city like Bologna. This argument is mainly based on our enormous ignorance of libraries at the time, and it is hard to see why the same books could not have been available at, for example, the Paduan faculty or the chapter library in Verona. More seductive is the centrality Dante placed on Bologna and its poets in *De vulgari eloquentia*, where he praised Bologna's dialect as the best in Italy, whereas his concurrent, derisive debasement of Tuscany and its language suggests that he had decided to burn all his bridges with his native region. No less suggestive is the fact that in the treatise he often mentioned the name of Cino da Pistoia and claimed to have a close friendship with him: this insistence, which Cino's poetic stature doesn't seem to justify, could be explained by his reputation as a legal expert – in other words, Dante was hoping that 'his name would open doors to the university and poetry circles in Bologna' (as Mirko Tavoni suggests in his introduction to *De vulgari eloquentia*).

So far all we have are clues, however intriguing, but Dante's residency in Bologna is also alluded to in the surprising evidence provided by his son Piero, who graduated in law at Bologna University after his father's death. *Messer* Piero wrote a song about astronomy, one of the liberal arts, in which he defines Dante as 'my master who read in Bologna'. This is a technical term for teaching at university. Dante scholars claim that Piero remembered incorrectly and at the very most Dante might have given a few private lessons, but it is a little baffling to dismiss such an explicit statement. Even Giovanni Villani asserted that Dante, once banished from Florence, 'went to the faculty in Bologna', and it is tempting to interpret this to mean that he went there not to study for the third time twenty years after his first stay, but rather to look for a position by obtaining the qualification of *magister* which some contemporaries attributed to him towards the end of his life.[2] Astronomy was considered to be part of philosophy, in that it was one of the ways of understanding how the universe was made and what it signified, and Dante in *De Monarchia* does not hesitate to use the verb *philosophari* in the first person when, starting significantly from astronomy, he discusses the parallel between the divine order of the heavens and that of the empire: something quite evident, he declares, to human reason, to those who syllogise and to 'us' who philosophise about it. While in his youth philosophers appeared to be men of another race, the older Dante considered himself to be one of them, and it is not unreasonable to suspect that such self-confidence reveals some experience as a teacher at the university.

Whereas the study of philosophy was the most profound intellectual passion of Dante's life, actually working in the faculty and teaching for money could at best have been something imposed by circumstances and contrary to his aristocratic idea of culture, and was such a pitiful exercise as to confirm his opposition to any form of selling one's knowledge and wisdom.

The ferocious contempt for the trade in knowledge that Dante expresses in *Convivio* is echoed years later in the sarcasm of Canto XII of *Paradise* directed at those who hope to make a career of studying canon law and medicine, and 'bustle along behind Ostïense and Taddeo'. The latter was the physician Taddeo Alderotti, a person of great importance in the faculty of arts and medicine during Dante's youth, whom the poet had already mocked in *Convivio*. The former was Cardinal Henry of Segusio (also known as Hostiensis), the leading expert in canon law in the thirteenth century. Dante was similarly negative in his veiled judgement on the intellectual aridity of the faculty in Bologna in his poetic correspondence at the end of his life with the teacher Giovanni del Virgilio, who had invited him to return to Bologna – if, as it appears, Dante really was alluding to those circles when he had the shepherds of his eclogues refer to the arid and stony slopes of Etna.

There is another difficulty, this time of a political nature, and it is that in the canto on Brunetto Latini, written shortly after the events, Dante clearly states that the White Guelphs were after his blood after he had broken away. It is not easy to reconcile this assertion with a peaceful life in Bologna, which was one of the places where the White Guelphs habitually resided in large numbers. Are we being asked once again to doubt the version of events Dante puts forward in the *Comedy*? In any event, if there was a sojourn in Bologna, it could not have lasted too long, as in February 1306 the Black Guelphs took power in Bologna as well and drove the White Guelphs and Ghibellines out of the city. Villani wrote that the people, who had been incited against them, appointed a superintendent of public order (*bargello*) and entrusted him with a troop of guards (*sbirri*) for the purpose of cleaning up the city, 'seeking them out and killing them'. Dante would have realised that it was time to leave and would certainly not have waited for the subsequent alliance of 5 April between Bologna, Florence and other cities of the same party, whose purpose was 'the killing, crushing, extermination and perpetual death of the Ghibellines and White Guelphs'.[3]

Another theory, which if accepted would have us shorten the duration of his stay in Bologna, is that of a residency in Treviso, which from March 1306 was governed by Gherardo da Camino. The main argument is that Dante spoke well of this man and spoke often. In *Convivio*, when he was busy attempting to demonstrate that nobility was nothing to do with ancestry, he chose for his example this *reductio ad absurdum*:

> Let us suppose that Gherardo da Camino were the grandson of the vilest peasant that has ever drunk from the Sile [a river running through Treviso] or Cagnano [a smaller river that joins the Sile in Treviso], and this grandfather of his had not yet fallen into oblivion: who would dare to say that Gherardo da Camino was a vile man? And who would not concede that he was a noble man? Nobody, of course.

In *Purgatory*, Marco Lombardo repeatedly calls him 'the good Gherardo', and takes him as an example of how the older generation in Lombardy was superior to the current one in valour and courtesy. The scene is quite bizarre, because Dante pretends that he doesn't know this Gherardo, and Marco Lombardo, stunned by his ignorance, refuses to make clear who he is talking about, and no one, from the very first commentators, has ever understood why.[4]

However, the theory that Dante lived for a while in Treviso also has problems. Gherardo was not only the Captain General of Treviso from 1283 until his death, but also was a Guelph and close friend of the Black Guelphs in Florence, particularly Corso Donati, who repeatedly held office in Treviso and according to a short story of the time, received considerable funds from Gherardo in that very period to sustain his ambitions to be the most powerful figure in Florence.[5] It is difficult to believe that a Florentine exile, who until then had been a leading figure among the White Guelphs and the Ghibellines, found refuge at a court where none other than Corso Donati was a regular visitor. However strange it may seem, this theory is not so implausible, because this period, in which disasters came one after another from every direction, led to the most embarrassing moment of Dante's life in exile. He attempted to contact the new regime in Florence, apologising for his wrongdoing and begging forgiveness.

Bruni placed this episode in the period when Dante was living in Verona, where Dante found himself for the first time alone and without a party to sustain him. According to Bruni, he became so disheartened there that he wrote to the Florentine government and to individual members of the Black Guelphs in power – a letter with the querulous opening line, 'My people, what have I done to you?' Bruni's portrayal of this Dante reduced to a turncoat, to use Marco Santagata's incisive definition, is truly upsetting: 'He abased himself, attempting through good works and good behaviour to acquire a pardon that would permit his return to Florence.' Bruni was a chancellor of the republic and therefore had access to this correspondence, which is now lost.[6]

All this has not prevented scholars from doubting Bruni when he stated that the letters had been written in Verona, because, so the argument goes, a Dante reduced to asserting pitifully his loyalty to the Black Guelph regime would not have been listened to while he was living in the Ghibelline capital. Leaving aside the fact that we don't exactly know what was written in these letters – and therefore we cannot be sure that Dante admitted to having been an ally of the Ghibellines and asked forgiveness for this betrayal – we need to free ourselves of the narrow stereotypes whereby Guelph cities and Ghibelline cities would have constituted two united fronts divided by an impassable abyss. This was not the case, and what has been called the 'false enmity' between the parties in the real world entailed such a dense tangle of compromise, turncoats and unnatural alliances as to render the argument unpersuasive. In any event, the point is not identification of the place, which Bruni may have got wrong; what matters are the various clues that suggest that Dante's attempt to approach the Florentine regime and plead for a pardon took place between the summer of 1304 and the beginning of 1306, and one of these clues must certainly be the esteem for and friendship with Gherardo da Camino that he was parading around.

If, on the other hand, we accepted that Dante, following his time in Verona, spent a long and fruitful period in Bologna, then a friend of the White Guelphs, and wrote most of *Convivio* and all of *De vulgari eloquentia*, sufficient for him to plan a new life there, only to have this torn away brusquely by a political turn of events in February 1306, when friends of the Black Guelphs came to power, then we would have to delay his moral collapse, albeit slightly. This coup definitively destroyed all the hopes of the White Guelphs, and Dante was obliged to flee once more, this time from Bologna, and could have descended into a state of despair and therefore contrition. Shortly afterwards this would lead him to write Canto X of *Inferno*, in which he tries to give credence to the idea that his ancestors were inveterate Guelphs and fierce enemies of Farinata degli Uberti, who had known them well and had driven them into exile. This is stretching the truth, to say the least, given that the Ghibellines were governing when Dante was born in Florence, but it was an indispensable attempt to tidy up his image with a view to changing sides. But only a few years earlier he had attended meetings with those same Ubertis and other Ghibellines and White Guelphs.

In spite of all the uncertainties over time and place, we can safely say that after a few years of exile Dante went through a period in which he had no qualms about contacting the Black Guelphs, now the masters of Florence, and asking for a pardon.

Giuliano Milani noted a change in his language between the years immediately following his banishment, when the Pact of San Godenzo and the letter to Cardinal Da Prato place Dante among the exiles who defiantly declared themselves to be at war with Florence, and the following period, in which he started to talk of himself as a 'guiltless exile' – complaining, that is, about the injustice inflicted on him and later even admitting his error and thus justifying his request for his sentence to be reviewed and struck down.

This is undoubtedly the immediate political meaning of one of his most famous songs, 'Tre donne intorno al cor mi son venute', in which, albeit in the context of a highly obscure reflection on the decline of justice and behind the screen of a supposed nostalgic love, he declares that he repents of his misdeeds which have kept him away from Florence: 'so if I had my faults, / many months have passed since they were extinguished / as long as guilt passes when a man repents.' In a conclusion, which some academics consider to have been added later, the theme is made even more explicit by the mention of the opposing parties, which Dante claims to be equidistant from: the song is invited both to go hawking 'with white feathers' and hunt 'with black hounds / from whom I had to flee, / but they hold the gift of peace'. The Black Guelphs could pardon him, 'but they won't, for they don't know who I am'. However, Dante invites them to be wise and not exclude the possibility of a pardon, because they have won and he surrenders ('for forgiveness is the pleasant victory of war').

Dante scholars diverge on the date of the song, and the truth is that we have no idea, except that it was transcribed by the customary and remarkably dependable notaries of Bologna in 1310, and from then on it circulated publicly. But he never received a response.

CHAPTER EIGHTEEN

'OTHER PEOPLE'S STAIRS'

No later than February 1306 Dante had to recommence the life of an exile in search of a roof and protection. Boccaccio claimed that he stayed 'for some time with Count Salvatico in Casentino, some time with Marquis Morruello Malespina in Lunigiana [a historic region part of which is now in Tuscany and part in Liguria], and for some time with the Della Faggiuolas in the mountains close to Urbino'.[1] It feels like he hid in the mountains and fled the world of the cities in the plain, where it was increasingly difficult to find a secure refuge. The landed properties of those lords in the Apennines would have been very different from the places he was accustomed to. To be clear, none of these lords was a stranger to the city; indeed, they were constantly offering the republics their well-paid services as specialists in warfare and taking command, but their courts didn't have organised parties capable of imposing ideological control and drawing up lists of political enemies. Each was free to offer hospitality to whoever they wanted, whatever their political colour, and Dante, who in the circumstances would not have been an expensive guest, could have been a precious asset to be deployed in the chancelleries, which must always have been short of qualified staff.

Fortunately Boccaccio's information is corroborated by one of the very few documents in the archives relating to the period of exile, and we learn from it that on 6 October 1306 Dante was in Sarzana, staying with the Marquises Malaspina and, even better, that he was in their service on a diplomatic mission. The cousins

Franceschino, Moroello and Corradino Malaspina, who had for some time been at war with the bishop of Luni, decided that the time had come to end the hostilities that were devastating Lunigiana. On that day Marquis Franceschino appointed 'Dante Alighieri of Florence' as his attorney to sign a peace treaty with the bishop on behalf of the entire family.

Thus Dante really was at home with the Malaspinas, and was considered to have sufficient abilities to represent the marquises in signing a peace treaty with their long-standing enemy. The treaty as a legal document does not, of course, demonstrate that Dante negotiated the peace, but only that he was sent to sign it. The power of attorney was given to him in Sarzana on 6 October 'before Mass', or 'in the first hour', and the treaty was signed on the same day two hours later 'in the third hour' in the bishop's chamber in the Castle of Castelnuovo Magra. It is clear that the treaty had been negotiated previously and the treaty specifies by whom: two Franciscan friars, one of whom was *fra* Guglielmo Malaspina, a relation of the marquises. Essentially Dante acted in place of the marquises, who for some reason didn't want to be present, and kissed the bishop of Luni on their behalf as a sign of peace. However, the *arenga*, or moralistic prologue, of the peace treaty is one of several documents in which philologists now tend to find Dantean phraseology, and some conclude that, before being nominated attorney, Dante must have been put to work in the Malaspinas' chancellery drawing up the text.

Even though on that occasion Dante was sent by Franceschino, it was Moroello who was his principal host. We know this not only from Boccaccio but also from Dante's son Piero in his commentary on the *Comedy*, and it is confirmed in a sonnet Dante wrote in the name of Moroello, which was a response to the one his friend Cino da Pistoia had sent to the marquis.[2] Writing poetry was not an unusual activity in the castles of an aristocracy eager for pastimes, and the fact that Dante and Moroello had joined together in this literary game demonstrates that between lord and guest there was a degree of intimacy. It should be pointed out that Moroello was a loyal ally of the Black Guelph government in Florence, and one of their most effective captains under whose command White Guelph Pistoia was taken following a long and tragic siege in 1305–6. And it was to him that Vanni Fucci referred when he announced to Dante, 'Mars took lightning from Val di Magra [another name for Lunigiana] ... so that every White Guelph shall be wounded' (*Inferno*, XXIV, 145–50). Dante's familiarity with the marquis, so shortly after events that Vanni Fucci thought would cause him distress ('And I said this so that it will pain you!'), is a clear indication that at this time Dante was looking for a rapprochement and would have been willing to change party if he had been pardoned.

The period when Dante lived as a guest of Marquis Moroello is linked to an episode previously mentioned, the supposed recovery of the first seven cantos of the *Comedy*. Boccaccio told the story of the manuscript found among Dante's things, which Gemma took to a monastery for safe keeping and which was shown to the poet Dino Frescobaldi who, having guessed that it was one of Dante's unfinished works, decided to send it to the author.

> And having investigated and found that Dante at the time was in Lunigiana staying with the nobleman of the Malespini family called Marquis Morruello, who was knowledgeable of such things and also a particular friend of his, he chose not to send it to Dante, but to the marquis so that he could show it to him. That is what he did and begged [the marquis] to do what he could to ensure that Dante continued with the enterprise and, if possible, finished it.

And so Dante, who according to Boccaccio believed the manuscript to be lost and had given up on pursuing the *Comedy*, decided to resume the undertaking.[3]

No one today believes that those early cantos, as we read them now, could have been written in Florence before he went into exile. Nor did Boccaccio really believe it. Yet academics are fascinated by the idea that Dante may have conceived a project, later abandoned, during the years he was engaged in Florentine politics, and that this early work then became part of an idea for the *Comedy* that was partly or entirely different. So the story Boccaccio told may have an element of truth. There is a further observation to be made on this matter: the decision to devote almost all of his intellectual energy to the creation of a formidable 'sacred poem' is obviously the most important single fact in Dante's life, and a biographer would pay any price to know more about the circumstances in which this idea came into his head. By dint of examining the chronological clues scattered around the *Comedy*, scholars have persuaded themselves that Dante started to write the poem in the form we're familiar with in 1306 or 1307, and I would have written about it in this chapter if we had had a little more hard evidence. Hence Boccaccio's narrative with Marquis Moroello in such a significant role could be another clue that this isn't perhaps an entirely invented story, and that Dante's family and his friends in literary circles recalled some connection between the *Comedy* and the period in which he lived with the marquis.

This raises the question of who were these Malaspinas in whose castle the first cantos of *Inferno* may well have taken on their definitive form. They were descendants of the Obertenghis, one of the most powerful families in northern Italy, and they took their name from an ancestor who lived in the first half of the twelfth century, Marquis Alberto (a contemporary of Cacciaguida). He was called Malaspina (Evil Thorn) very much as some of his peers were called Guerra (War), Guastavillani (Peasant-Destroyer) or Non-ti-giova (Doesn't-Help-You) to emphasise their ferocity and the little advantage that could be gained from their proximity. Powerful over a wide area of transit between the Ligurian coast, the Apennines and the Po Valley from Bocca di Magra (close to La Spezia) up through Lunigiana and the Cisa Pass and as far as the Piacenza area, the Malaspinas belonged to the rural aristocracy that in vast areas of Italy had been marginalised or even wiped out by the expansion of urban republics. However, they were still very strong in mountainous regions, where the possession of fortresses and castles, the loyalty of rural communities and the control of roads and passes turned them into forces to be reckoned with, which powerful cities near by could only oust with considerable difficulty. The lords in the mountains didn't ignore the cities (no one in Italy could do that), but they cultivated their own way of life, which was very distant from the ideals and practices of a republic governed by the people, like the one Dante had served a few years earlier. As was made very clear by the series of frescoes such families liked to have adorning their castles, their values were the chivalric ones of courage, loyalty and virility, displayed on horseback with a sword in hand – all values, for that matter, which weren't completely alien to Dante either, even though he was a citizen and the son of a money-changer.

Choosing the hospitality of those families and those castles – and it seems unlikely that Dante had any choice – did not therefore mean entering a world radically different from the one he knew in the city (after all, those chivalric frescoes teeming with helmets, swords and horses also decorated the municipal halls and loggias in the city-states). However, it did mean a surgical separation, cutting himself off from everything that belonged to politics in the city: the life of the party and faction, the competition for office, the counting of votes in the councils, the official condemnation of the pomp associated with the magnates and knights who were the enemies of the commoners in order to maintain the values and practices of an exclusive, criticised but nevertheless influential elite. It meant abandoning the language of the citizenry and adapting to that of lordships and their subjects. It has to be said that Dante found no difficulty in doing so. Shortly after leaving the court of the Malaspinas he sent a letter to Marquis Moroello in which he addressed him as *dominus*, his lord, and called himself *servus*, and expressed his nostalgia for Moroello's court, which he had had to leave and in which he had the good fortune to 'fulfil the offices of freedom'. Some interpret this as carrying out the honourable services requested by his lord, and others as Dante's freedom to devote himself to his studies and his writing: *Convivio* and *De vulgari eloquentia*, always supposing that he had not completed them in Bologna, but above all *Inferno*.[4]

The encomium to the Malaspinas that Dante places in Canto VIII of *Purgatory* is also steeped in the ideology of nobility and knighthood. On recognising Marquis Corrado, the traveller exclaims there is nowhere 'in all of Europe' that does not know his family, and the fame of its lords reflects well on their country, Val di Magra, which however he has never visited – in the 1300 of the poem's narrative, of course. Within a dozen lines Dante manages to deploy the lexicon of honour twice, that of courtesy once and that of esteem, the *pretz* of the Provençal troubadours, recalling the fame 'which honours your family' and defining the Malaspinas as 'honoured people', because they both spend generously and are formidable in war ('esteemed for their purses and for their swords'). Obviously gratified, the marquis prophesies that within seven years Dante shall experience in person what up till then will have only been hearsay ('let this courteous opinion / be nailed into the middle of your head / with larger nails than other people's speech'). The least we can say is that the image is singularly forceful, and Dante's admiration for the Malaspinas had become an obsession.*

Boccaccio, it appears, was well informed about the

---

* In *Purgatory*, XIX, 142–5, he finds a way to flatter even Alagia Fieschi, the niece of Pope Adrian V and Moroello's wife.

Malaspinas. Then we have Count Salvatico ('the uncouth count'). He was one of the Counts Guidi, a princely family with very many branches which owned an enormous quantity of castles, villages, mountain pastures and livestock from Casentino to Romagna, and whose title of count, like that of marquis for the Malaspinas, gave them the authority of descendants of holders of high imperial office in the kingdom of Italy. For instance, the Guidis owned Poppi Castle, under whose shadow the Battle of Campaldino was fought and which was so famous as a place of aristocratic pleasures that a contemporary expression for affluence was 'living like the count in Poppi'. Although they too had difficulties with the expansion of the republics, the Guidis were still powerful in Dante's times, and they were anything but unaccustomed to life in the cities, where they often accepted appointments such as supreme magistrates and captains in war. In Florence, in particular, the Guidis had owned a palace in the *sesto* of Porta San Piero where Dante lived, although those *nouveaux riches* Cerchis had bought it when he was a boy, causing a great deal of envy and gossip. The fact that Dante, like any other Florentine, knew them is demonstrated by the wisecrack he attributed malignly to his friend's mother-in-law in the exchange of sonnets with Forese: unhappy with the husband she had found for her daughter, the woman complained that with less expense she could have organised a more prestigious marriage which would 'have had her in with Count Guido'.[5]

A closer relationship with another branch of the Guidi family is referred to in the second of the letters traditionally attributed to Dante. It is an undated letter of condolence sent to the Counts Oberto and Guido da Romena on the death of their uncle Alessandro, who in 1302 was the first captain nominated by the White Guelphs in exile. In the letter the author wrote that Count Alessandro 'was my lord', and that he would be loyal to his memory for the rest of his life, because for many years the munificence of the count had convinced him to become his subject. Dante declared that he shared in the mourning of the greatest family in Tuscany and its friends and subjects, and counted himself as one of the latter, having been driven from his country without any guilt, and accustomed to seeking consolation and hope in the company of Count Alessandro. Finally he addressed the bereaved nephews, calling them 'my lords', and apologised for not having attended the funeral because of the unexpected poverty he had been reduced to, so that he had neither arms nor horses, and in spite of all his efforts he had not yet been able to recover his position.[6]

In truth, this is a very strange letter. We don't know when Count Alessandro died, but the event is usually attributed to the early years of Dante's exile. Why did he claim to have been the count's subject for many years? Strictly speaking, a friendship would not have been impossible when Dante had been a prominent advocate of the popular regime that ruled in Florence, but the expressions used in this letter go far beyond that, further than what we have already encountered in the letter to Malaspina. It is a letter that fully espouses the values of the rural aristocracy, pride in their lineage (against which Dante argued so forcefully in *Convivio*) and loyalty to one's lord in exchange for his generosity. The reference to arms and horses is evocative: of course the funeral of one of the Counts Guidi would have been a magnificent ceremony worthy of a knight at which you had to present yourself in the appropriate style. But the urban elites also had a taste for such practices. There was rather less, however, of the pride in being subjects and the joy in serving the great lords. Was it possible that in such a short time Dante had adopted so completely the style and values of the military aristocracy?

There is another oddity! In Canto XXX of *Inferno* the traveller in hell meets Master Adamo, who was burned at the stake for having falsified gold florins in 1281, when Dante was sixteen years old, and had committed this crime at Romena Castle ('there's Romena, where I counterfeited / the sealed alloy of the Baptist') on the orders of his lords, the three brothers Alessandro, Aghinolfo and Guido ('they persuaded me to mint the florins'). And Master Adamo, who is the only one to have paid such a high price, hopes to see before not too long the other villainous souls who instigated his crime ('but if I were to see the wretched soul / of Guido or Alessandro or their brother ...'). There's no denying it, Dante remained loyal to the memory of Alessandro. Understandably, doubts have been raised in the past about the authenticity of this letter; it could have been an imitation or a scholastic exercise. If, on the other hand, it really is Dante's letter, we are faced with yet another blatant contradiction between judgements about someone he should have been grateful to, expressed in different periods and above all in different contexts.

According to Boccaccio, the Count Guidi who hosted Dante during the years of exile was not Count Alessandro da Romena but Count Guido Salvatico, who was already an old man at the time. He had been a knight and active in politics when Dante was born – and had always been a friend of the Guelphs. He was very involved in conflicts in the Italian cities, as on several occasions he had been the supreme magistrate in Prato and Siena, and *condottiero* in the pay of the republics of Bologna and Florence. He was the one who gave up his palace in Florence to the Cerchis in 1280. He was obviously someone well known to Dante, and there would have been nothing strange about him taking in the exile. It would not have been an impediment that in the early years of the century Count Guido Salvatico was so closely linked to the Black Guelphs who governed Florence that he took part in the defence of the city when Emperor Henry VII was besieging it. As we have seen, Marquis Moroello Malaspina had been a captain in the Black Guelph alliance and had commanded the terrible siege of White Guelph Pistoia during the years in which Dante had a close relationship with him. In this phase, the time of contrition and hopes of returning to his home city, Dante seemed to be going out of his way to seek the protection of the aristocrats in the mountains and friends of the Black Guelphs in Florence who could help to get his pardon.

It seems certain, then, that Dante moved in with the Counts Guidi after he left the Malaspinas, partly because in the above letter to Marquis Moroello he declared that, after he had left his court, he had moved close to the source of the Arno. In his song 'Love, since it pleased you that I should suffer' ('Amor, da che convien pur ch'io mi doglia'), which most academics believe was attached to the letter, he addresses Love and laments because it has attacked him 'in the midst of the mountains / in the valley of the river / along which you always move me so strongly'. Thus Dante is certainly in the Arno Valley, but upstream among the mountains, so that when he addresses his song itself, he calls it 'my little mountain song'. In other words, he was in Casentino, which was the land of the Counts Guidi. The song confirms that in that moment Dante was tired and longed to give up the struggle and return home. He concluded with the hope that the song would reach 'Florence, my land / which locks me out, / devoid of love and sincere pity', and repeats once more to his fellow citizens who are so deaf to his appeals that he is no longer an enemy:

> If you go in there, say as you go: 'Now
> my maker can no longer make war.'

Dante continued to call Florence *Fiorenza*, because he was a learned man, but also because that was what all the rest of Italy called it. Remigio del Chiaro Girolami, the great Dominican preacher at Santa Maria Novella during those years, recorded not without some irritation that by that time only foreigners used that name: the citizens in their own corrupted language called it *Firençe*. Without realising it, Dante was turning into a foreigner.[7]

Boccaccio also wrote of a sojourn with the Lords della Faggiola, one of the great families that dominated the region known in the Middle Ages as Massa Trabaria, covering a huge stretch of the Apennine mountain range from the Metauro in the north to the upper reaches of the Tiber in the south. The head of the family in Dante's time was Uguccione della Faggiola, one of the most celebrated figures of the time and an exemplary representative of the military aristocracy in the mountainous regions who knew how to exploit skilfully the tensions between factions in the cities to carve out an important political role for himself. Usually considered to be a passionate Ghibelline, he was in fact an unscrupulous politician whose sole aim was to construct a territory under his own personal rule. If on many occasions he found himself at the head of a Ghibelline coalition, this in no way impeded him from entering into relations and alliances with the Church and the Guelphs. He was the supreme magistrate of Arezzo in 1302, and the White Guelphs driven from Florence chose that city as the place in which to gather in the hope of obtaining his support. At that particular moment, however, Uguccione had his own reasons for seeking the favour of Pope Boniface VIII, and consequently he decided to support the Black Guelphs. Hence he gave his daughter in marriage to Corso Donati, who during the years he was exiled from Florence had been appointed the rector of Massa Trabaria by the pope. Uguccione had no interest in helping the exiles and taking part in their war; indeed, as Dino Compagni wrote, 'corrupted by the vain hopes Pope Boniface had given him that he would make his son a cardinal, he responded to the [pope's] petition by abusing [the White Guelphs] so often that it was better for them to depart'.[8]

The fact is that there is absolutely no corroboration of the idea that Dante stayed with him, and the information probably came from another source. In a commonplace book written in Boccaccio's hand there is a transcription of part of a letter to

Uguccione della Faggiola, signed by a Friar Ilaro of the monastery of Santa Croce del Corvo at Bocca di Magra. The friar told of 'a man' travelling to France who stopped at the monastery and gifted as a keepsake the first part of a work he was writing. On taking a look at it, the friar was shocked to see that it was written in vernacular and not in Latin, and the man, who of course turned out to be Dante, explained to him that this had been his original intention but then he had reflected that Latin poets were held in little esteem by his contemporaries, and he had preferred to write in vernacular. On leaving the monastery, the man had asked the friar to write a comment on that first part of his work, which could be none other than *Inferno*, and send it on to Uguccione della Faggiola, who was his close friend and to whom he intended to dedicate the work. He also informed him that the second part would be dedicated to Marquis Moroello Malaspina and the third to Frederick of Aragon, king of Sicily. Friar Ilaro's letter was without question of doubt a fake, a literary exercise or pastiche, even though today it is not believed to be the work of Boccaccio himself. Given the nature of the commonplace book into which it was transcribed, where Boccaccio gathered his material on Dante, and that he used the biographical details contained in the letter in several other works, it seems clear that the author of *Decameron* believed that it was authentic and that this letter was what made him think that there had been a degree of familiarity between Dante and Uguccione.

Whatever the case, we can be sure that during these particular years Dante frequented the great aristocratic families who dominated the mountainous regions of Central Italy, and he could even delude himself that there, rather than in the cities drowned in corruption, the seed of virtue capable of resurrecting the destiny of Italy lived on. This explains his declaration in *Convivio*, which is directed at those who have most to gain from reading it, 'and these nobles are princes, barons, knights and many other noble people, not only men but also women'.

And it explains his frosty observation that it is pointless to approach those who are busy with their own affairs, because they would not in any case be able to understand ('commoners … busy throughout their lives in some trade or profession concentrate their minds on this livelihood … so much that they pay heed to nothing else').[9] Even if he kept faith with his assertion in 'Le dolci rime' that true nobility is that of the mind, Dante was developing a vision of the world that left little room for the crowd of traders, money-changers, usurers and contractors – mostly peasants who had moved to the cities and become rich only recently – and they were the people of the republics. This too, in its own way, was contrition and something more lasting: while the contrition he displayed when pleading with the Florentines for a pardon looks contrived and would not survive the new hopes raised by Emperor Henry VII's journey into Italy, the rejection of republican ideology by an ex-member of the Council of the Hundred is radical and definitive.

In a subsequent phase after the sojourns in the aristocratic castles of the Apennines, fourteenth-century writers insert a journey Dante is supposed to have made to Paris. This was asserted by Villani, according to whom Dante, once banished from Florence, 'went on his way to the faculty in Bologna, and later to Paris', and by Boccaccio in his *Brief Treatise in Praise of Dante*, in which he declared that, after Dante had wandered from one city to another and one Italian court to another, he lost all hope of being able to return to Florence and 'went to Paris, and there he devoted himself to the study of philosophy and theology', until Henry VII's march south rekindled his hopes and convinced him that he should return to Italy. In the second version of the *Treatise* he added a detail that has the feel of an account from someone with information acquired directly. It was that Dante did not stay long in Paris and had serious financial difficulties, which seems entirely logical given that there were no powerful protectors willing to maintain him.[10]

When Boccaccio examined Dante's intellectual education in another passage, he pointed out that 'close to his old age, he went to Paris where to his considerable glory, he delivered his own disputations and on various occasions revealed the loftiness of his genius, so much so that his listeners still marvel at it'. In short, Dante, who in his youth had attended the 'disputations of philosophers', would become in Paris the protagonist of these intellectual tournaments. As evidence of Dante's extraordinary memory, Boccaccio told the story of how:

> he was in Paris and was performing an 'as-you-please' disputation which was taking place in the schools of theology, and various gifted men asked fourteen questions on various subjects with the arguments for and against being delivered by the opponents. Without interrupting, he took it all in, and once they had all said their piece, he spoke to the arguments following the same order in which they were put, and resolving the questions with subtlety and responding to the counter-arguments. This was reputed to be almost a miracle by everyone who was there.

This exploit was the equivalent of a chess grandmaster who plays and wins a dozen games at the same time.[11]

For various reasons, including the novelistic tone that pervades the episode, not all Dante scholars are persuaded by this detailed report, and many are sceptical about Dante ever getting to Paris, preferring to suggest that, if he ever went to France – as it appears that he may have done from the manner in which he describes the necropolis in Arles and the marshes created by the Rhone – he only went as far as the papal court in Avignon. In truth it doesn't seem amiss that Dante could have decided to visit in person the most important centre of studies in the world, where the great Sigieri di Brabante had taught before he was murdered at the papal court in Orvieto, when Dante was seventeen. The poet would meet him in Canto X of *Paradise* with stupefied admiration. Here he evokes the rue du Fouarre, which still exists today, not far from the Sorbonne, in which the most prestigious schools were to be found ('this is the eternal light of Sigieri, / who reading in rue du Fouarre / demonstrated truths that provoked envy and hate'), and develops a theory about the truths that create enemies – an idea that must have been close to his heart. Ultimately, it appears that there is no evidence that precludes a journey which all the earlier biographers confidently claimed to have happened. It is quite likely that Dante did visit the rue du Fouarre in person – siding with those who decided in nineteenth-century Paris that the southern part of that road, which had been modernised in the style of Haussmann's renovations, should be renamed *rue Dante*. Thus a Parisian Dante was enthusiastically welcomed into French culture.

Boccaccio spoke of another residency, this time in Padua, which just for a change is without any corroboration, and yet it is not implausible because it was, it's true, a smaller city than Bologna or Paris – though its 30,000 inhabitants were not a small population for the time – but it was also a very important university city, full of students from all over Europe, particularly Germans, Poles and Hungarians. During those years Padua was one of the liveliest cultural centres in Italy: today we tend to attribute to it a role in the history of Italian literature that is second only to that of Florence. Above all, together with Bologna, it was the most important centre of Aristotelian scholarship in Italy. The great Pietro d'Abano taught there, and there Dante could have found some of the books he used in *Convivio* and *De vulgari eloquentia*. Moving outside Padua, he could have come to know in person the places and dialects in that part of Italy, from the Arsenal (shipyard) of Venice to the dikes along the Brenta as far as the Roman cemetery in Pula, which crop up so often in his works.

Benvenuto da Imola added his anecdote about a meeting between Dante and Giotto, whom the poet was supposed to have visited while the latter was painting the Scrovegni Chapel in Padua, but it is a brief short story with a decidedly literary flavour, entirely contrived to arrive at the punchline, and unquestionably invented. Scholars in the nineteenth century felt certain that they had got their hands on documentary proof that Dante had lived in Padua, because in a contract dated 27 August 1306 there is a reference to a Dantino of the late Alighiero of Florence, and yet an inhabitant of Padua at the time. However, a Dantino of the late Alighiero, resident in Verona, was recorded in many documents between 1336 and 1350, when Dante had been dead for some time. Evidently he was someone else, the son of a Florentine exile who, like so many others, had created a new life in the city of the Della Scalas, and who in 1306 was still young and living in Padua, possibly as a student. The thirty-year interval between the first document and the second does raise questions, but the theory that these were the same person is more likely than the one that claimed that the person mentioned in 1306, who for some reason was called by the diminutive Dantino, was our Dante.

However, it would be strange if Dantino of Alighiero from Florence was not a relation of Dante di Alighiero degli Alighieri from Florence, even though they weren't the same person. Neither the fathers' name nor the sons' were common. Dante had several uncles we know almost nothing about, any one of which could have named his own son Alighiero, and this Dantino could have been Dante's nephew. When there were two men with the same name in a family, it was the custom for the younger one to be called with the diminutive, which he was often stuck with for the rest of his life, something that did not happen if the person bearing the name was the only one in the family. We could therefore be in the presence of yet another cousin about whom we know little or nothing.

Clearly Dante was constantly on the move during the barely five-year period from the banishment of the White Guelphs from Bologna in February 1306 and Emperor Henry VII's arrival in Italy at the end of 1310. If in the period immediately after his break with the White Guelph faction he felt like 'a ship without a sail and without a helm', these years must have been even harsher, especially when you consider that he had reached the fateful age of forty-five, the threshold of old age.

And we still haven't covered all the possibilities! We have to add Lucca, a city not mentioned by Boccaccio, to the list of places where he might have lived, and for which we have a couple of clues. The first clue is Dante's meeting with the poet from Lucca, Bonagiunta Orbicciani, in Canto XXIV of *Purgatory*, who speaks to him of a teenage girl, also from Lucca, and tells him that in the future she would please him. 'She was born a woman, and doesn't yet wear a wimple', he said, and therefore wasn't married in 1300 (it should be noted that in Dante's world a married woman would never be seen in the street without a wimple to cover her hair: this was so much part of life that in the silent language of monks they would indicate a woman by drawing a finger across their foreheads from one eyebrow to the other). The fellow poet from Lucca gave Dante prior notice that this young woman 'will make you like my city'. Very sadly, this is all we know of her, but just knowing of this young anonymous woman whom Dante liked so much, it seems probable that he also lived in Lucca.[12]

The other clue is the previously mentioned document of 21 October 1308, in which Dante's son Giovanni acted as a witness in a contract involving merchants from Lucca and Florence, and signed in Lucca. Given that the son was living there, it has been inferred that Dante could also have been there, and yet Lucca was ruled by the Black Guelphs and two and a half years earlier had adhered to the treaty between Bologna and the Guelph cities in Tuscany in which they undertook to annihilate the Ghibellines and White Guelphs. It seems hardly possible that Dante could have lived there. As a few years later Giovanni returned to

the territory of the Florentine republic, the destinies of father
and son may well have already diverged at the time. But it is
also true that the contract involved Florentine merchants of
the company of the Maccis, who were White Guelphs. Indeed
one of them was the son of Tignoso de' Macci, who died while
being tortured after being arrested by the supreme magistrate
of Florence, Fulcieri da Calboli, together with other 'citizens of
the White party and Ghibellines'. Villani recorded that when
he was put on the rack, he died 'while tied by the hemp ropes,
because of his weight'. All the others who were arrested were
decapitated.[13]

The presence of the Maccis suggests that at the time the
faction in Lucca had slackened their repression of the White
Guelphs or just diminished their checks. This seems to have
been confirmed by the fact that a few months later, on 31 March
1309, the Republic of Lucca thought it necessary to restate its ban
on Florentine exiles entering its territory. On the other hand, it
should also be said that the act at which Giovanni was present
involved changing money for the Maccis, who were on their
way to the Fair of St Ayoul of Provins, one of the great Cham-
pagne fairs which attracted merchants from all over Europe.
They purchased from the Moriconi of Lucca 600 pounds in small
tornesels, which were a denomination minted in France, and paid
them 762 pounds in good *denari* or pennies minted in Lucca. In
other words, the Maccis were just passing through, and they
acted in concert with one Micheluccio of the late Fredo Gentile,
'citizen and merchant of Lucca', with whom they were staying.
Their presence is not sufficient to guarantee that even someone
who had been condemned to death, like Dante, could live per-
manently in Lucca in complete safety. It is also true, however,
that in 1306 the Captain of the People of Lucca was none other
than Marquis Moroello Malaspina, a very close friend of the
Black Guelphs but also of Dante. In short, there was no shortage of reasons for the exile to stay there for a while, particularly

in a period in which he appeared to be seeking a rapprochement with the Black regime. In the vast range of theories over the places in which Dante could have found the books he needed to write *Convivio*, there are also those who have suggested the library of the monastery of San Romano in Lucca.

CHAPTER NINETEEN

HENRY VII

Wherever he was in 1308, Dante learned shortly after the events, because such news travelled fast, that on 1 May the king of Germany, Albert of Hapsburg, had been assassinated, and by the end of the year Count Henry of Luxembourg had been elected king of the Romans by the German princes, which meant that he was their candidate for the empire. His election cut short the ambitions of Charles of Valois, the brother of King Philip IV of France, also known as Philip the Fair, who had hoped to gain the title with the support of Pope Clement V. Dante must have been overjoyed, because Charles of Valois was the man who had allowed the Black Guelphs to take power in Florence and expelled the White Guelphs. Henry (whom Dante called Arrigo, in the Tuscan manner) was crowned king of Germany on 6 January 1309, and by July the pope, partly under the influence of Cardinal Niccolò da Prato, an old friend of the Ghibellines, decided to confirm his election. From that moment, Giovanni Villani assured his readers, there was talk of the new sovereign coming down into Italy for an imperial coronation.[1]

Luxembourg was a small principality on the western borders of the empire, whose name not even the German chroniclers could spell (they produced many versions: Lüczelburk, Luscelenborg, Luzzillinburg), but their counts descended from Charlemagne himself, or at least this is what modern Luxembourgish genealogists claim, though they may not be entirely impartial. Henry was a German prince but was imbued with the i-+++++For a long time any attempt to have done this was considered fanciful and anachronistic, and perhaps even pathetic because of its naivety. Today a greater knowledge of that world suggests that this was not the case, and that Henry was a talented, flexible and pragmatic politician, whose project was not destined to failure from the start. It's true that for a long time emperors had ceased to intervene in practical terms in the Italian peninsula – in effect, not since the death of Frederick II in 1250. During Dante's childhood two European princes who weren't German had claimed the title of king of the Romans, after having been elected by two opposing factions: Richard of Cornwall, a son of King John of England, and Alfonso X of Castile. In 1272, when Dante was seven, Richard died, and a year later the German princes finally elected a German king, Rudolf of Hapsburg. Rudolf, who technically was never emperor, did all he could to re-establish imperial power in Germany, which attracted a great deal of hostility ('King Rudolf judges well and hates false counsellors,' a poet sang in German – and he meant it sarcastically), but he always avoided the Italian morass, which merited a harsh judgement from Dante, who placed him in Purgatory among the negligent princes:

> The one sitting up high who seems
> to have forgot his obligations, ·
> and moves not his mouth to others' cries,
> was Emperor Rudolf, who could have
> healed the sores that murdered Italy.
>
> (*Purgatory*, VII, 91–5)

Rudolf lived until 1292, when Dante was twenty-seven, and his successor, Adolph, count of Nassau, held the crown until 1298, when he fell in battle against his rival Albert of Hapsburg, Rudolf's son. 'Albert the German' was king in the fateful year of 1300, in which the fictional Dante journeys into the next world, and he too is a beneficiary of the poet's fierce invective in Canto VI of *Purgatory*, where Dante accuses him of abandoning Italy and Rome, 'the garden of the Empire', and wishes an exemplary punishment to be inflicted on his descendants by the heavens. This is yet another prophesy after the event: when Dante was writing, he knew very well that Albert's son would die before him, and that on 1 May Albert himself would be assassinated and that the crown would elude his dynasty.

Dante's preoccupation with imperial absenteeism had greatly increased, and it seems that it only made its presence felt when he ceased to be a leading figure in an arrogant and victorious Guelph regime and became an exile who was not quite sure whether the Ghibellines had not been right after all. It is entirely understandable that Dante was overjoyed by the news of Henry VII's election and perhaps even more by the pope's approval – which undoubtedly opened the way for the king of the Romans to travel south in order to be crowned emperor for the first time since anyone could remember. The cantos of *Purgatory* in which he meets Rudolf and curses Albert were definitely written in those months, when his thoughts were focused on the newly elected emperor, who, Dante openly declares, would do well to remember Albert's fate and be fearful of it.

The king of the Romans did not disappoint him. In September 1309, having just received the papal benediction, Henry was in Berne, intent on assembling the army that would accompany him to Italy. He had already sent his ambassadors to notify the princes and republics in Italy of his intention to march into the country and have himself crowned king of Italy in Milan and emperor in Rome. Two more diplomatic missions followed in the spring of 1310, one to Lombardy and the other to Tuscany, and finally in October of the same year the emperor passed Mont Cenis and made his first stop at Susa, followed by Turin and Asti, on the way to his main objective, Milan. There he was crowned with the iron crown on 6 January 1311, which is associated with the *Befana* (a popular name for epiphany), as Villani wrote. For Germans, 6 January was the festival of the Three Kings, the very same festivity that had been chosen for Henry's coronation as king of Germany two years earlier.[2]

In Florence they had decided for some time that the new king of Italy was their enemy. His ambassadors appeared in July 1310, according to Villani, and asked for the city to acknowledge their sovereign, and *messer* Betto Brunelleschi, who had been charged by the republic with delivering the message, 'replied with haughty and dishonest words'. They must have thought that he had gone beyond his remit, because the government was so dismayed that they replaced him with another orator, *messer* Ugolino Tornaquinci, who this time replied 'wisely [...] and courteously'. The ambassadors believed him and, given that they had ordered the cessation of all wars, and in particular that the Florentine siege of Arezzo be lifted, they proceeded to that city convinced that on their arrival there would be no more siege. The Florentine army wouldn't even think of obeying, with the result that the imperial ambassadors were 'greatly indignant with the Florentines'. The anxious government talked of sending a magnificent diplomatic mission to Henry, who at that time was in Lausanne, to assure him of their good intentions, but the Guelph magnates incited the people by spreading the word that, if they heeded the emperor, the Ghibellines would return to the city. As ever, ideological hatred blinded people, the mission was cancelled and Florence was the only city in Italy that did not send anyone to Lausanne to greet and honour the emperor on the eve of his journey. On the other hand, the exiles lost no time in convincing the sovereign that the Florentines distrusted him.[3]

We don't know if Dante was among them on that occasion. Biondo Flavio, relying as always on the writings of his fellow countryman Pellegrino Calvi, argued that in the summer of 1310 Dante was in Forlì, where he found out about the Florentine response to Henry VII's envoys, and in a letter to Cangrande della Scala, written in his own name and on behalf of the White Guelphs, he denounced the arrogance, temerity and folly with which they had responded to the emperor. To be honest, there is the suspicion that Biondo got his notes muddled up, because if such a letter really had been sent to Cangrande, the fact that Dante was once more writing on behalf of the entire White Guelph party would have been a very remarkable event: the terrible things he would say against them in the canto of Caccia-guida were yet to come, but he had already written the canto of Brunetto Latini, where he accuses the White Guelphs of being after his blood. We have seen that Biondo had previously spoken of Dante's journey to Forlì back in 1302 in order to negotiate on behalf of the White Guelphs with various lords in the north and, mistaking the chronology, had included Cangrande as one of their number at a time when he was only eleven years old: such an unreliable witness is not enough to be certain that, with the arrival of Henry VII, Dante had agreed once more to be the spokesman for the White party.

It is, however, true that the political confrontation was a breeding ground for declarations, open letters and manifestos, and this was the environment in which Dante, the acknowl-edged master of oratory and rhetoric, could be of greatest use to Henry VII. In the summer or autumn of 1310 he published the manifesto known as Epistle V, which announced the arrival of the emperor in Italy and invited everyone to submit to his justice. The letter, in Latin, was addressed 'to all the kings of Italy [there were two of them, mortal enemies both claiming the title of king of Sicily, the Angevin in Naples and the Aragonese in Palermo] to the senators of the generous city [the Republic of Rome was the only one which prided itself in calling its mag-istrates senators, rather than consuls and supreme magistrates, like everyone else] as well as the dukes, marquises, counts and commoners' – that is to say, republics. 'The lowly Italian Dante

Alighieri Florentine and guiltless exile' (for some time 'guiltless' had been an adjective he was fond of applying to himself) wished everyone peace and invited them to rejoice in a new day and the arrival of a new Moses, and he exhorted the descendants of Longobards to remember that first of all they were Trojans and Romans. He called on them to stop repeating like sleepwalkers 'We have no lords', a vain boast of absurd liberty, to try to be worthy of Latium rather than Scandinavia (where learned men of the time believed the Longobards to have come from) and to implore the mercy of Caesar Augustus, who was coming with the benediction of the pope.

On 31 March 'of the first year of the most propitious arrival of Henry Caesar in Italy', namely 1311, Dante sent another open letter to the 'iniquitous inner Florentines'. For some considerable time 'inner' and 'outer' had become widely used terms in Italian politics to define the faction holding power in a city and the opposing faction that had been thrown out. The letter exhorted the 'iniquitous' Black Guelphs to surrender to the emperor to avoid inflicting a terrible punishment on the city. As it was loaded with insults, the letter obviously did not aim to convince them, but rather was a manifesto that joined the duel of opposing propagandas. The era of contrition and entreaties to the Black Guelphs to grant him a pardon was evidently a thing of the past, and Dante was once more on a war footing – though this does not authorise us to conclude that he had become a Ghibelline, because the pope at that time was supporting Henry VII and any orthodox Guelph could have done the same without feeling guilty.

By proposing submission to the emperor, the 'king of the world, and the minister of God', Dante was introducing the same themes developed in *De Monarchia*, which was written during those years. The only liberty was spontaneous obedience to the law of Caesar, who by divine will must govern humanity and represents the only truly public power, which is the guarantor of civilised co-existence. All other powers that were currently governing Italy, whether they were principalities or republics, represented nothing more than private interests. This was a stunning U-turn for a man of the republic. The letter was sent 'in Tuscany near the springs of the Arno' and therefore in Casentino, where Dante – we will discuss the evidence shortly – was once again a guest of the Counts Guidi.[4]

Two weeks later, on 17 April, he wrote another open letter from the same place, but this time to Henry VII, who was besieging Cremona, explaining that he was mistaken to remain in the Po Valley, where, once Cremona was subdued, Brescia, Pavia, Bergamo or Vercelli would certainly rebel. Thus he should stop wasting time on these trifles and come to destroy his true enemy in its lair, the viper ready to turn against its maternal womb and the plague-stricken sheep that could infect the whole flock – in other words, the city of Florence. Like the previous ones, this epistle is full of biblical references and displays a prophetic tone that has always caught the attention of Dante scholars, so it is customary to refer to the Dante of this period as the 'prophet Dante'. These are the years in which he put aside the writing of learned treatises such as *Convivio* and *De vulgari eloquentia* and was immersed in the composition of the *Comedy*. In the letter to the emperor the prophetic tone is so pervasive that it also became obvious to Villani, who wrote that Dante directed his reproaches to Henry 'almost by prophesising'. *Almost*: the chronicler is not suggesting that Dante wanted to present himself as one of the true or false prophets who every now and then appeared on the scene, enjoying various degrees of success, but his intention was to employ a language that was similar to theirs.[5]

The idea that Dante did feel that he had a little bit of the prophet in him would explain an episode in his life that, untypically, he alludes to in Canto XIX of *Inferno*. Having compared the round holes into which the heads of simoniacs have been thrust downwards to the holes 'in my beautiful San Giovanni', the baptistery in Florence, which held amphoras full of the water used in the baptisms, Dante added:

> ... not long ago, one of these I broke
> to save a child drowning inside: let this be
> the last word and every man be undeceived.
>
> (*Inferno*, XIX, 19–21)

So Dante broke one of the amphoras to save a child who had slipped inside, and considered it important enough to mention in his *Comedy*, stressing moreover that it contained a precious message that would sweep away some misunderstanding (but he was wrong about that: scholars have never ceased to wonder vainly about the meaning of that 'last word' which should have been 'undeceived'). Mirko Tavoni has argued that, while he was writing his *Comedy*, the memory of that episode convinced Dante that God had invested him with prophetic powers, as he identified with the prophet Jeremiah, whom the Lord had ordered to break a clay vase before the elders and priests of Israel to warn them of the misfortune that awaited the Jewish people. The fact that this episode is narrated in Chapter 19 of the book of Jeremiah just as it is in Canto XIX of *Inferno*, and that in both cases the context is one of brutal polemic against the profanity of priests, does suggest the plausible idea that Dante, who very often refers to the book of Jeremiah in his works, was struck by the parallels between them and saw this as a confirmation of his own prophetic spirit.

Returning to the letter to Henry VII, Dante reminded the emperor that he had already met him and had kissed his feet, as the ceremony required, and this raises the question of whether he had been present at the coronation in Milan. As usual, it is impossible to be certain. There is another point that merits some examination: in this letter of April 1311 Dante declares that he is writing not only on his own behalf but also on behalf of others.

Of whom? In spite of what we have thought so far, we have to ask whether he really had made peace with his old comrades. Even then, as Marco Santagata observes, politics was the art of the possible and experienced continuously changing alliances. Something of this kind could have been behind Biondo Flavio's impression that Dante had written to Cangrande in the name of the White Guelphs, albeit in the changed circumstances sparked off by the arrival of Henry VII, which created new political configurations and less formal ones. If Dante was admitted to kiss the emperor's feet, he was certainly part of a network of supporters in the enterprise, which was not necessarily a revitalised party of Florentine White Guelphs.

As for the proof that Dante stayed with the Counts Guidi during those months, a manuscript of the late fourteenth century attributes to him a letter conserved in three versions – probably two drafts and one final copy – which Countess Gherardesca da Battifolle is supposed to have sent the Empress Margaret, the wife of Henry, to thank her for having written. It is worth noting that the wives of kings and princes had their own parallel diplomatic network which supported that of their husbands. Countess Gherardesca assured the empress that her husband was in good health and both of them rejoiced at the emperor's successes, and she dated the letter 18 May 1311 from Poppi Castle. Count Guido da Battifolle, about ten years older than Dante, was one of the many Counts Guidi who was close to the Guelph party. At the time of the clash between White and Black Guelphs, he unequivocally sided with the latter, giving one of his daughters in marriage to one of their leaders, *messer* Musciatto Franzesi, and when Henry VII besieged Florence in 1312, he intervened in defence of the city, for which the emperor condemned him for treachery. It could seem rather strange that Dante was his guest at Poppi and was acting as the secretary for his wife, Gherardesca, a daughter of Count Ugolino of unhappy memory, were it not that the Dominican monk Niccolò da

Ligny, bishop of Butrinto, a fellow countryman and aide of the emperor, who was sent to visit the Counts Guidi in October 1311, reported that all of them had by then declared their loyalty and were ready to follow him to Rome for the coronation, although those of them who were Guelphs went back on their promises. Openly aligning themselves against the emperor was a risk that no Italian lord living at the time had ever had to take, and understandably Count Da Battifolle had sought at the beginning to keep a course that was not overly dangerous. It may well have been a prudent measure in such circumstances to host and employ a famous poet and orator full of zeal for the imperial cause.

Prudence was not a characteristic of Florentine politics: following some initial vacillations, Florence decided to resist at all costs the emperor's requests. To consolidate the regime and remove support for the enemy, an amnesty was decreed in August–September 1311 granting those banished or in internal exile permission to return to the city, as long as they were 'true Guelphs'. The provision was linked to the name of one of the priors in office, the judge, *messer* Baldo d'Aguglione, and Dante, who always had a good word for everyone, insulted him in Canto XVI of *Paradise*, when Cacciaguida sympathised with contemporary Florentines who, with their city full of immigrants, had to 'put up with the smell / of the peasant of Aguglione'. The amnesty contained many restrictions on the return of the magnates, who remained the real bugbear for the government of the people. But there was also a list at the end of the document of condemned men who could not benefit from these provisions. It contained a hundred or so names, both of entire families and of individuals. In the *sesto* of Porta San Piero the list, which appears to have been drawn up more or less in order of importance, starts with the Adimaris, Abatis, Cerchis, Maccis, Portinaris and goes on until, about half-way down, we find 'the sons of *messer* Cione del Bello and Dante Alighieri'.

It is useful to have the confirmation that, although they didn't have the surname Alighieri, the Del Bello cousins continued to be seen as Dante's confederates, but what is more important is that they were considered to be among the regime's implacable enemies whom they had no intention of pardoning.

Dante proved to be a good prophet – in fact, an excellent one. Having taken Cremona in April 1311, the emperor had to face a rebellion in another city, which was Brescia, as he had expected. There was another siege, and it did not surrender until September. At the end of October, Henry VII was in Genoa, where the empress died, and where all the Florentine merchants were ordered to leave. In March 1312 he reached Pisa by sea, the most loyal city in Italy, whose citizens 'gave him the government of the city and provided him huge gifts of money to supply his people, which he had great need of'.[6] It is very probable that Dante, together with other exiles, was in his retinue, and possibly collaborated in the imperial chancellery from which documents were issued that seemed to echo in several points his open letters to Florentines and the emperor.

The most specific allusion to the place where Dante was staying during those months is to be found in a letter that Petrarch wrote many years later to Boccaccio, and is compatible with the theory that he was at the imperial court, except that the interpretation of this particular passage comes with some quite difficult problems. According to his own writings, Petrarch was still a child when he met Dante, as he was in exile together with Petrarch's grandfather and father, *ser* Parenzo and *ser* Petracco dall'Incisa, having been driven from Florence on the same day and for the same reason. Dante was younger than one and older than the other, and as happened with exiles, they developed a strong bond of friendship, partly because they had the same tastes. Later however, *ser* Petracco, who had to provide for his family, resigned himself to exile and got on with his business, while Dante insisted on continuing his fight.

Leaving aside some inevitable mistakes – for instance, that *ser* Petracco was condemned many months after Dante – Petrarch's memories are confirmed by the documents: the names of his father and uncles come almost immediately after Dante's in the list of condemned men who hadn't been beneficiaries of Baldo d'Aguglione's amnesty. Petrarch claimed that these events coincided with his early *pueritia* and, given that *pueritia* at the time followed infancy (*infantia*) and started after seven years, he must have been seven or eight years old. He was born on 20 July 1304, when his father was with the other White Guelphs in Arezzo, and therefore his period of friendship with Dante has to be dated after 20 July 1311, in the midst of Henry VII's campaign.

Given his business commitments, *ser* Petracco was constantly on the move between Padua and Avignon, where his protector, Cardinal Niccolò da Prato, lived, and it is difficult to imagine that there was much time for a baby Petrarch already capable of remembering things not only to become Dante's intimate friend but also for Dante to be 'living' with *ser* Parenzo and *ser* Petracco. In another of his letters Petrarch claims that he spent more or less all of his infancy – up to his seventh year – in Incisa, and then his eighth year in Pisa, after which *ser* Petracco moved his family to Avignon. We could infer that it was precisely in that Pisan period between July 1311 and July 1312 that Dante appeared – as did the emperor, who, as we have seen, landed in Pisa in March 1312. But it would be dangerous to base any chronology on an old man's memories of childhood: at other times Petrarch variously asserted that he lived in Pisa during his seventh year, remembered being torn away from it when he was seven years old (which appears to mean shortly after his seventh birthday in July 1311) and claimed that he arrived in Avignon just before turning eight years of age (and therefore just before July 1312). Moreover he declared that the sea journey took place in winter and involved a sojourn in Genoa. When Petrarch claimed that he had spent his eighth year in Pisa, did he mean 1311? If so,

While we don't know where he was, we can attempt to guess what he was up to: he was engrossed in the business of writing *De Monarchia*, the important political treatise in which, as a Guelph distrustful of the papal court and a supporter of the republic terrified by the fratricidal struggles that were bleeding Italy dry, he extolled the emperor and held him up as the only guarantor of peace. There is an autobiographical assertion in the treatise, in which Dante, who is discussing free will, recalls having spoken about it in his *Comedy*. Given that this particular canto in *Paradise* must have been written much later, some scholars infer that *De Monarchia* could not have been written during the period Henry VII was in Italy, but it is much more likely that the clause – a unique example in the whole of Dante's oeuvre and contrary to the rhetorical precepts of the time – was not written by Dante but started as a gloss by one of the commentators, and then switched to the first person and inserted by error in the manuscript tradition. In any event, an author who takes on such a demanding literary project while also committed to such a bagatelle as the *Divine Comedy* must have taken his time, and we can assume that quite a few years passed by between the concept and the final stylistic reappraisal. The underlying idea and the first draft of *De Monarchia* unquestionably went back to the years in which the emperor, having come to Italy to bring peace, found himself at war with everyone and Dante, hopeful that his arrival was a gift from God, was, in his own words, enraged 'to see kings and princes agree on only one thing: their opposition to their lord, their anointed one and their Roman prince'.[9]

The emperor remained in the vicinity of Florence until All Saints' Day without achieving anything. So he lifted the siege and spent the following months destroying the countryside and taking castles, but with increasingly unfavourable prospects as his knights died or returned to Germany and money started to become scarce in spite of the generous funding he had received

CHAPTER TWENTY

OTHER PEOPLE'S BREAD

The story that Boccaccio tells is that, after the death of Henry VII, Dante was desperate, like all the emperor's followers, and lost all hope of returning to Florence. Instead he fled to Romagna, where, on learning of his arrival, Guido Novello da Polenta, the lord of Ravenna, offered him hospitality, which he gratefully accepted.[1] This narrative appears to be corroborated by a letter in the vernacular dated 30 March 1314 and written by Dante while on a diplomatic mission to Venice on behalf of Guido da Polenta. Dante wrote sarcastically of how he had given an oration in Latin in the presence of the Doge, Giovanni Soranzo, but had almost immediately had to switch to the vernacular because no one could understand him. Published in 1547 by the Florentine writer Anton Francesco Doni, the letter is definitely a fake, which typifies the rivalry between Florentine and Venetian humanists. But Boccaccio is also wrong, because he declares that, having been welcomed and courteously taken into Guido Novello's household, Dante remained there until his death. In other words Boccaccio, who knew that Dante died in Ravenna and for some strange reason didn't know where had been previously, filled the gap in his knowledge by deciding that Dante had immediately travelled to Romagna. This cannot be true, if only because Guido at that time had a secondary role within the Da Polenta government of Ravenna, which was still ruled by his uncle.

In the meantime, another sudden death had modified the

political landscape of Christendom. Clement V died on 20 April 1314 in Carpentras, where the papal court had established his residence, and within ten days the conclave which should have elected his successor was in session. Dante, now in the habit of making public statements, wrote a harsh open letter to the Italian cardinals in which he compared Rome, abandoned by the pope, to the desolate and widowed Jerusalem in a passage by the prophet Jeremiah. This excerpt was dear to the poet, who quoted it twice in *Vita Nuova* to describe the desolation of Florence following Beatrice's death, but now he was putting it into the service of a political cause. He had never liked the dead pope, and in *Inferno* he accuses him of being 'a lawless shepherd' (*Inferno*, XIX, 84), but he probably gave him a little credit at the time when he supported Henry VII. However, Clement V did not lose any time in betraying the emperor's trust and, indeed, in deceiving him, as Dante would say in Canto XVII of *Paradise* ('but before the Gascon [Clement V] deceives high-minded Henry'). Dante was furious with Clement and full of contempt for his foreign origins, but he was no less furious with the Italian cardinals who nine years earlier had played their part in electing him. The only way to make up for the enormity of what they had done, he warned, was to fight vigorously in the combat that had already commenced 'for the Bride of Christ, for her Holy See that is Rome and for our Italy' so as to put the Gascons to shame and bring triumph to Latin glory. We can imagine Dante's mood when the news spread that on 24 July 1314 Clement V's nephew had burst into the conclave and driven out the Italian cardinals by force. The proceedings were suspended!²

Boccaccio's claim that Dante had given up on his chance of returning to Florence on the back of a defeat of the existing regime cannot be taken as read. In spite of Henry VII's death, the city, governed by the Black Guelphs, still found itself in a fairly precarious situation. The Pisans, stunned as they were by the demise of the emperor and abandoned by their ally, Frederick

III, who after a brief appearance in Pisa had returned to Sicily, were still determined to pursue the war and had managed to keep in their pay 1,000 German, Brabantian and Flemish knights. Another orphan of the great enterprise, our old friend Uguccione della Faggiola, who had been Henry VII's deputy in Genoa, accepted the seigniory of Pisa 'and subsequently achieved very great things in Tuscany along with the German knights who had remained', Villani admitted, thus honouring a formidable enemy with the merit he deserved. Florence responded by conferring the lordship of the city on King Robert for five years: it was a measure the republics considered possible in emergencies, even if we may find it surprising that they could so easily renounce their independence and submit themselves to the protection of a king. 'And this was the saving of the Florentines', the chronicler commented dryly.[3]

However, it took some time for them to save themselves: in the short term, the Pisans and the Germans under Uguccione's command scared the wits out of the Florentines. In June 1314 they took Lucca and plundered it, among other things taking possession of the treasure of the Roman Church which Pope Clement had attempted to transfer to France but which, because of the uncertainties of a journey by sea, which was dominated by the Pisans and Genoese, had ended up in Lucca under the custody of the abbot of San Frediano. 'In the heat of such a victory' Uguccione and his Germans spread out over the whole of Tuscany from the countryside around Pistoia to Maremma, besieging and taking one castle after another.[4] When the campaign of the following year was approaching, in May 1315, the Florentine government approved yet another amnesty to all exiles who presented themselves by 24 June, St John's Day. Friends wrote to Dante to inform him and explain the conditions. The poet replied to one of them affectionately but clarifying that he did not intend to accept them. He could have paid a fine and undergone a humiliating procedure, which involved entering the republic's prison symbolically and then coming out to be offered as a penitent to the patron saint in the baptistery: all things, Dante explained, that were incompatible with his honour and the fame that he now enjoyed.[5] We do not know who these friends were, but in the letter Dante addresses his unknown correspondent as 'my father' and thus someone of authority, probably a member of the clergy, and assures him that many other friends had written to him, including a nephew. Likely candidates for this relationship could be Bernardo Riccomanni, a Franciscan monk at Santa Croce and Tana's son, or Andrea the son of Leone Poggi and another of Dante's sisters, or even Niccolò the son of Foresino Donati, who was Gemma's brother, who in subsequent documents proved to be very close to the aunt and cousins.[*]

As for the confidence with which Dante spoke of his fame, it should be said that, although we don't know the dates of the composition and publication of his *Comedy*, by this time some people knew of the work in progress and had read the first cantos. The very first mention is in a manuscript by Francesco da Barberino, who was the same age as Dante and, like him, a Florentine exile. In the second half of 1314 he found himself in Mantua, Virgil's home town, and noted down that Dante praised the ancient poet in his work called the *Comedy*, which spoke of hell and many other things. Among Dante scholars there are those who think that not only *Inferno* but also *Purgatory* had been completed and copied extensively by the time of Henry VII's death, having met with immediate success. Others are not so sure, but the translations of the *Aeneid* into Tuscan by the Sienese writer Ciampolo degli Ugurgieri and the Florentine notary Andrea Lancia, both completed by the end of 1316, repeated lines from *Purgatory* word for word, so the second canticle must have been published by then. The poem's success

---

[*] There is still an ongoing debate on Dante's correspondents involved in the affair.

must have given Dante the powerful and heady confidence that eventually dictated those lines in Canto XXV of *Paradise*, in which he hopes that his literary fame will one day permit him to return to Florence and be crowned with laurels in the baptistery of San Giovanni:

> If it ever happens that the sacred poem
> in which both heaven and earth have had a hand,
> such as to reduce me for many years to skin and bones,
> overcomes the cruelty that locks me out of
> that pleasant sheepfold where I slept like a lamb,
> the enemy of wolves who wage war against it;
> now with another voice, another fleece
> I shall return a poet, and at the font
> of my baptism shall I have my crown.
>
> (*Paradise*, XXV, 1–9)

It is difficult not to detect in this a sarcastic reversal of the self-serving offer of amnesty in exchange for returning to Florence as a penitent of St John.

Immediately after his rejection of the amnesty, Dante must have had the impression that his prophetic curses against his native city were coming true, because in the summer of 1315, to the bewilderment of the terrified Florentines, which many years later was clearly still fresh in Giovanni Villani's memoirs, 'Uguiccione da Faggiuola with his bands of German knights, lord of Pisa and Lucca and triumphant throughout Tuscany', had put Montecatini under siege. The Florentines, under the command of the prince of Taranto, who was the brother of King Robert, had put together a powerful army of 3,200 knights and marched on Montecatini, where Uguccione inflicted the most catastrophic of defeats on them on 29 August 1315. It was one of those defeats that could easily have caused a regime to collapse, and unsurprisingly Dante had hoped for it, but the Black Guelph regime withstood the blow. The terms of the amnesty granted in the spring were definitively terminated, and on 6 November Dante and his sons were included on one of the long lists of exiles, 'Ghibellines and rebels', who were condemned to death for not having presented themselves. Dante was completing *Purgatory* at the time, and there was little he could do but have Forese Donati, whom he chose to meet there, predict with bitter satisfaction the screams of the Florentine women whose husbands, sons and brothers would be killed in Montecatini.[6]

We do not know where Dante was during this period of years immediately after the death of Henry VII, which stubbornly remain in complete darkness. Boccaccio thought that he was in Ravenna, where he remained until his death, but he was mistaken because, when Cacciaguida prophesies in *Paradise* that Dante would benefit from Cangrande's generosity, he was evidently referring to a stay in Verona of some importance which must have come after 29 November 1311, when Cangrande, following the death of his brother Alboino, became the sole ruler of Verona. Filippo Villani must have known more about this: in the 1380s he wrote a brief biography of Dante in which he followed Boccaccio slavishly, but when in the following decade he wrote his commentary on the *Comedy*, he clarified that, following his sojourns in Lunigiana and Casentino, Dante went to Verona, where he stayed for as long as four years and worked very hard, before accepting the hospitality of Guido Novello in Ravenna.[7]

Some of the scholars interested in this obscure period of Dante's life have recently come up with another hypothesis, which is not backed up directly by any of the sources but is nevertheless not without a degree of plausibility, namely that, on reaching Pisa along with Henry VII's retinue, Dante could have stayed there under the protection of Uguccione della Faggiola. However odious he may have found the Pisans when he wrote the canto on Count Ugolino – so much so that he hoped that the River Arno would drown them all – ultimately their city was the safest possible place for a prominent enemy of the Florentine regime. Dante could have stayed for some years in that still great city capable of competing with Florence, enclosed in the almost perfect quadrilateral of its walls and crossed by the River Arno full of docks and warehouses, under the disdainful scrutiny of unfinished buildings such as the magnificent cathedral and its tower, which had already started to incline. It was a city full of construction sites, which included the government building and the palaces of rich merchants along the riverside. It may well have been here that Dante completed his *De Monarchia*.

The idea of a prolonged period in Pisa, perhaps interspersed with further sojourns with the Malaspinas who lived near by, contrasts with another theory that regularly comes up, according to which Dante very soon left for Verona, where he stayed with Cangrande for more than the four years referred to by Filippo Villani. Recently Paolo Pellegrini perceived the hand of Dante in a letter sent by the lord of Verona to Henry VII in August 1312, and concluded that the poet must have been in that city since he decided not to accompany the emperor to the siege of Florence. If so, all the other hypotheses concerning Dante's movement between 1312 and 1316 have to be rejected, including the one that had him in Pisa as part of the emperor's retinue. Could this be the case? The academic in question observes that the theory that Dante lived in Pisa is essentially supported 'by the school that gravitates around the University of Pisa'; it is not out of malice that we could add that Pellegrini, the exponent of a long and happy stay in Verona, happens to teach at the University of Verona.

The fact is that the sojourn at the court of Cangrande della Scala, which everyone takes for granted and, to repeat ourselves, appears undeniable in the light of Cacciaguida's prophecy, is based on very little documentation. The evidence of the so-called letter to Cangrande is disputed: it is a long and extremely erudite text which takes up ten printed pages, and in reality it is an introduction to the *Comedy* itself and, more specifically, the first canto of *Paradise*. The authenticity of this text, which in truth is extremely uninspired, has split Dante scholars. Dante declared to the 'magnificent and victorious lord, Lord Cangrande della Scala', Imperial Deputy of Verona and Vicenza, that he had wanted to come to Verona to verify whether his fame, which resounded around the world, was merited. Having ascertained in person that this was the case and experienced his beneficence, he had decided to be his devoted friend and dedicate to him the most important canticle of his work, which was *Paradise*. We will examine just one of the many doubts that challenge the authenticity of this letter. It was the custom to dedicate literary works when they had been completed and the works were made public, so the letter – if authentic – must have been written after the completion of the *Comedy*, but we know that when he wrote the last cantos of *Paradise*, Dante was no longer in Verona but happily the guest of another lord, Guido da Polenta, in Ravenna

Marco Santagata has rightly emphasised the false notes that echo through all the references Dante made to Cangrande and the Della Scalas: both the dubious ones and the reliable ones. In the letter he says – or someone has him say – that he had long believed that Cangrande's fame had been exaggerated. He who excuses himself accuses himself, and this reminds us that in *Purgatory*, a few years earlier, Dante had been rude about Cangrande's father, Alberto, accusing him of having appointed to the position of abbot of San Zeno his illegitimate son, who was crippled and led a scandalous life. Early commentators convinced themselves that Dante was demonstrating his fearlessly independent judgement, unconcerned about offending his powerful protector, but it is much more likely that, when he wrote those lines, Dante was not in Verona and could not have imagined that soon he would need to implore the assistance of Cangrande. Still more improbable is that Cangrande, as someone has suggested with great optimism, 'had clearly demonstrated his lack of involvement in the appointment of the disreputable abbot', given that in 1321 Cangrande went on to appoint the latter's own illegitimate son to the same position: the management of ecclesiastical benefices was a political question in which considerations of this kind had no place.

A clue that Dante may have feared that writing those lines could have lost him the chance of gaining Cangrande's protection is to be found in his strange reply to Cacciaguida, after the latter has prophesied his exile, the courtesy of the great Lombard and the beneficence of Cangrande. Dante comments that he knows that hard times are coming, and must be more careful about what he writes,

> thus if my dearest place has been taken from me,
> I must not lose others with my poetry.

He feared that, with his overly sincere verses, some people would bar his way to some safe haven. Cacciaguida's only response was to warmly invite him to tell the truth without worrying whether someone might take it badly. More than one academic perceives this appeal as a laborious attempt to justify Dante to some circles in Verona who found some of his writings to have the 'flavour of bitter fruits'. The high praise of Cangrande in Cacciaguida's prophecy was clearly designed to remedy these errors, and it is no coincidence that shortly afterwards and without any apparent motive Dante introduces an extremely violent invective against John XXII, the pope based in Avignon who 'only wrote [excommunications] to cancel them [against payment of large sums of money]' and who of all the saints was only interested in John the Baptist – the saint who appeared on gold florins. He was a pope who had never harmed Dante personally, but on 6 April 1318 he excommunicated Cangrande.

And then there is the letter Dante sent to Cangrande – always supposing that he was the author – in which he argued that his poverty leaves him no time to complete the commentary and makes it clear that he can only do so if he receives adequate funding. This seems odd if the letter was written when Dante was in Ravenna as a guest of Guido da Polenta, but it would also have been extremely inappropriate if it had been written while he was living in Verona. It would be easier to understand if the letter, which has been circulating in its current form since the middle of the fourteenth century, included excerpts from an original letter composed before arriving at the court of Cangrande. Would it be stretching the point to argue that this desperate struggle to guarantee assistance from a powerful person, the most humiliating Dante ever encountered, occurred during a particular period of economic disruption? The years of bad weather and hunger in Italy began in 1311 and culminated in the terrible European famine which lasted from 1315 to 1317, in which we can detect the death knell of the long cycle of medieval economic prosperity. In any case, we should remember that during those years it was probably more difficult to find hospitality and get financial assistance.*

The fact remains that we are unable to fix the dates of when his stay in Verona started and ended with any certainty. It is true that there's a brief work of possible attribution to Dante, *Questio de aqua et terra*, which claims to be a transcription of his speech at the close of a cosmological dispute of the kind favoured by intellectuals of the time, which was held for an audience of clergy in Verona on 20 January 1320. This is the only text that provides a date for his stay in the city, but its authenticity is

---

* The chronology of the famines in northern Italy only partially coincides with what was happening in the rest of Europe, but it seems certain that the entire decade was characterised by extremely serious crises of famine and high mortality.

anything but reliable, and in any case we cannot eliminate the possibility that Dante had returned to Verona, after moving his residence elsewhere: Dante scholars are sometimes reluctant to admit that people of that time were constantly on the move, just like us, albeit with fewer comforts.

The importance of the time he lived in Verona is demonstrated by the very close relationship his sons maintained with the city after his death. In 1326 Iacopo returned to Florence, and the bishop of Fiesole gave him his tonsure and accepted him into the clergy. There is no evidence that he ever became a priest, and in fact he would get into trouble many years later for breaking a promise of marriage. However, he did succeed in being allocated a canonry in the diocese of Verona with the assets of seven different churches, which paid him 60 pounds a year once he had rented them out.[8] Piero, who in 1320–21 held benefices in Ravenna and was therefore a clergyman as well, decided to study law. In 1332, when we come across him again, he had graduated and was a judge in Verona, where he would live a rich and respectable life for another thirty years.[9] Both the conferment of a canonry and the appointment as judge were very difficult to obtain without the support of the local rulers of a city-state. After the death of Cangrande in 1329 there would have been his nephews Alberto and Mastino; Dante had evidently established a lasting bond with the family, in spite of the initial embarrassments.

Why, then, did Dante leave Verona in the end? It may have been that at some stage his position at the court of the Della Scalas was becoming somewhat ambivalent. At the time people were used to those figures known as 'men of the court' or, not without irony, 'knights of the court', who were half entertainers and half scroungers, not that different from the court jesters, although with a higher tone socially. They lived at the expense of princes and potentates, well received for their pleasant company and always ready with a joke or some gossip but also sometimes used for confidential missions. Quite a few of them appear in the *Comedy*. The first is Ciacco, whom Dante meets in Canto VI of *Inferno*, but he is a peculiar kind of 'man of the court' and of a higher social rank than the others. Boccaccio wrote, 'that man was not entirely of the court', but as he loved to eat well more often that his means permitted, he frequented the homes of gentlemen more accustomed to good living, 'to whom he went to eat if invited, and equally if not invited, he invited himself all the same'. He was well received because he was always ready with some witticism. In other words, a man of the court was above all someone who knew how to entertain his hosts, and so he ate and drank at another man's expense. Besides, Boccaccio insists that Ciacco could have lived off his own income, and was not a professional man of the court, but another fourteenth-century commentator, Ottimo, who didn't understand such subtleties, cut to the quick: Ciacco 'was a man of the court, that is to say a buffoon'.[10]

The next was Guglielmo Borsiere, whom Dante placed in Canto XVI of *Inferno*, where he distressed the other damned souls by lamenting the decline in valour and courtesy in modern Florence. Of him Boccaccio observed: 'he was a knight of the court, a very well-bred man of praiseworthy manners, and it was his duty and that of his peers to negotiate peace between magnates and gentlemen in the matters of marriages and lineages.'[11] 'Negotiate peace': this reminds us of something and we will return to it, but not before presenting the last 'man of the court' in the *Comedy*. This is Marco Lombardo, whom Dante imagines himself meeting in Canto XVI of *Purgatory*, and with whom he lingers in elevated conversation, and to whom he shows both respect and affection ('o Marco mio'). We don't know exactly who he was, but his name was legend. We find him as the protagonist in the *Novellino*, a text that came out in Dante's youth, in which Marco Lombardo was defined as 'a man of the court who was the wisest of his trade', and which emphasised that he was poor and yet ashamed to ask. Villani defined him as 'a wise and gifted man of the court', and spoke of his terrible and prophetic reply to Count Ugolino in Pisa shortly before his fall. At a sumptuous banquet to display the count's wealth Lombardo was reputed to have said that there was nothing lacking except the wrath of God. Ottimo knew something else: Marco had lived in Paris and, before ending up in poverty, and 'while he had his own things, had been prized for his fighting skills and his courtesy'. When there was no other choice, he had the powerful maintain him but always made sure that his honour was upheld.[12]

The analogies are impressive: depending on 'those better off than him' when he could no longer maintain himself, and the insufferable poverty that deprives him of indispensable things such as arms and horses; then there is shame of asking (which recalls Dante's comment that the 'great Lombard' gave things before the poet could ask for them), but on the other hand the powerful entrusted Dante with negotiating peace as had occurred in Lunigiana in distant 1306. There is even the trip to Paris! There is enough here to glimpse a Dante who is shocked to discover that he too has become a figure not that different from a 'knight of the court', and he consoles himself by making of Marco Lombardo and Guglielmo Borsiere two champions of valour and courtesy, and guaranteeing that their lives were honourable, even if they did eat at other people's tables. However, it may be that keeping up appearances became an arduous task. Petrarch's absolutely apocryphal anecdote about a sharp exchange of words with Cangrande does, however, conjure up the potentially humiliating aspects of Dante's situation: a permanent guest was constantly at risk of becoming a 'man of the court', maintained by the powerful because he amused them.

In the second half of the century Petrarch observed that Dante had been freer and more insolent with his language than could be tolerated by the easily offended princes of his own time, and it is true that by Petrarch's time the rulers of the cities had so thoroughly consolidated their positions that they had effectively become principalities, and they were surrounded by flattering courtiers worthy of *Rigoletto*. At least in the mellowed perception of the past Petrarch felt that it hadn't always been like that, and perhaps it was true, because in Dante's time the lords must have had fewer illusions about the legitimacy and sacred nature of their own power, and more awareness of having to build consent in republican society. According to the anecdote, when Dante was welcomed into Cangrande's household he was initially extremely agreeable, but gradually the ruler tired of him. One day a jester (but Petrarch calls him a *demens*, a madman, although the English translate it better as a 'fool') was entertaining the company with his obscene jokes, and Cangrande, having noticed that Dante was not amused, wanted to tease him: how come everyone liked the fool and not the wise man? Dante is supposed to have replied that everyone appreciates those who resemble themselves. In truth, the quip was an old one, had done the rounds in the previous century and was attributed to none other than Marco Lombardo. In his commentary, the Anonymous Florentine reported that Lombardo uttered this witticism on his return from festivities at the court of the Della Scalas in Verona. There is a revealing parallel in all this, because in the final years of his life Dante came close to adopting precisely this lifestyle.[13]

could well have worried about living in a city where it was not certain that he would have access to the sacraments and decided that, should the opportunity arise, he would move elsewhere. What is certain is that at some stage he abandoned the court in Verona and accepted the invitation from Guido Novello da Polenta, a loyal supporter of the Church, to go and live with him in Ravenna.

A little younger than Dante and a descendant of the lords of the Polenta Castle near Bertinoro in Romagna, Guido belonged to the highest level of the military aristocracy of the Apennines, which for some time had been imposing its will on the republics in Romagna. He had undergone his political apprenticeship as a counsellor and wise man in the Republic of Ravenna, and as both Captain of the People and Supreme Magistrate in Reggio and Cesena, and in 1316 he inherited from his uncle the position of Supreme Magistrate for Life, which to all intents and purposes made him the ruler of Ravenna. Today historians tend to emphasise that in this era the power of such personal government was still perceived as deriving from the republic and dependent on the consent of the people, which envisaged a regulated interaction with republican bodies. Nevertheless contemporaries perceived it as a disturbing innovation. A few years earlier Dante himself, while writing Canto XXVII of *Inferno*, had been brutally frank in describing the plight of the cities of Romagna to Guido da Montefeltro. In that country, Dante the fictional character asserts, tyranny, the government of a single man, had replaced liberty, the state of freedom. Governed by tyrants accustomed to expanding their power through force of arms, Romagna had lost all memory of what peace was ('Your Romagna is not and never was / without war in the heart of its tyrants'), and of those cities in the clutches of dictators the first one that came to Dante's mind was none other than the Ravenna of the Da Polentas, where autocratic government had been established for a long time ('Ravenna remains as it has been for many years / the mark of the eagle of Da Polenta is lurking there ...'). More recently, in Canto XIV of *Purgatory*, Dante lamented Romagna once more and railed against its nobles. He only mentioned Ravenna in order to complain about it, because all the families who practised 'love and courtesy' were extinct. Dante may have recalled those lines with embarrassment when he received the invitation from Guido da Polenta. But the Lord of Ravenna was also a poet – the author of songs, some of which have survived – and he may have judged with the sensitivity of a poet the cantos in which his city and his family appeared, starting with the third canto of *Inferno*, in which the starring role belonged to his aunt Francesca, who was murdered by her husband when Guido was a child.

At the time Ravenna was an important ecclesiastical capital and the see of one of the richest archbishoprics in Italy, as well as home to the extremely wealthy abbeys of San Vitale and Sant'Apollinare in Classe. The archbishop was the Milanese Rinaldo da Concorezzo, who in his time had been an influential adviser to Boniface VIII, on whose behalf he had almost got himself killed when he was the rector of Romagna. To be precise, he had been attacked and very badly wounded in Forlì during disorders instigated by the Ordelaffis on 1 September 1302, at more or less the same time that Dante and other leading advocates of the White Guelphs were in the city. Later still he had conducted the trial against the Knights Templar in Italy in masterly fashion, which led him to absolve them and declare their confessions null and void because they had been obtained under torture. By now however, the archbishop was old and rarely seen in the city. Like other powerful members of the clergy unwilling to subject themselves to living in a city under the control of a republic or a lord, he preferred to stay in his own residence, Argenta Castle, where he died on 18 August 1321, a few weeks before Dante.

But Ravenna was also a prosperous centre of trade, the

capital of a hinterland rich in pastures and vineyards, which was close to the sea and surrounded by salt pans and fish markets, and this guaranteed considerable revenues for the republic through customs duties, although the trade mainly consisted of the export of salt, fish and wine and was mainly in the hands of Venetian merchants. The local currency was Venetian, but, as in other places where money changed hands a great deal, the city surrounded by earth and water was also home to Florentine entrepreneurs who were active in trade, money-lending and the management of Church properties. So we should not allow ourselves to be guided by D'Annunzio's definition of Ravenna as a dead city: in Dante's time it was an extremely lively urban hub and teeming with foreigners.

So it does not seem strange that, once Dante arrived in Ravenna, he lost no time in creating a network of contacts. This must have happened in other cities in which he stayed, but in the case of Ravenna we know much more about it because of the *Eclogues*, the correspondence in Latin verse during those years between Dante and the humanist in Bologna *maestro* Giovanni, also known as 'del Virgilio' or Virgiliano – it seems that he was such an admirer of the Latin poet that he named his son after him. It is the only time, after Dante's exile from Florence, that we know exactly when he was writing one of his works. In a sense it was an epistolary work, but also literary in every sense. There are four texts, two by Giovanni and two by Dante in response, which were transcribed by Boccaccio in the same Laurentian Codex XXIX, 8, in which the monk Ilaro's letter has been conserved. The information that Boccaccio gathered from friends of Giovanni and Dante, along with references to contemporary events, suggests that the first and second texts went back to the winter of 1319–20, the third to the spring and summer of 1320 and the fourth to the summer of 1321.

The correspondence started with an attempt by Giovanni – victim of what we can now only perceive as the obtuseness and insensitivity of humanists – to convince Dante to write only in Latin. High-minded Giovanni had some suggestions for Dante – themes for an epic poem that commemorated the great events of their times. When we attempt to decode his abstruse and allusive language, it appears that he was speaking of Henry VII's venture into Italy, Uguccione della Faggiola's victory at Montecatini, Cangrande's victory over the Paduans and Matteo Visconti's siege of Genoa, which was still going on, the city having been taken over by the Guelphs and defended by the fleet of King Robert of Naples. Giovanni gave in to Dante's well-argued refusal, but insisted that his friend, this Virgil reborn, should come to Bologna, where he would find many admirers. Dante replied that he was doing just fine in Ravenna, and besides he didn't want to fall into the hands of Polyphemus, who is usually identified as the ever-present nobleman of Forlì, Fulcieri da Calboli, who was the supreme magistrate of Florence when Dante was banished and defeated his fellow-citizen and rival Scarpetta degli Ordelaffi at Puliciano. He had been a ferocious persecutor of the White Guelphs, and for this reason he was appointed Captain of the People in Bologna in 1321.

In the first letter Giovanni attempts to seduce Dante by suggesting the possibility of obtaining the crown of laurels in Bologna, which in Canto XXV of *Paradise*, coincidentally being composed at more or less that time, was precisely what Dante was hoping to receive in the baptistery of San Giovanni following his long-dreamed-of return to Florence. Literary figures of the time were persuaded that in antiquity it was the custom to crown the victors of poetic performances with laurels in the Capitol, and they believed that this honour had been granted to Statius, the author of the *Thebaid*, to whom Dante devotes a great deal of space in *Purgatory*, using it to present him as one of the greatest poets of antiquity. The aspiration to be crowned for his poetic brilliance had already manifested itself in the first canto of *Paradise*, where Dante turns to Apollo to express his hope to be worthy of the 'beloved laurel'. The crowning of the humanist Albertino Mussato in Padua in 1315 undoubtedly fuelled this desire, and it must have been public knowledge if Giovanni del Virgilio thought that it would persuade him. In his reply Dante insisted that it was on the banks of the Arno that he wanted to be crowned, and in describing the scene that he dreamed of, he informed us that his hair was now white (Dante would never realise his desire; instead Petrarch, more of a society person, would achieve this in 1341, when he was crowned by King Robert of Naples in the Capitol).[1]

Thanks to the indefatigable Boccaccio, who managed to speak to many people who had known Dante personally and recovered a commentary on the *Eclogues* written in Bologna shortly after his death, we can identify the people referred to in the correspondence with Giovanni del Virgilio and hidden behind the inevitable pastoral pseudonyms – some of whom were friends the poet had made in Ravenna. The shepherd Melibeo was the Florentine notary *ser* Dino Perini, who assured Boccaccio that he had been 'as much of a friend to Dante as he could possibly have been'; we have in fact already met him, because he was one of the two people – the other being Dante's nephew Andrea Poggi – who claimed to have found the first seven cantos of the *Comedy* in Gemma's famous strongbox. In the guise of Alfesibeo, his most intimate and trusted friend, *maestro* Fiduccio de' Milotti, was to be found: he was a doctor, and the son and brother of doctors, and related to the rulers of the city because his daughter Caterina had married Guido Novello's brother. Boccaccio also knew – and we have already come across him – 'a worthy man called *ser* Piero of *messer* Giardino da Ravenna, who was one of the most intimate friends and servants that Dante had in Ravenna'.[2]

Finally, one of the letters by the late fourteenth-century humanist Coluccio Salutati recalls a 'friend and relation of our Dante', who was another notary and writer, *ser* Menghino

Mezzani, whose epitaph of Dante and a summary in verse of the first two canticles have survived. In reality *ser* Menghino (which is a diminutive of Domenico), who commenced his notarial career in 1317 and would die in 1376, must have been quite young at the time; Salutati only provides us with imprecise information about him, given that he erroneously believed that he had been a canon of the church in Ravenna. We could therefore have a few doubts about whether his friendship with Dante was of any great importance.

Altogether, we have at our disposal some exceptional personal accounts that allow us for the first time since his youth to reconstruct on the basis of reliable information the environment of the new city in which Dante now lived: doctors and above all notaries, all members of well-established families who were personally influential and not without contacts with both the city's government and the extremely wealthy local clergy – but they were all well-educated men who shared literary interests and who, after Dante's death, contributed to the rapid rise of his glory by publicly boasting of their own friendship with him.

However, Dante also engaged in correspondence with distant friends while he was living in Ravenna. The astrologist Cecco d'Ascoli, who six years after Dante's death would meet with a terrible death, wrote in one of his books about the influence of stars on the nobility of the spirit, and remarked that Dante, evidently sceptical of such a thing, sent him a letter posing the problem of two twins born more or less in the same moment but of a very different mindset:

> But then Dante, doubtful, wrote to me:
> 'Two boys are born of single birth,
> and nobler the first one proves to be,
> and vice versa, as you already see.
> I return to Ravenna, from where I never move:
> tell me, Ascolano, what think you of that?'[3]

We can infer from this that Dante, during his latter years, had continued to reflect on the question of nobility in which he had shown a keen interest throughout his life, and every now and then he left Ravenna, although he promised never to do so again at least until he got Cecco's reply. Where was Dante when he wrote to Cecco, who in that period was teaching astrology in Bologna? Some might reply that he was in Verona, where he was resolving the *Questio de aqua et terra*, but we cannot possibly know.

We do know, however, that in Ravenna Dante managed to secure a future for two of his children: Piero, to whom two profitable ecclesiastical benefices were assigned – the churches of Santa Maria in Zanzanigola and San Simone al Muro – and Beatrice, who became a nun in the convent of Santo Stefano degli Ulivi. This is a clear sign that Dante had been accepted with great acclaim because these were accommodations that required connections in high places. The granting of a benefice often came though the support of a lay patron who had the right to nominate the candidate. In this specific case, the church of San Simone al Muro, which came with a hospital, was in the gift of Guido Novello's wife, Caterina Countess of Bagnacavallo, and her cousin Idana, the wife of Count Aghinolfo da Romena, who had been one of the first captains of the White Guelphs in exile. To obtain all this for his son, Dante must have had protection at the very highest level which linked the ruler's hospitality to connections made fifteen or twenty years earlier and majestically overlooked the copious invectives the poet let rip unsparingly in his *Comedy*. These included one against the counts of Bagnacavallo, whose extinction as a family Dante charitably hoped for in order that another generation wouldn't end up dishonouring them.[4]

As for the date of his arrival in Ravenna, it could have been no later than 4 January 1321, when Piero appears in the list of clergy in Ravenna excommunicated by the papal legate in

Lombardy for not having paid their share of a tax. We should not imagine that this excommunication was a very serious sanction because Piero was in good company: like him, the abbot and the Cistercian monastery of San Severo and the cantor of Ravenna Cathedral had paid nothing, and four monasteries, including Sant'Apollinare in Classe, had paid only part of the sum. However, the tax had been requested in July 1320, which means that Dante's son was already in possession of the benefices on that date. It should be remembered that residency was not required in order to profit from a benefice, so it is not certain whether Piero was there. At the age of twenty he could just as easily have been at Bologna University, where he would complete his law studies quite a few years later. But we have further proof that by that date Dante's move to Ravenna must have become an established reality.*

Equally, no document demonstrates that Iacopo had lived in Ravenna with his father, but it seems that he was there at the moment of Dante's death. By then Dante was a public figure, and Piero and Iacopo knew that they were sons of a genius, the author of a masterpiece that was spoken of throughout Italy. Boccaccio tells us that immediately after their father's death the sons went through his papers in search of the last thirteen cantos of *Paradise*, which had not yet been published. When they could not find them, in their desperation they were almost persuaded by their friends to complete the poem themselves, given that they both knew how to write poetry. Who knows what they would have made of it! Then, eight months after Dante's death, Iacopo, 'who was much more thorough in such matters', saw his father in a dream, who led him to his own room and showed him a secret compartment. Iacopo rushed

---

* The idea that Dante's wife, Gemma, joined him in Ravenna is gratuitous speculation, which contrasts with the affirmations of Boccaccio, who was well acquainted with Dante's friends in Ravenna, but it is still dear to some academics.

to the home of Dante's friend *ser* Piero Giardini, and told him everything. They then searched the room and discovered the hiding-place, where they found a bundle of papers which 'would have rotted if they had stayed there much longer, due to the humidity of the mouldy wall'. Once they had removed the mould, they recognised the cantos they had been so desperately searching for.[5]

If it were true, this story would have demonstrated that Dante's house in Ravenna was very damp, but it is difficult to give any credence to Boccaccio, who apparently got it from Giardini himself. It is, however, plausible that Iacopo was in Ravenna during that period and sent Guido Novello his verse description of the *Comedy*, along with a sonnet which the manuscripts date very precisely to 1 April 1322. Iacopo appears to have been writing a commentary on the poem right from the beginning, a challenge that his brother would take up much later and with greater success (if it is true, as one of the leading experts on Dantean commentaries has observed, that Iacopo's is characterised 'by an embarrassing lack of content').

While Dante was in Ravenna, his name came up in Avignon in rather terrifying circumstances. Those were the years in which unwarranted fear of witchcraft was starting to take hold in Western Christendom, where it would continue to cause great harm for the rest of the Middle Ages and a large part of the modern era. In that climate there were frequent trials for witchcraft, which were clearly staged to frame people for political purposes. There were interrogations of witnesses willing to confess anything, and this was widely used by the sinister King Philip IV of France, who even instructed such legal proceedings against Pope Boniface VIII. Now Pope John XXII was setting up a trial for witchcraft against his arch-enemy Matteo Visconti, the ruler of Milan: the accusation was that he had attempted to kill the pope by means of an evil spell. Dante was mentioned by a key witness, and the declarations of what today we would call a supergrass and undercover agent constituted the basis of the prosecution's case.

Bartolomeo Cagnolati was a clergyman from Milan, and in the first interrogation, on 9 February 1320, he declared that he had been approached by Matteo Visconti for his expertise in necromancy. The ruler of Milan was supposed to have shown him a silver statuette on which the name of John XXII had been engraved, and told him that this pope was no more a pope than he was. Visconti went on to explain that this pope had to be eliminated and therefore Cagnolati had to use the statuette to cast a spell on him. The clergyman assured the commission in Avignon that he refused, at which Visconti let him go but ordered him not to speak of it to anyone; but instead he got in contact with the enemy of the Viscontis, Simone della Torre, as soon as he could, begging him to inform the papal court of this danger. Later Matteo had summoned him a second time and charged him with taking the statuette to Verona and giving it to another necromancer, Pietro Nan, which was the nickname of *messer* Pietro da Marano, a close adviser of Cangrande, who was effectively a dwarf (*nano*). Cagnolati refused once more, claiming health problems, with no further consequences other than upsetting his lord. When he received a summons from Avignon, he happily went there to be questioned, but not without stopping once more in Milan and speaking to Scotto da San Gimignano, a judge who knew everything about the affair. He asked if he knew the whereabouts of the statuette. The judge replied that the statuette was in a fine state, and the evil spell had been completed by smoking poisonous herbs for nine nights.

After he had submitted this stupefying deposition without batting an eyelid, the two cardinals who were conducting the investigation sent Cagnolati back to Milan, where he was promptly arrested and interrogated under torture by Scotto da San Gimignano himself, who wanted to know the reasons for his trip to Avignon, and after being held in irons for a month and a half he was released on bail. At this stage he was summoned by Matteo Visconti's son Galeazzo, the ruler of Piacenza, who treated him very well and revealed that the evil spell had not worked. He asked Cagnolati if he was responsible. The clergyman repeated that he hadn't spoken to anyone in Avignon and suggested that perhaps the sorcery had been carried out incorrectly. Visconti asked him if he was willing to try it himself, assuring him that freeing the world of 'this diabolic pope' would be an act of charity, and then he added that he had summoned 'maestro Dante Alighieri of Florence' for this very purpose. Cagnolati was relieved by this news and said that in his opinion it would be excellent if Dante could cast the spell. On hearing this, Galeazzo incomprehensibly replied that he would not tolerate Dante getting involved at any cost; indeed he didn't even want to let him know the reason for which he had been summoned to Piacenza. Cagnolati was the one who had to do it. The clergyman pretended to agree, but as soon as he was given the statuette he slipped away and found refuge in Avignon, where on 11 September 1320 he revealed all these wonders in his second deposition, while also producing the statuette and three letters from Galeazzo Visconti that proved his involvement.[6]

Whether or not you believe in this extravagant account, you cannot deny the logical conclusions. If the clergyman's story was authentic, Galeazzo Visconti, the lord of Piacenza, thanks above all to the position of imperial deputy granted him by Henry VII, must have known Dante well and thought seriously enough about involving him in the business to have him summoned to Piacenza, except that when Dante appeared he changed his mind and decided not to tell him anything. If, on the other hand, Cagnolati's deposition had been entirely invented, then Dante must have been well known in Avignon circles, where he was considered to be a confidant of the hated Viscontis and someone wanted him involved in the trial. But perhaps this was reconsidered at the last moment, his part in the affair was eliminated and Cagnolati was told to say that, however unlikely it appeared, Galeazzo decided to keep him in the dark about why he had been summoned. The alternatives, I think the reader will agree, are both fascinating, unless of course the *maestro* conjured up in Avignon was the Dantino Alighieri, also from Florence, whom we know to have lived at that time between Padua and Verona!

This involvement in a plot put together by Ghibelline lords clearly flies in the face of the fact that Dante had definitely moved to Ravenna and was the guest of Guido da Polenta, a Guelph, so everything points to an attempt by the Avignon court to frame their enemies. It may have been that they weren't well informed about his recent movements, and for years they had been in the habit of thinking of him as a resident of Verona and a protégé of Cangrande.[7] This did not mean that Dante never moved from Ravenna, as he had assured Cecco d'Ascoli. Almost certainly he never went to Bologna, even though he discussed it in the last eclogue, which was written in the summer of 1321. That summer, however, Guido Novello sent him on a diplomatic mission to Venice. We know this from Giovanni Villani, according to whom the poet's death (which the chronicler incorrectly places in July) occurred 'on his return from an ambassadorial journey to Venice in the service of the Lords Da Polenta, with whom he resided'.[8]

Relations between Ravenna and the great city of islands were always a little tense for inevitable geopolitical reasons. The Venetians wanted a monopoly on all the trade leaving the port of Ravenna, particularly the goods of strategic importance like the Comacchio salt, and there were frequent conflicts between the two republics, accusations of smuggling, and agreements repudiated or not complied with. In that summer Cecco Ordelaffi, who had taken over the government of Forlì some years earlier, was threatening war against Ravenna, and Venice was willing to finance it. We don't know what Dante's business was in Venice, but his trip to that city probably served to get more time and to notify the government there that another proposed agreement was on its way, and in fact one was presented by another delegation from Ravenna on 20 October 1321.

By then Dante had been dead for more than a month. It is generally thought, hazarding a guess, that he was killed by a sudden attack of malaria contracted during the journey over the marshlands. The burgeoning case history of Florentine hatred for Venice did not fail to adopt Filippo Villani's invention, according to which the Venetians, unprepared to take on Dante in the field of eloquence and terrified of his fame, refused to let him speak, and when the poet, who was suffering from fevers, requested permission to return to Ravenna by sea, that too was refused because they feared that he might convert the admiral. Thus he was forced to take the uncomfortable journey back home overland, which would come at a very high price.[9]

As with all the small amount we know of Dante's life, the date of his death relies on contradictory sources. According to Boccaccio, he died on the day of the Elevation of the Holy Cross, which comes on 14 September, but the epitaphs that men of letters wrote in competition with each other to mark the occasion of his death dated it as the ides of September, which is the 13th.[10] As one of the epitaphs was written by Giovanni del Virgilio and transcribed by Boccaccio himself, it would appear that the biographer did not detect the discrepancy. And perhaps there wasn't one. We should remember that Christian feast days, continuing the Jewish tradition, started at sunset on the day before, and we could thus conclude that Dante must have died during the early hours of the night between the 13th and the 14th. That night the prophet went off to discover how much truth there was in the afterlife he'd imagined over a period of many years.

NOTES

Chapter 1: St Barnabas's Day

1. Leonardo Bruni, 'Della vita, studi e costumi di Dante', in *Le vite di Dante*, ed. G. L. Passerini (Florence, 1917), para. 2; Leonardo Bruni, 'Vita di Dante', ed. M. Berté, in *Nuova edizione commentate delle opere di Dante*, vol. VII, tome IV, in *Le vite di Dante dal XIV al XVI secolo: iconografia dantesca*, ed. M. Berté, M. Fiorilla, S. Chiodo and I. Valente (Rome, 2017), para. 1. Bruni was keen to clarify that the notice affixed to Palazzo Vecchio to celebrate the victory stated that it was over the Ghibellines and not the Aretines, because 'all the Guelph gentlemen and commoners exiled from Arezzo were fighting alongside the Florentines in that battle'.

2. Dante Alighieri, *Convivio*, IV, vi, 6. See also *Convivio*, I, viii, 5, in which he provides examples of useless gifts, 'such as when a knight gives a doctor a shield or when a doctor gives a knight such writings as the *Aphorisms* of Hippocrates or Galen's *Ars Medica*'.

3. According to Bruni's quoting or paraphrasing of Dante's letter in Latin, Dante wrote, 'wherever I am, I never play with arms', because for Dante *iuvenis* meant an adult age which started at twenty-five. If, however, he really wrote *iuvenis* in the letter, he was lying because he had only just turned twenty-four!

4. Franco Sacchetti, *Novella VIII*. See also Cecco Angiolieri's sonnet 'Dante Alighier, if I'm a good charlatan', in which Cecco jokingly accuses Dante of giving himself totally inappropriate airs of nobility, now that he's in exile.

5. Summarised in Guido Castelnuovo, *Être noble dans la cité: les noblesses italiennes en quête d'identité (XIIIe-XVe siècle)* (Paris, 2014), pp. 48–59. For the operational practices of citizen knights, the fundamental text is still Cesare Paoli, *Le cavallate fiorentine nei*

secoli XIII e XIV (Florence, 1865). The obligations amounted to the provision of a horse and a knight, or just the horse. In the first case the owner could pay for a substitute, but this was not common: at Montaperti, 111 of the 127 horses relating to the *sesto* of San Pancrazio (the only *sesto* for which we have a list) were ridden by the owner or by a close relative (C. Lansing, *The Florentine Magnates: Lineage and Faction in a Medieval Commune* (Princeton, NJ, 1991), p. 151).

Chapter 2: Dante and the Nobility

1. Among the city's powerful families, very few had taken the name of an ancestor who had lived in the eleventh century: Giandonati, Caponsacchi, Visdomini, Nerli and perhaps Brunelleschi. An ancestor of the same name who lived in the first half of the twelfth century is the case for Adimari, Amidei, della Bella, Buondelmonti, Cavalcanti, Cipriani, Donati, Fifanti, Gherardini, Giudi, Infangati, Sacchetti, Scolari, Tosinghi, Vecchietti. Even more recent were the names Abati, Acerbi, Ardinghi, Chiarmontesi, Galigai, Gianfigliazzi, Lamberti, Macci, Pigli, Sizi and Tornaquinci. A comparison with the list that Dante has Cacciaguida come up with in *Paradise*, XVI, will suggest that the poet overestimated the antiquity of most of these families.

2. Giovanni Villani, *Nuova cronica*, II, 4, ed. G. Porta, 3 vols (Parma, 1990–91), He argued, 'we find that this is not an authentic chronicle, because for us there is no proof.' His nephew Filippo Villani claimed that in the opinion of his forebears, which in effect meant his uncle Giovanni, Dante descended from a patrician family who came from Rome when Julius Caesar founded Florence (*De vita*, 12), but he heard these things when Dante was already famous and everyone knew the references to the Roman origins of Florence in his works. Bruni is wisely sceptical of all this: 'Dante's forebears were of an ancient lineage in Florence and he occasionally suggests that they were among those Romans who founded Florence, but this is very doubtful and in my opinion nothing more than conjecture' (Bruni, *Vita di Dante*, ed. Passerini, para. 2; Bruni, *Vita di Dante*, ed. Berté, para. 1).

3. Many scholars have gone through the history of this debate: see Lansing, *The Florentine Magnates*, pp. 212–28.
4. When Dante wrote *Le dolci rime*, the Ordinances of Justice had already come into law in April 1293.
5. Dante Alighieri, *De Monarchia*, II, iii, 4–7.
6. N. Rubinstein, 'Dante and Nobility', in *Studies in Italian History in the Middle Ages and the Renaissance*, vol. 1, *Political Thought and the Language of Politics. Art and Politics*, ed. G. Ciappelli (Rome, 2004), pp. 165–200, at p. 190.

Chapter 3: Cacciaguida and the Others

1. *Paradise*, XVI, 98–120.
2. It should be noted that in *Convivio*, I, xiii, 4, Dante mentions his parents, without naming them, while listing the merits of the vernacular: 'This vernacular of mine was what brought my parents together, as this is what they spoke.'
3. This matter should be seen in the light of Umberto Carpi's timely reminder 'that the Alighieris as a family had no social standing in Florence during the thirteenth century'.

Chapter 4: The Alighieri Clan

1. The first mention of the coat of arms with a golden wing was probably by the sixteenth-century man of letters Alessandro Vellutello, who claimed to have seen it used by the Alighieris of Verona.
2. The conventional division of the ages of man handed down from antiquity – for example, by St Augustine in *De genesi contra Manichaeos*, I, 23.35–40, and further clarified by Isidore of Seville in *Etymologiae*, XI, ii, 1–8 – was as follows: *infantia* up until seven years of age, *pueritia* until fourteen, *adolescentia* until twenty-eight, *iuventus* until fifty, *senioris aetas* until seventy, and finally *senectus*, which concludes with *senium*, decrepitude. Dante in *Convivio*, IV, xxiv, preferred a division into four parts, preceded by infancy, and placed adolescence as from eight to twenty-five, followed by youth until forty-five, *senettute* until seventy, and finally *senio*, which in his opinion can last for ten years (see also *Purgatory*, XXX, 124, in which

Beatrice says that she died 'on the threshold ... of my second age', or in other words when she was about to turn twenty-five).

3. *Inferno*, XXIX, 18–36.
4. Zorzi has demonstrated that, contrary to a widely held belief, vendettas were not a specifically noble practice, but in fact universally accepted (pp. 142–3). According to Umberto Carpi, on the other hand, Dante mentions Geri's murder and the obligation to take revenge which was acknowledged by the Alighieris, because that was an indirect way to claim their nobility. There is often misunderstanding about this episode, because people are unaware that this was both a moral duty and perfectly legal, and therefore do not want to admit that Dante was openly demanding the vendetta had to be carried out (not even Bruni, who bases his interpretation on the clear-cut distinction between Dante the author and Dante the character). Marco Santagata comes closer to this opinion about Geri del Bello, but is concerned about taking things too far: Dante 'almost appears to hope that someone will finally decide to wash away ignominy that weighed upon the family'. A current theory put forward by Renato Piattoli and recently taken up by Giuseppe Indizio is that, while the murder was avenged thirty years later according to the commentators, the vendetta actually took place around 1305. This oddity is explained by the mistaken idea that Cione's sons, who were actually in exile at the time, were banished as a result of the vendetta, which was in fact a legitimate act and could not have been pursued under the law. Equally erroneous is Giorgio Inglese's inference that Dante had written the episode after the vendetta had already been carried out, 'as though to excuse the deed'. The Sacchettis only made peace with the Alighieris, represented by Francesco, in 1342, when the government of the duke of Athens promoted a series of reconciliations in the city.

Chapter 5: Infancy and the District
1. *Paradise*, XXII, 110–17. Filippo Villani, in one of his works written in his own hand, asserted that Dante was born on 1 June. E. Brilli (*Dante Studies*, 136 (2018), p. 141) observes that 'the invocation to Gemini (*Paradise*, XXII, 115–17), a milestone for all biographers, is

also a capital testimony to an attention to one's date of birth that was rare in Dante's time'. This is not the case: Dante was not at all interested in his birthday, which we do not know; his interest was astrological, and this was not at all unusual at the time. (On the other hand, Villani spoke of a huge party organised in Pisa 'for the day of his birth': this could have been an apocryphal anecdote or it could be that wealthy citizens really did celebrate their birthdays in the context of a progressive sacralisation of their own person.)

2. Dino Compagni, *Cronica*, ed. D. Cappi (Rome, 2000), and translation by Daniel Bornstein as *Dino Compagni's Chronicle of Florence* (Philadelphia, PA, 1986), II, 8. For the other quotations see *Convivio*, I, iii, 4, and *De vulgari eloquentia*, I, vi, 3. A. R. Bloch, in 'The Two Fonts of the Florence Baptistery and the Evolution of the Baptismal Rite in Florence, ca. 1200–1500 (in *The Visual Culture of Baptism in the Middle Ages*, ed. H. M. Sonne de Torrens and M. A. Torrens Alzu (Farnham, 2013), pp, 77–104), argues that Dante's description of the baptismal font in *Inferno*, XIX, 13–21, suggests that at the time baptisms were also carried out individually using amphoras and not in collective ceremonies on Easter Saturday, for which the central pool had to be filled with water; Giovanni Villani, *Cronica nuova*, II, 23, further clarified the way things were evolving when he wrote that on that day 'the baptismal water in the said fonts was consecrated' – evidently this water would be used for the rest of the year.

3. Boccaccio, *Trattatello*, I, 13.

4. *Vita Nuova*, XXIII. See Marco Santagata, *Dante: il romanzo della sua vita* (Milan, 2002), pp. 32–4, 197–201, 348–50, 398, who develops the theory that Dante suffered from epilepsy. On Dante's clinical history, we can add his disease of the eyes due to excessive studying, which is mentioned in *Convivio*, III, ix, 14–16.

Chapter 6: Love and Friendships

1. The presence of Folco di Ricovero at the oath in 1280 is covered in *Delizie degli eruditi toscani*, IX (Florence, 1777), p. 92. Its interpretation is controversial: for Diacciati, he is one of the neutral guarantors (neither Guelph nor Ghibelline) who took an oath on behalf of the guilds; for D. Medici, he is 'one of the

guarantors for the Ghibellines'. The document does not provide any evidence for this, and I think it more significant that Folco appears in fifth place in the brief list of twelve witnesses, after four members of the Cerchi family (the fourth being *messer* Ricovero de' Cerchi, whose relatively rare name suggests a degree of kinship).

2. Boccaccio, *Trattatello*, I, 30–31. Bartuschat argues that the build-up of realistic details 'nullifies the spiritual meaning the *libello* [short work of literature, in this case] attributes to his love for Beatrice' and ends up 'diminishing the importance of this love both for Dante and for his poetry'. It has been argued, not unreasonably, that Boccaccio could not have known anything about it and invented the scene.

3. S. Vegetti Finzi and A. M. Battistin, *I bambini sono cambiati: la psicologia dei bambini dai cinque ai dieci anni* (Milan, 1996).

4. This is an ongoing debate. It is certainly curious that the French humanist Laurent de Premierfait (d. 1418), who translated the *Decameron*, asserted that in Paris Dante 'wanted to live up to the beautiful book of the Rose'.

5. Bruni, ed. Passerini, paras. 10 and 14; ed. Berté, paras. 36 and 62. For St Catherine, *Legenda maior*, pp. 866–7. Marco Santagata is doubtful (*Dante: il romanzo della sua vita*, p. 9) and imagines the Dante who was the protagonist of *Vita Nuova*, already married and possibly a father, and constructs a whole theory out of the meaning behind his claim – invented, in Santagata's opinion – to have had his own room in the house, which he defines insistently as 'small' and 'modest' without any justification. D. Wallace, 'Lives of Dante: Why Now?', *Forum: Dante and Biography*, ed. E. Brilli, *Dante Studies* 136 (2018), pp. 213–22, at p. 216, observes that here Dante is drawing on Matthew 6: 6 ('But you, when you pray, go into your room, and when you have shut your door, pray to your Father who is in the secret place; and your Father who sees in secret will reward you openly'), but the fact remains that Dante obviously had a room of his own.

6. *Vita Nuova*, III; on the vernacular poets in *Vita Nuova*, XXV, 4. When he refers to taking up the challenge of poetry, he was probably referring to his first sonnet, 'Savete giudicar', sent in

response to Dante da Maiano. Gragnolati and Lombardi claim that here Dante was only recreating the past and that originally the sonnet 'probably didn't even refer to Beatrice at all'; if this were the case (that 'probably' is disarming), this short account of Dante's adolescence would have to be scrubbed.

7. *Vita Nuova*, XL, 2; *Purgatory*, VIII, 3. See Teodolinda Barolini, 'The Poetic Exchanges between Dante Alighieri and his "amico" Dante da Maiano: A Young Man Takes His Place in the World', in *'Legato con amore in un volume': Essays in Honour of John A. Scott* (Florence, 2013), pp. 39–61, Barolini suggests that in the youthful poetic challenges, *amico* ('friend') had a more aggressive meaning, 'a word that signals posturing and rivalry masking as friendship', which was later abandoned from *Vita Nuova* onwards.

8. See *Vita Nuova*, XXXII, 1. Manetto also appears to have been a friend of Guido.

9. *Vita Nuova*, V, 1–2.

10. *Vita Nuova*, XIV.

11. *Vita Nuova*, VIII, 1, and XXII respectively.

12. Quotations from Compagni, *Cronica*, I, 20. Folco Portinari was the owner of a 'palace with a tower' and had built at his own cost a 'new house' adjacent to the tower.

13. *Vita Nuova*, XXVIII–XXIX, and XLII, 2, for the date, which can be inferred from the complicated clues provided by Dante's calendar.

14. Compagni, *Cronica*, I, 20. Beatrice supposedly married Simone in 1280, according to an archival discovery about which there are some serious doubts. Del Lungo believes her to have already been married at the time of her meeting with Dante in 1283, and, given the average age of marriage for Florentine girls of the time, this is almost certain.

Chapter 7: Dante's Studies

1. See Giovanni Villani in *Cronica nuova*, XII, 94.

2. *Convivio*, II, xii, 1–7. Here he says that he applied himself to those readings, after having been inconsolable over Beatrice's death 'for quite some time' and having then started to imagine philosophy as 'a noble woman'. He immersed himself so deeply in his philosophical studies that 'in a short time, perhaps thirty months'

his love of philosophy had driven every other thought from his mind.

3. *Convivio*, III, ix, 15–16.
4. Bruni, *Vita*, ed. Passerini, para. 11; ed. Berté, para. 44.
5. Boccaccio, *Trattatello I*, 21–4. The classical list of the seven liberal arts – the Trivium and the Quadrivium – is presented by Dante as follows: 'Grammar, Dialectic, Rhetoric, Arithmetic, Music, Geometry and Astrology' (*Convivio*, II, xiii, 8). In *Esposizioni sopra la Comedia di Dante*, ed. G. Padoan (Milan, 1965), p. 7, Giovanni Boccaccio wrote that 'from his childhood in his native land he devoted himself to liberal studies', and 'as well as the first art, he was, as we shall soon demonstrate, a marvellous logician and he knew rhetoric, as can be clearly seen in his works. Therefore in this work it appears that he was an astrologer, and you cannot do that without arithmetic and geometry. I consider him to have mastered similarly all these arts.' The list is the same, given that the 'first art' is grammar and that in scholastic usage, logic and dialectic could be considered synonymous, except that for some reason Boccaccio omits music.
6. Grassi has clearly demonstrated that in the world of the Italian republics the determination to suppress sodomy became systematic only at the end of the Middle Ages, but even then the penalties continued for a long time to be relatively mild. Also significant is the relaxed manner in which Boccaccio observed that homosexuality between 'clergymen and men of letters' was very common and even that in their circles 'their treatment of young men did not seem unbecoming to any honest man', whereas association with women was considered a more serious distraction: Boccaccio, *Esposizioni*, p. 679, and see the following note.
7. Boccaccio, *Esposizioni*, p. 680.
8. Boccaccio, *Esposizioni*, pp. 7 and 678.
9. Boccaccio, *Trattatello*, I, 26. The Faculty of Arts and Medicine in Bologna co-existed with the more famous Faculty of Civil and Canonical Law. It is worth noting that in *Fiore*, XXIII, Dante (through the voice of Jealousy) expressed his enormous respect and admiration for the university teachers in Bologna. If this was Dante just after his first experience of life in

Bologna, then it has to be said that he changed his opinion later.

10. Giovanni Villani, *Cronica nuova*, X, 136.

11. 'As my teacher Aristotle says in the first chapter of *Ethics*': *Convivio*, I, ix, 9. There are in all thirty-eight references to *Ethics* in *Convivio*, and Dante was very keen to let everyone know that it was his favourite book – so much so that Virgil, when chatting about those guilty of violence, calls it 'your *Ethics*': *Inferno*, XI, 80.

12. In Bruni's famous dialogue in which Niccolò Niccoli, Coluccio Salutati and Bruni himself discuss the greatness of Dante, Niccoli ridicules his familiarity with this kind of culture, which the humanists then considered outdated, and he unquestionably identifies it with the religious orders: Leonardo Bruni, *Opere letterarie and politiche*, ed. P. Viti (Turin, 1996), p. 108. See also Bruni's criticisms of *De Monarchia*, 'this book is written in a monkish manner, without any nobility of style' (*Vita di Dante*, ed. Berté, para. 60). On the other hand, in Bruni's *Vita di Dante*, ed. Passerini, para. 13, the wording is described as 'in an unembellished manner'.

13. See *Convivio*, I, ix, 3; III, xi, 10. In *Paradise*, XII, 83, there is also a contemptuous reference to the teaching of Taddeo Alderotti, who had a decisive role in the foundation of the Faculty of Arts and Medicine in Bologna and in instilling a philosophical approach into the faculty. This contrasts with the fondness he expresses for the language of Bologna and Bologna in general in *De vulgari eloquentia*, which gave Tavoni the idea that the treatise was written in Bologna for Bologna: that is to say, the city and not the faculty. In any event, Dante's attendance at the faculty in Bologna is the subject of radically opposing views among Dante scholars. Gargan argues that the entire period of philosophical study in the 1290s mainly took place in Bologna, with irregular spells at the Florentine monasteries, whereas Barański categorically declares that 'the suggestion that Dante frequented Bologna University, even briefly, is unfounded'.

Chapter 8: A Mysterious Marriage

1. Unfortunately the identification of the notaries does not help. *Ser*

Uguccione di Baldovino, who drew up the contract, is only known for one other document, which was enacted in 1282. His nephew *ser* Ranaldo, the author of the copy presented by Gemma, drew up another act in 1297; thus anything is possible. Petrocchi has the idea that the transcription error merely consisted of mistaking a 'MCCLXXXVI' for a 'MCCLXXVI' which is not impossible but does not resolve the problem of the indiction, which was the fourteenth in 1286.

2. Boccaccio, *Trattatello*, I, 44. In *Trattatello*, II, 37, 'his parents' became 'his friends', but these were synonyms.

3. We should add here that in *Paradise*, XV, 103–5, Cacciaguida, among his other criticisms of contemporary Florence, states that girls are made to marry too young and with excessive dowries. However, the tone is very measured and almost indifferent: perhaps Dante would not have expressed himself in such an anodyne manner if he had himself been the groom in a marriage to a wife who was still a child.

4. According to a scrutiny of the documents in the seventeenth century, Tana is supposed to have had a dowry of 366 gold florins. To be clear, a 'pound in small florins' was the equivalent of 20 shillings or 240 pennies in *small* Florentine currency – that is to say, mixed currency. Its value in relation to gold florins decreased during Dante's lifetime: the gold florin was worth 20 shillings in small florins – i.e., a pound – when it was coined for the first time in 1252, but worth 36 in 1289, 39 in 1295, 46 in 1300 and 58 in 1305.

Chapter 9: Dante's Business Dealings

1. Bruni, *Vita*, ed. Passerini, para. 10; ed. Berté, paras. 35–6. Those furnishings definitely included terracotta plates, of modest value, and pewter ones, of higher value, though not comparable with those made of silver and gold which princes and kings were in the habit of eating off: this is undoubtedly the meaning in *Inferno*, I, 103, 'he shall not eat [off] earth or pewter', which even the first commentators misunderstood as a reference to wealth and landownership.

2. The *Libra* was a property tax in Florence. According to Barbadoro, who has examined how assessments were made, the estimated

sum at the time could approximate to expected income from capital. The unjustifiable opinion that Dante found himself in financial difficulties has even led some to be stunned that he could have followed a 'political career' (a term that was inherently unsuited to the reality of popular republican government, which involved a wide range of citizens in offices of state) because 'his socio-economic status did not suggest that it was possible'. The reality was that in Dante's time it was normal to find artisans, notaries and shopkeepers at the top of the republic's government, and these were certainly less wealthy than him.

3. Giovanni Villani, *Cronica*, XII, 94.

4. Boccaccio confirmed that Dante's wealth was inherited (see *Trattatello*, I, 5), and he described the confiscation as 'the seizure of the paternal assets'.

5. Bruni, *Vita*, ed. Passerini, para. 10; ed. Berté, para. 36.

6. For the extent to which property was held in shared ownership by siblings, see Lansing, *The Florentine Magnates*, Chapter 1.

7. In 1348 the gold florin was worth 3 pounds and 3 shillings.

8. We should remember that in 1332 four plots of land were in the same place, of which one bordered with the farm, and they were sold for 55 gold florins. In 1356 *messer* Piero di Dante sold his rights to the farm at Pagnolle to Nese, the widow of Biliotto Alfani and the mother of Iacopa, for 30 florins. On the matter of prices, it should be noted that when in 1312 Francesco sold a cottage with adjacent land in the parish of Sant'Ambrogio, the price was only 59 pounds, but it is possible that this was security on a loan and therefore a value very different from the market price.

9. By studying the administration of real estate confiscated in Bologna, G. Milani discovered 'that in this sector decisions did not aim at maximising profit' and the prices of houses were estimated at levels that were clearly much lower than the market ones. By analysing the management of rural properties, he encountered enormous problems in their management and the recurrence of fraud, and this was likely to have halved the estimated value of a farm. He concluded that 'the prices for renting the land were considerably lower than the market ones': for arable land, 'the highest figures were one third of the ordinary price'.

Chapter 10: Politics: The Magnates and the People

1. *Vita Nuova,* XXX.
2. Giovanni Mario Filelfo, in his *Vita Dantis,* attributes him with two diplomatic missions to Naples, but this detail has little value, given that he was a totally unreliable biographer, who also invented ambassadorships to Venice, Hungary and France.
3. J. Najemy, *Corporatism and Consensus in Florentine Electoral Politics, 1280–1400* (Chapel Hill, NC, 1982), pp. 46–8, firmly points out that restricting the priorship purely to the professions threatened the participation of not only those who had registered with a guild for procedural purposes but also the many members of well-established families who frequently invested in trade without practising a regular profession.
4. Giovanni Villani, *Cronica nuova,* IX, 8, wrote that after Giano della Bella was driven from the city, 'the artisans and common people had little power in the republic, but the fat commoners and the wealthy remained in government'.
5. Giovanni Villani, *Cronica nuova,* IX, 12, recalls that those priors, at the termination of their mandate, were subjected to a stoning by hotheads who accused them of betraying the spirit of the Ordinances of Justice and the interests of the common people.
6. See G. Milani, 'Dante politico fiorentino', in *Dante attraverso i documenti,* vol. 2, ed. G. Milani and A. Montefusco, pp. 11–12, for the matters presented to the Council while Dante was a member, and P. Gualtieri, *Il comune di Firenze tra Due e Trecento* (Florence, 2009), p. 129, for the frequency of the sessions.

Chapter 11: Politics: The White Guelphs and the Black Guelphs

1. Compagni, *Cronica,* I, 20.
2. Giovanni Villani, *Cronica nuova,* IX, 39; Dino Compagni was of a similar opinion.
3. Giovanni Villani, *Cronica nuova,* IX, 39. The prevalence of priors favourable to the White Guelphs has been confirmed by the trials instigated against the priors in office after the Black Guelphs' coup, which commenced on 15 December 1299.
4. Compagni, *Cronica,* I, 22; see also Giovanni Villani, *Cronica nuova,* IX, 39.

5. Compagni, *Cronica*, I, 21.
6. Compagni, *Cronica*, I, 21. On the other hand, the chroniclers who sympathised with the Black Guelphs did not think for one moment that the cardinal was acting in bad faith; they felt that the White Guelphs were the ones who rejected his mediation.
7. Bruni, *Vita*, ed. Passerini, para. 5; ed. Berté, para. 16.
8. It seems to me that the decisive information required to resolve this question, which is still debated, is whether Dante meant the date of 25 March as the anniversary of Jesus' death, as reported by Tertullian, and which other ancient Christian authors thought was also the creation of the world, or Good Friday, which in 1300 fell on 8 April. The very fact that Dante even brings the hours into the calculation (*Inferno*, XXI, 112–14) suggests that he was thinking about a set date and not that of a movable feast day like Good Friday. According to Florentine usage, 25 March commenced the year of 1300, and this too added to the suggestiveness of that date. I confess, however, that I cannot resolve the mystery of the full moon which Dante imagines to have lit up the wood during the first night of his journey to the other world (*Inferno*, XX, 127): the full moon took place on 6 March and then on 5 April in 1300, whereas it occurred on exactly 25 March of the following year, 1301. Was the journey supposed to have taken place in 1301 rather than 1300? No other date would fit.
9. Bruni, *Vita*, ed. Passerini, para. 6; ed. Berté, para. 23–4. Giorgio Inglese considered this particular event to be a good example of the tendency by which 'Dante's words are still shrouded in a sacred aura, and in the case of counter-evidence, scholars seem to believe that their task consists in tracking down the liar'.
10. Someone came up with the idea that Dante went to Rome in November 1300 on a diplomatic mission and was therefore able to witness the Jubilee on that occasion, but it is difficult to understand why Dante, like so many others, could not have simply gone on a pilgrimage to Rome of his own volition.
11. *Messer* Neri de' Giandonati was one of the two captains of the Guelph party: Compagni, *Cronica*, II, 5.

Chapter 12: Banishment

1. Compagni, *Cronica*, II, 5, 10 and 13.
2. Bruni, *Vita*, ed. Passerini, para. 7; ed. Berté, para. 27; Giovanni Villani, *Cronica nuova*, IX, 49. Also Boccaccio, *Trattatello*, I, 67: 'having rushed to the houses of those who had been driven from the city, the rabble furiously robbed and emptied them', and I, 180: 'the ungrateful and disorderly plebeians tumultuously ran to the house, more desperate for booty than justifiable vendetta.' In his *De bono comuni*, written shortly afterwards, Remigio de' Girolami added to the portrait of a city devastated by factional struggles by adding that of the desolate countryside.
3. Compagni, *Cronica*, II, 21 and 26. Also Boccaccio, *Trattatello*, I, 165.
4. Compagni, *Cronica*, II, 4, and see also II, 11. The current consensus is to take this information as genuine. Milani stressed that Boccaccio and Bruni had been in agreement on this, as did various early commentators, and also attributed to this mission to Rome something that appeared in *Centiloquio* by Antonio Pucci (d. 1388), a poetic version of Villani's chronicle ('then he went to the court … and the pope wanted to keep him in his presence'). There is no doubt that Dante went to Rome, just as we know that he did not like it there, as he was irritated by the Romans' habit of addressing everyone with the informal 'tu' form (*De vulgari eloquentia*, I, xi, 2), but he may also have been there in the previous year for the Jubilee.
5. Compagni, *Cronica*, II, 15.
6. In 1302, 5,000 pounds in small florins was the equivalent of around 2,000 gold florins, and not 170, according to Marco Santagata. The exchange rate for one gold florin in 1301 ranged between 47 shillings and 6 pennies and 48 shillings and 5 pennies, and in 1303 it rose to 52 shillings.
7. Giovanni Villani, *Cronica nuova*, X, 136. I also refer to Lana's commentary on *Paradise*, XVII: Iacomo della Lana, *Commento alla 'Commedia'*, as interpreted by D. Cappi.

Chapter 13: An Exile's Family

1. Boccaccio, *Trattatello*, I, 72, and I, 58, respectively.
2. Boccaccio, *Esposizioni*, pp. 449–50, observes that Ciacco's prophecy

in Canto VI must have been written after the banishment of the White Guelphs. It is made clear that the safe place was in a monastery in *Trattatello*, I, 180–82, where Boccaccio had recorded the first version of the same story, and attributed the discovery of the seven cantos to someone who for his own reasons was rummaging among 'Dante's possessions in some strongboxes hurriedly hidden in sacred places' (in *Trattatello*, II, 117, the 'someone' becomes 'some relation of his').

3. In 1312 Francesco and his mother, Lapa, sold the cottage with adjacent land in the parish of S. Ambrogio, and Francesco took possession of his part (it may, however, still have been distrained). Definitive proof came in 1343, when Iacopo paid 15 florins to redeem from confiscation his share of the farm at San Miniato a Pagnolle (also referred to in the 1305 contract) which had belonged to Dante. On all other occasions the farm at Pagnolle is referred as just that, a farm on its own. In the 1343 contract, on the other hand, it is clear that Iacopo is redeeming not the whole farm but only Dante's part, which had been seized.

Chapter 14: The Fate of Dante's Wealth

1. Boccaccio, *Trattatello*, I, 73. The documents tell us that, even eight years after Dante's death, Gemma still had to request the income from her own dowry every year. In 1343 her son, Iacopo, would redeem part of the assets in Pagnolle in his capacity as Gemma's heir.

2. The cottage in Sant'Ambrogio is perhaps the same one that Francesco and his mother, Lapa, sold to the Peruzzi brothers in 1312, and the sale may have been security for a loan, by which the cottage would be returned to the Alighieris once it had been paid off.

3. As we have seen, Francesco's share also included the reimbursement of two loans Dante had taken out with his brother in 1300 for a total of 215 florins, and which were never paid back. If Dante's sons had paid off the debt, then half of the land in Sant'Ambrogio would have become their property. Francesco was not to be troubled about the debt he and Dante took out from Iacopo del fu Lotto Corbizzi, for which Dante's sons remained entirely liable.

4. In 1336 one of the Portinaris rented Dante's properties in Camerata from the Office of Rebel Assets for 48 bushels of grain, so the 30 bushels paid by the grandsons probably corresponded to their share of the reimbursement of this rental. On 12 March 1341 Francesco officially renounced this rent, which should have coincided with the definitive cancellation of the farm from the list of rebel assets.

5. The document in question is the one that refers to 'burned and not burned' houses, and the only one in which Dante is called Durante.

6. Three years later, in 1339, Goccia would respond to a summons sent out to all the tenant farmers renting rebel assets on behalf of Niccolò di Bocchino, who was in possession of Dante's assets in Sant'Ambrogio. Goccia was heir to Pera. In 1342 Goccia was one of the witnesses to the peace agreement between the Alighieris, represented by Francesco, and the Sacchettis.

Chapter 15: Keeping Company with the Wicked

1. Compagni, *Cronica*, II, 29.
2. Giovanni Villani, *Cronica nuova*, IX, 53. Bruni also wrote (*Vita*, ed. Passerini, para. 8; ed. Berté, para. 29): 'Once Dante knew of his ruin, he immediately left Rome, where he was an ambassador and, travelling at great speed, he arrived in Siena. There he understood the full extent of his calamity and decided to join up with the other exiles. The first gathering took place in Gargonsa ...'
3. See Giovanni Villani, *Cronica nuova*, IX, 53.
4. Compagni, *Cronica*, II, 28.
5. Compagni, *Cronica*, II, 30; Giovanni Villani, *Cronica nuova*, IX, 60.
6. Giovanni Villani, *Cronica nuova*, IX, 68–9, where he observed that the cardinal 'was born of Ghibelline stock, and he demonstrated this by favouring them greatly'.
7. Quotations respectively from Compagni, *Cronica*, III, 4, and Villani, *De vita*, IX, 69 (according to whom, there were fourteen representatives).
8. Bruni, *Vita*, ed. Passerini, para. 8; ed. Berté, para. 29.
9. Giovanni Villani, *Cronica nuova*, IX, 59 and 68 for 1302–4.
10. Giovanni Villani, *Cronica nuova*, IX, 71–2.

11. Compagni, *Cronica*, III, 10–11; Giovanni Villani, *Cronica nuova*, IX, 72 and 82.
12. Bruni, *Vita*, ed. Passerini, para. 8; ed. Berté, para. 31.
13. *Inferno*, XV, 70–72.

Chapter 16: The Mysteries of Verona

1. Boccaccio, *Trattatello*, I, 74: 'when he first fled, he went to *messere* Alberto della Scala, who received him with kindness.'
2. *Convivio*, IV, xvi, 6.
3. *Convivio*, I, iii, 4.
4. Gian Maria Varanini claims that Dante's first stay with the Della Scalas coincided with the shift in that family's power which had previously been based exclusively on the support of Veronese citizens of middle social standing to a new phase, embodied by Cangrande, by which power became increasingly 'internationalised' and took on a decidedly lordly and aristocratic flavour. Areli Marina emphasises the formidable transformation of Verona's urban space imposed by the Della Scalas' architectural polices before Dante's arrival.

Chapter 17: Turncoat

1. Boccaccio, *Trattatello*, I, 74–5; Bruni, *Vita*, ed. Passerini, para. 9; ed. Berté, para. 33.
2. Giovanni Villani, *Cronica nuova*, X, 136. The title of *magister* was attributed to Dante in the final years of his life at a trial in Avignon and by the professor in Bologna Giovanni del Virgilio (*Egloghe*, I, 51). But Boccaccio, *Esposizioni*, p. 8, rejected this: Dante died 'without having gained any title or honour for his artistry, in spite of his desire to be crowned with laurels in his own city'.
3. Giovanni Villani, *Cronica nuova*, IX, 83.
4. *Convivio*, IV, xiv, 12, and *Purgatory*, XVI, 124–40.
5. The story that Gherardo da Camino, shortly before dying, 'gave *messer* Corso four thousand pounds to assist him in his war', is told in one of the novellas in Vincenzo Borghini's collection, *Cento novelle antiche*, published in 1572, which replaced a hundred censored novellas. In the fifteenth novella, the figure has undoubtedly become 'four thousand florins'. Corso was

appointed the supreme magistrate of Treviso at the end of 1307, after Gherardo's death, but the contemporary chronicler Ferreto de' Ferreti tells us that he had been there two years earlier as Gherardo's right-hand man.

6. Bruni, *Vita*, ed. Passerini, para. 8; ed. Berté, para. 31. Giovanni Villani, *Cronica nuova*, X, 136: Dante sent a letter 'to the government of Florence lamenting his exile and his innocence'. The first lines are a quotation from the Bible (Micah 6: 3).

Chapter 18: 'Other people's stairs'

1. Boccaccio, *Trattatello*, I, 74–5.
2. The sonnets are respectively 'Cercando di trovar minera in oro' and 'Degno fa voi trovare ogni Tesoro'. *Messer* Piero Alighieri's account appears in the third version of his commentary, when he examines *Purgatory*, VIII. As is well known, the attribution is not reliable. The kinship of the Malaspinas is extremely complicated, and it is not clear if the Marquis Moroello Malaspina di Giovagallo we're referring to is the same Moroello who appears with Franceschino and Corradino in the peace agreement with the bishop of Luni.
3. Boccaccio, *Esposizioni*, pp. 448–9; a similar narrative already existed in *Trattatello*, I, 180–82.
4. Epistle IV.
5. The Counts Guidi owned 4,600 head of livestock in 1239. 'Living like the count in Poppi': Giovanni Villani, *Cronica nuova*, VIII, 140.
6. Epistle II. It has been argued that the White Guelph party was only organised in 1303, and if that is true, Alessandro could not have been the captain, but the author does not exclude 'the existence of some kind of ad hoc coordination between the exiles' around him.
7. As for the reasons why Dante had left Lunigiana for Casentino, Casadei helpfully reminds us about the hopes that were raised among the exiles by Cardinal Napoleone Orsini's peace mission in the spring and summer of 1307, followed by yet another disappointment which more than justified Dante's attitude in the song.
8. Compagni, *Cronica*, II, 28.
9. *Convivio*, I, ix, 5, and I, xi, 6. See Chapter 2 for the debate between

Dante scholars on nobility, and how the question of the readership Dante was aiming at for his *Convivio* is perhaps too easily associated with that debate. Tavoni considers Dante's first stay with the Della Salas to be decisive along with his experience of castles of the rural nobility. An important popular republic like Verona, albeit one ruled by an overlord, seems less suited to inspiring the idea of such an exclusively noble readership.

10. Giovanni Villani, *Cronica nuova*, X, 136; Boccaccio, *Trattatello*, I, 75; *Trattatello*, II, 56. They were followed by Benvenuto da Imola, who wrote *Comentum super Dantis Aldigherii Comoediam* and knew nothing of a sojourn in Bologna after his youth but stated that, in middle age and already in exile, Dante went to study theology at the Sorbone. Francesco da Buti, who almost copies the *Trattatello* to the letter in his *Commento di Francesco da Buti sopra la Divinae Commedia di Dante Alighieri*, and Filippo Villani (*De vita*, 32) declared that in Paris Dante gained complete command of the 'theological science'.

11. Boccaccio, *Trattatello*, I, 123. Boccaccio, *Esposizioni*, p. 8, puts it slightly differently: 'he went to Paris, there to devote himself to listening to [lectures in] natural philosophy and theology. In a short time, he advanced so far in these [disciplines] that, having carried out on various occasions certain scholarly deeds, such as sermonising, reading and disputing, he merited enormous praise from talented men.'

12. In their desperation, Dante scholars have got into the habit of thinking that the woman from Lucca was called Gentucca, a mysterious murmur that Dante barely understands when Bonagiunta speaks to him. Actually this name has been documented as a woman's name used in Lucca, but the text suggests that this was not her name, and most of the fourteenth-century commentators did not think it was either. Boccaccio, *Trattatello*, II, 35, identifies it as that of a 'small girl' to whom Dante dedicated two ballads, a sonnet and a reference in *Purgatory*, XXXI, 59.

13. Giovanni Villani, *Cronica nuova*, IX, 59.

Chapter 19: Henry VII

1. Giovanni Villani, *Cronica nuova*, IX, 102.
2. Giovanni Villani, *Cronica nuova*, X, 9.
3. Giovanni Villani, *Cronica nuova*, IX, 120, and X, 7.
4. Bruni was certainly referring to this letter, Epistle VI, when he wrote that after Henry VII's election Dante 'could no longer keep to his resolve to await destiny, but having risen with his proud spirit, he started to speak ill of those who ruled the land (Florence), calling them villainous and wicked, and threatening them with their due punishment' (*Vita*, ed. Passerini, para. 9; ed. Berté, para. 32).
5. Giovanni Villani, *Cronica nuova*, X, 136.
6. Giovanni Villani, *Cronica nuova*, X, 37.
7. The main text is Francesco Petrarch, *Letters on Family Matters*, XXI, 15.7, to be compared with *Letters on Family Matters*, I, 1.24 and *Letters of Old Age*, X, 2.
8. 'Destroying and burning': Giovanni Villani, *Cronica nuova*, X, 45. Bruni, *Vita*, ed. Passerini, para. 9; ed. Berté, para. 32. P. Pellegrini, 'De profundis per l'Instant Book', pp. 176–86, especially p. 185. Dante's name 'does not come up in the list of over 400 Florentines involved in Henry's siege of the city, which was drawn up by the Guelphs in Florence on 7 March 1313 and kept in the *Libro del chiodo*'. For the various theories about where Dante was living during this period (Verona? Pisa?), see Chapter 20 below.
9. *De Monarchia*, II, I, 3.
10. Giovanni Villani, *Cronica nuova*, X, 44–53.

Chapter 20: Other People's Bread

1. Boccaccio, *Trattatello*, I, 79.
2. Epistle XI. See *Vita Nuova*, XXVIII and XXX.
3. Giovanni Villani, *Cronica nuova*, X, 54 and 56.
4. Giovanni Villani, *Cronica nuova*, X, 60 and 68.
5. Epistle XII. Boccaccio, *Trattatello*, I, 163, describes the humiliating conditions. The Statute of the Captain of the People of 1322–5 clarifies that this custom was generally applied to prisoners who were released after obtaining a pardon.
6. For the events at Montecatini, see Giovanni Villani, *Cronica nuova*,

X, 70–72. Concerning the meeting with Forese in *Purgatory*, XXIII, it can be argued that *Purgatory* was completed and circulated before Henry VII's death, and Forese's prophecy could not refer to Montecatini but must rather refer to the terrible vendetta that the emperor had to bring down on Florence. Dante did not modify the text after the emperor died without having inflicted that vendetta; readers at this stage will have thought of Montecatini, and we can only infer that Dante confirmed this interpretation by his silence.

7. Filippo Villani, *Vita*, 57.
8. Iacopo returned to Florence profiting from the amnesty of 1325. As he was only a curate, he could get married, and in fact he had children by his first wife. As a widower, he agreed to a second marriage in 1346 with Iacopa of the late Biliotto Alfani, and the break-up of this engagement would become an unpleasant and long-drawn-out legal proceeding.
9. A student in Bologna in 1327 and living in Verona from 1332 according to legal documents, Piero died in 1364. In the early years of his life in Verona he also gained a canonry at the parish church of Sant'Andrea di Sandrà, which was one of the seven that made up his brother's benefice, but in 1335 '*dominus* Piero Alighieri, cleric and beneficiary of the said churches' renounced his benefice: it has been argued that this was a condition for permission to marry, but the example of Iacopo suggests that the possession of benefices did not always constitute a problem.

Chapter 21: Ravenna

1. Statius' association with the poetic coronation is motivated by some of the opening lines of his *Achilleid*, I, 15–16, in which he declared that laurels were the prize. According to Dante, however, Statius was crowned with myrtle (*Purgatory*, XXI, 90), while Dante was undoubtedly thinking of laurels for himself: see *Purgatory*, I, 25–6.
2. Boccaccio, *Trattatello*, I, 186–9; *Esposizioni*, p. 20.
3. Cecco d'Ascoli, *L'Acerba*, ed. M. Albertazzi (Trento, 2005), p. 108.
4. *Purgatory*, XIV, 115.
5. Boccaccio, *Trattatello*, I, 185–9.
6. The minutes, which are undoubtedly authentic, have been

published by Gerolamo Biscaro, and the academic observes that a payment of 100 florins was made out to Cagnolati a few days later by the Camera Apostolica (Papal Treasury) on the orders of the two cardinals who interviewed him, as well as a generous pension, along with some other gifts, which was paid up till 1328. The title of *magister* could strengthen the argument that Dante did actually obtain some kind of académic qualification and taught in Bologna.

7. Giuseppe Indizio appears take the deposition at face value and not pose the problem of the various consequences that could have arisen should it have been a set-up. He doesn't realise that Galeazzo, according to the deposition, is supposed to have asserted that he had Dante brought to him and then concludes that Galeazzo *believed* that Dante was still in Verona, whereas in reality he was already in Ravenna, albeit for only a short while.

8. Giovanni Villani, *Cronica nuova*, X, 136.

9. Filippo Villani, *Vita*, 65–68. M. Alberani, a doctor, finds the diagnosis of death from malignant malaria to be improbable.

10. Boccaccio, *Trattatello*, I, 86, and, for the epitaphs, 89–91.

INDEX